the complete
Wild Game
cookbook

Includes **165** recipes

Jean-Paul Grappe

Robert
ROSE

The Complete Wild Game Cookbook
Text copyright © 2015 Jean-Paul Grappe
Recipe photographs copyright © 2015 Pierre Beauchemin
Cover and text design copyright © 2015 Robert Rose Inc.
Translation copyright © 2015 Robert Rose Inc.

Published originally under the title: *Gibier à poil et à plume* @ 2008, Les Éditions de l'Homme, division du Groupe Sogides Inc., filiale de Québecor Media Inc. (Montréal, Québec, Canada)

For complete cataloguing information, see page 384.

Disclaimer
The recipes in this book have been carefully tested by the author. To the best of our knowledge, they are safe and nutritious for ordinary use and users. For those people with food or other allergies, or who have special food requirements or health issues, please read the suggested contents of each recipe carefully and determine whether or not they may create a problem for you. All recipes are used at the risk of the consumer.

We cannot be responsible for any hazards, loss or damage that may occur as a result of any recipe use.

For those with special needs, allergies, requirements or health problems, in the event of any doubt, please contact your medical adviser prior to the use of any recipe.

Design and Production: Daniella Zanchetta/PageWave Graphics Inc.
Editor: Carol Sherman
Translator: Donna Vekteris
Associate Translators: Myriam Birch, Kristin Cairns
Recipe Consultant: Christophe Measson
Copy Editor: Karen Campbell-Sheviak
Indexer: Gillian Watts
Food Photographer: Pierre Beauchemin
Food Stylist: Myriam Pelletier
Prop Stylist: Luce Meunier
For a complete list of photo credits, see page 375.

Cover image: Cubes of Braised Neck with Fall Vegetables, page 238

The publisher gratefully acknowledges the financial support of our publishing program by the Government of Canada through the Canada Book Fund.

Published by Robert Rose Inc.
120 Eglinton Avenue East, Suite 800, Toronto, Ontario, Canada M4P 1E2
Tel: (416) 322-6552 Fax: (416) 322-6936
www.robertrose.ca

Printed and bound in Canada

1 2 3 4 5 6 7 8 9 TCP 23 22 21 20 19 18 17 16 15

This book is dedicated to cooks.

Art serves to embellish life. It should help us live longer and better. It can only fully achieve this objective if it allows us to experience intellectual satisfaction in addition to physical well-being. Satisfaction and well-being must play off of each other, resist each other and strike a balance in order for each to preserve its own specificity. Otherwise, it is mysticism on the one hand, and excess on the other, that will prevail. It is precisely this fine balance between body and mind that must be respected in food tasting if we wish to elevate it to the realm of art.

Contents

Foreword

I had the pleasure of discovering Jean-Paul Grappe a few years ago on an expedition to Quebec's Great North where, in the company of my fellow chefs, we travelled more than 1,200 miles (2,000 km) by snowmobile.

Each night found us in a different encampment where Jean-Paul presided over the cooking, concocting recipes from local products usually fished or hunted by our Inuit guides. This was our introduction to some astonishing and highly original dishes.

I have read with keen interest the enormous manuscript on hunting and all things related, which served as the inspiration for this book. I seldom have had the opportunity to hold in my hands such a comprehensive work on the subject. This book, richly illustrated with photographs, brimming with information and highly detailed explanations, is more like an encyclopedia than a simple book of recipes.

Canada is not only a very beautiful country, but also a country well stocked with game. There is much to be said on the subject, and our friend has more than risen to the occasion, coloring his discourse with his deep sense of humanity and respect for nature.

Just as in his previous book, *Poissons, Mollusques et Crustacés* (Fish, Mollusks and Crustaceans), Jean-Paul Grappe has produced a monumental pedagogical work on a subject for which he has a profound attachment. Reading this book is like attending a lecture on the different ways of cooking game and all matters related.

My congratulations are in order. This book is surely destined to become bedside reading for hunters and nature lovers alike, and its success is assured.

Paul Bocuse

Paul Bocuse

Hunting and Respect

When the first Frenchmen arrived on these shores, they were surprised (and reassured) to find such an abundance of game. In their homeland, by contrast, the staple diet was far from rich in meat products. A number of historians would say that people ate better in New France than in France itself.

In this vast territory, where forests, lakes and rivers were home to an abundance of wildlife, the native people lived in harmony with their environment. They drew from this ample reservoir all that was necessary for them to eat, dress and trade without depleting their resources. They exhibited the care inherent in their culture for preserving the cycle of life. Animals and humans alike contributed to maintaining this equilibrium.

Many years later, we no longer hunt for our livelihood, food or clothing. We hunt for pleasure—for the thrill of collecting trophies and tasting wild meat.

Often enough, what we refer to as "game" is only that in name. We talk of farmed game, without acknowledging the fact that these words are opposite in meaning. The sale of "genuine" game meat is forbidden by law. Caribou is the only meat that does not fall under this regulation, along with muskox under certain conditions. Hunters alone can access this resource and share their good fortune with others.

Hunting is a privilege. An honor code should accompany it. Killing to collect only a few pieces of meat is an insult to nature. It shows a lack of respect and community spirit. Just as a hunter should know how to handle a weapon, so should he be able to handle a butcher's knife!

With the publication of this book, nobody will ever have an excuse again. All the coveted prey, from the smallest to the greatest, have been meticulously identified here. They will thus make their way to our tables, accorded the proper respect due to them. Happy hunting and bon appétit.

Françoise Kayler

Introduction

Since time immemorial, hunting has been a way to put food on the table. Grimod de la Reynière, Brillat-Savarin, Escoffier, Paul Bocuse and many other famous chefs have praised the delights of game meat, whose flesh is more substantial and flavorful than that of domestic animals. Wild animals live in complete freedom and eat whatever suits their needs. This in turn imparts their meat with flavors that transform a meal into a gastronomic delight.

Before tasting game meat, however, one must learn to respect it. Among other things, this means giving it a chance to escape death: this is what makes the hunter wait patiently to kill his prey only once it has ventured into proximity. And if the hunter wins, he must use every part of the animal.

In this book we will discuss all kinds of game animals and game birds (water or land), along with their different methods of preparation. While some recipes are simple, others call for marinades or larding. Small game here is limited to hares and squirrels, for which many recipes have been created.

In the recipes in this book, we use animals that have been bred locally and elsewhere. Since the hunting of certain species is allowed in certain regions, while in others these species are protected, it is important to check that the animal you want to hunt is not prohibited in your hunting territory.

Game Birds

When it comes to game birds, several questions arise. Should one eviscerate game birds before cooking? Some specialists will tell us that we must remove the insides of birds with short, fat beaks (such as quail), and leave birds with long and thin beaks (such as the woodcock) as they are. One will also find enthusiasts who, for the sake of hygiene and cleanliness, see the need to eviscerate even the smallest birds.

Some birds are so small that one needs to count several in a serving (quail, woodcock, thrush or lark, for example); others are large enough to feed two or more people (pheasant, partridge, ptarmigan, wood grouse, wild goose and duck). The different species of game birds are presented in families that are either completely distinguishable or that resemble each other. They will be cooked in a traditional or progressive fashion, always with the objective of preserving their flavor.

Game Animals

We will now deal with animals that are rarely found at your local butcher's. Should you be fortunate enough to know some hunters, on the other hand, the adventure of tasting muskox, beaver, bear and even seal will prove to be a wonderful culinary experience.

In Quebec, which is a paradise for hunting and fishing, we have had the opportunity to develop our own culinary art, using the products of our forests, lakes and rivers. This art has turned some of us into "gastronomic chefs." But what is gastronomy?

Gastronomy

To say that gastronomy is an art will raise criticism from those who claim that "one must eat to live and not live to eat." For them, the art of eating should not be allowed to exist.

Art is nothing but the cause and effect of the refinement of certain senses such as sight, hearing and touch. So then why shouldn't the sense of taste have its place in the artistic process and in artistic achievement?

As we will see in this book, the fact of appreciating the pleasure that comes from a good meal does not only stem from taste; the other senses come into play as well. Gastronomy is not only an art that addresses the palate; it also affects the psyche and all of the senses. Gastronomy should be considered an art in its own right.

Gastronomy is also a science, an applied science. Some will tell you that it is no more than a technique. If one admits this is true, it is a technique stemming from actual science, and one that shares common points with all the other sciences.

One could certainly attribute artistic value to cooking while refusing to recognize all scientific value. A chef who blindly executes the recipes in his cookbook will never invent new technology; he will remain confined to his infinitely small circle, never imagining that there are new ways of combining the ingredients that he uses in his kitchen on a daily basis. This chef will forever remain a poor one.

Brillat-Savarin once said that, "the discovery of a new dish does more good for humanity than the discovery of a new star." While stopping short of those claims, we will admit that although it is difficult for an astronomer to discover a new planet, it is also relatively difficult for the gourmet to find a new dish. The chef, just like the gourmet, must be cultivated and educated. Think of the famous combinations of foie gras and truffle attributed to Rossini, or Meyerbeer's idea of using kidneys to heighten the flavor of certain dishes.

The gourmet, always a chef at heart, should understand the how and the why of his actions. From that day forward, cooking becomes a science in his hands.

To understand how and why a well-prepared dinner fills us with such delight is to presuppose that we have an elementary understanding of foods, digestion, harmony and consistency, even the psyche.

Do you really need to know the chemical composition of an oyster's tissues to appreciate its flavor and unctuousness? No. One can be an artist without being a scientist. One can admire a Gothic cathedral without knowing anything about the strength of the materials that went into building it. It is fair to say, however, that an observer who has basic notions about the construction of vaulted roofs and the strength of pillars will discover, in the apse of a church, elements to admire that would certainly escape the attention of a wandering tourist equipped only with his Baedeker travel guide.

Every art form has its own scientific dimension. Architecture would not exist without the science of the builder. Sculpture would amount to nothing without the field of anatomy. Painting would mean very little without the notion of color. In the same way, gastronomy is coupled with gastrotechnology.

Gastrotechnology is the science of food preparation. Food should be rendered digestible and presented as a culinary art in a way that will maximize the diner's spiritual pleasure and stimulate the secretion of digestive juices. This is very important, since once food has been digested, it becomes an active agent in our tissues and matter. Among other things, food is the source of our natural heat, our muscle strength and our intellectual abilities. In short, it is the source of our energy.

Land of Gastronomy

You will notice that some of my recipes often pay homage or are dedicated to a great chef or a personality in the hotel and restaurant industry.

These are the very people who have established the solid foundation of our cuisine over the past 50 years. Of course, there have been others, but the people I have named in this book are those I have worked with and who have been models of professionalism to me.

While some of them have left us, others are enjoying a well-deserved retirement. It is thanks to these people that Quebec gastronomy is known the world over.

Other capable generations who honor this reputation now carry the torch. They include André Besson, Alain Pignard, Dominique Crevonnier, Marc Decan, Jean-Pierre Curtat, Normand Laprise, Claude Pelletier and Jean Soulard. Their succession ensures a bright and promising future. Some of my former students are distinguishing themselves abroad, in Shanghai, Hong Kong, Ho Chi Minh City, Lausanne, Kuwait, Paris, Munich, Amsterdam, and in Toronto and Vancouver. These young Quebecers are a credit to us. Others have made a name for themselves in Quebec: Martin Picard, Myriam Pelletier, David McMillan, Karen Anderson, Eve Rozon, Martin Boucher, Ian Perreault, Pierre Tétrault, Marie Sophie Picard, Steve McCandless, Colombe St-Pierre, William Chiasson, Nelson Boucher and many others.

Structure and Tenderness of Meat

Christina Blais, Department of Nutrition, University of Montreal

All meats, whether derived from livestock or wild game, have the same structure. They essentially consist of muscle fibers, adipose tissue (fat) and connective tissue (collagen). The proportion of these different components, however, along with their color and texture, may vary.

Arrangement of Muscle Fibers

Muscles are made of very long specialized cells called muscle "fibers" or "cells." These cells can measure up to several inches (cm) in length. They contain fluid as well as the proteins actin and myosin, which are required for muscle contraction. These two proteins, sliding against each other inside the cells help the muscles to contract and relax.

Each muscle fiber is coated in a thin layer of collagen called endomysium. Muscle fibers are grouped together by the hundreds to form sheathed bundles. These bundles are coated in a layer of collagen called the perimysium. The bundles are joined together to form the muscle, which itself is coated in a sheath of collagen called epimysium. These three levels of collagen (endomysium, perimysium and epimysium) help attach the muscles to the bones and joints and allow movement. The extent of this layer of connective tissue largely determines meat's tenderness, while the arrangement and size of the bundles of muscle fibers determine the grain of a piece of meat.

The Role of Collagen

Collagen is made up of long networks of proteins wound like strings. These strings, called fibers or fibrils, are entangled like the fibers in a piece of felt and are thick and resistant. Collagen fibers are joined together by chemical bonds that vary in number according to age and exercise. The more tightly wound together the fibers, the tougher the meat. The muscles used most contain more collagen and are more resistant than muscles that are used less. Age also has an effect: over time, the number of chemical bonds that join the collagen fibers together increases, which explains why the meat of older animals is always tougher than the meat of young animals.

In its raw state, collagen is elastic and tough. Fortunately, under the right conditions, cooking breaks down the chemical bonds that hold the collagen fibers together, allowing them to "solubilize," or transform into gelatin. The collagen of young animals is more easily transformed into gelatin than that of older animals. As we will see later, the cooking method should be adapted to the collagen content of meat in order to bring out its tenderness.

The Role of Fat

It is the fat, or adipose tissue, and not the lean tissue, which is mainly responsible for making meat tasty. Fat content varies from 5 to 30 percent of the muscle weight. Game meat, however, contains less fat than livestock, so it is leaner meat that tends to dry out during cooking. The texture (firmness) of the fat and its color vary according to the species of an animal, its age and its diet. We can differentiate between the cover fat, which coats the outside of the carcass, the intermuscular fat that surrounds the muscles and the intramuscular or "marbled" fat that we find between the bundles of muscle fibers.

Well-marbled meat is considered juicier than lean meat because fat stimulates salivation and also helps to separate the muscle bundles.

The Color of Meat

Muscles contain three types of muscle fibers: the red fibers, which are rich in myoglobin, are found in the muscles responsible for long and slow movements (walking and balancing, for example); the white fibers in the muscles, which do not contain myoglobin, are responsible for sudden and swift movements; the intermediate fibers provide muscle stamina. Migratory birds have many intermediate fibers in their muscles. The proportion of red and white fibers in a muscle explains the difference in color between white and dark meat in poultry.

The red color of muscle fibers is mainly due to myoglobin, a pigment whose role is to transport oxygen within the muscle cell. If an animal is properly bled after slaughter, the hemoglobin (the pigment that gives blood its red color) barely alters the color of the muscle.

The brightness of the muscle color varies according to the species, gender, age and type of physical activity of an animal. The muscles used most often by an animal are the most pigmented, and the muscles of younger animals are paler in comparison to those of older animals. In different species, the color of the muscles varies according to the physiological needs of the animal and the way it moves. Seals, for example, have dark, almost black meat that is very rich in myoglobin because they have a large capacity for storing oxygen in their muscle cells. This characteristic gives these marine mammals the ability

to remain underwater without breathing for long periods of time. Rabbit meat, on the other hand, is rather pink because it contains a lot of white muscle fibers that favor short and swift movement.

Meat color also depends on the acidification in muscles that takes place in the hours following death. After the slaughter, the pH level (measure of acidity) of the muscles changes from neutral (7) to slightly acid (between 5.5 and 5.7). Acidification causes tightening of muscle fibers and a modification in the chemical form of the myoglobin. This change in the pH balance is beneficial to meat conservation and takes about 48 hours to occur in a large animal. If an animal suffers stress shortly before death (flight, fear, pain), its glycogen reserves (the sugar present in the muscles that is transformed into lactic acid following death) will be depleted and acidification will not be sufficient. The color of the meat will therefore be very dark.

After skinning, the color of the meat will depend on the presence or the absence of oxygen. In fact, the color of myoglobin varies according to its degree of exposure to oxygen. The surface of freshly cut meat is bright red because the myoglobin reacts to the oxygen in the air. The inside of a piece of meat remains a darker purple color because of a lack of oxygen (the oxygen does not penetrate more than a fraction of an inch (a few millimeters) beneath the surface. If cut surfaces of meat remain exposed for long periods of time, the myoglobin will oxidize and turn an unappealing brownish color. Vacuum-packed meats progressively lose their bright red color and turn purple because of a lack of oxygen in the packaging. However, when the package is opened and the meat comes into contact with air, it regains its red color as a result of the reaction of the myoglobin to oxygen.

Transformation of Muscles into Meat

Immediately following the slaughter, the muscles are flexible, but they soon turn harder: this is the onset of rigor mortis, commonly called "rigor." The stiffness sets in one to two hours after a small game animal is slaughtered, and approximately 12 hours after a large game animal is slaughtered. The stiffness is caused by a series of biochemical changes in the muscle, the most significant being the transformation of glycogen (energy reserve in the muscle) into lactic acid. The action of hanging the carcass (or quarters) soon after the slaughter allows certain muscles to stretch and prevents them from contracting too much. The rigor period lasts a few hours in small game and from 24 to 48 hours in large game. After a certain amount of time, the muscle fibers will tenderize as a result of the maturation process.

Two phenomena linked to the drop in temperature of a carcass before the appearance of rigor can occur: contracture (shortening of the muscle fibers) caused by the cold, commonly known as "cold shortening," and contracture due to defrosting, called "thaw rigor" or "thaw shortening."

Contracture due to cold will occur if the temperature of the carcass drops below 50°F (10°C) in the span of a few hours. This phenomenon can occur in small game hunted in cold weather (outdoor temperature below the freezing mark). In this case, a powerful muscle contraction can occur that ultimately compromises the tenderness of the meat, even after a normal period of maturation.

Contracture due to defrosting occurs when the meat is frozen before the appearance of rigor. At the time of defrosting, the meat will contract powerfully, which will make it extremely tough.

Aging

Following the rigor stage, meat will continue to tenderize. It is a well-known fact that large livestock such as beef becomes more tender and flavorful when the meat is aged under refrigeration between 35 and 40°F (between 1 and 4°C) for a period of 10 to 14 days. The meat can be aged as a carcass, but it is more often aged in quarters that have been vacuum-packed. This period, called "maturation," is not required for farm-raised birds (poultry) nor for pork or the meat of young animals like veal or lamb, since the few days that elapse between the slaughter and the sale of the meat are usually sufficient to ensure the tenderization of the meat.

One must not confuse maturation with hanging, a procedure once used for game birds. During hanging, the bacterial fermentation of the intestinal contents gave meat a pronounced flavor. This phenomenon does not occur when the bird is eviscerated.

During the maturation process, enzymes called proteases naturally present in the meat fragment the muscle fibers and tenderize them. Flavor is also enhanced thanks to the formation of aroma and flavor precursor molecules. Contrary to popular belief, however, the maturation process has almost no effect on collagen, which retains its resistance. Even though the enzymes remain active for about 28 days, their effectiveness decreases significantly after 10 to 14 days of maturation.

The Maturation Process in Large Game

Should we age large game? Ideally, yes, but the practice might pose sanitary risks depending on hunting and climatic conditions as well as the hunter's means of cooling the carcass.[1] Here are some considerations:

- Young animals do not require a period of maturation: the meat is naturally tender. The time that elapses between the harvest, the trip home and the preparation for refrigeration or freezing will suffice.

- If the animal is slaughtered in mild weather (outdoor temperatures above 60°F/15°C) and there is no access to a cold room, it is neither necessary nor desirable to age the carcass. As a matter of fact, under these conditions, rigor is less significant and the action of the enzymes responsible for the aging of the meat is much faster. The carcass is as tenderized in three to four days as it would be in about 10 days of refrigeration. A longer maturation period is not recommended because the risk of bacterial growth is too high.

- If the animal was hurried or stressed by running, or if it was fearful or wounded before being killed, its glycogen reserves will be depleted. Under these conditions, there will not be enough glycogen left to allow acidification in the muscles due to increased production of lactic acid, which compromises conservation during the aging process. The acidification of meat actually impairs the growth of microorganisms. In this case, maturation is not recommended. Moreover, the meat of such animals will often be dark and sticky (see the section on meat color, page 18) and will not display the qualities that are sought in game meat.

To safely age large game, it is essential to follow a few ground rules:

- Eviscerate the animal as quickly as possible.

- Cool the carcass as soon as possible. Under ideal conditions, the meat temperature should be lowered to 45°F (7°C) or less in the 24 hours following the kill. Hanging the carcass by the hind legs while keeping the thoracic cage wide open can accelerate cooling. Ensure adequate air circulation around the carcass. If the game animal is immediately quartered, hang the pieces and provide good ventilation around them. A long metal stem thermometer inserted in the buttock or shoulder is very useful for monitoring changes in the temperature of the muscle.

- Do not skin the animal. Whether the animal is to be preserved as a carcass or in quarters, the skin serves as a natural protection against contamination and reduces loss through dehydration later on during maturation.

- Maintain adequate temperature and aeration conditions during transportation.

If these conditions are respected, the meat can be aged in a cold room (35 to 40°F/1 to 4°C) for 7 to 10 days. Note that this period will be shorter if the carcass or quarters have been exposed to less than optimal conditions between the time of the harvest and the start of the maturation period.

Finally, instead of aging the entire carcass, it may be more practical to quarter it and age only the tender parts (ribs, loins), taking care to vacuum pack them to minimize losses. It is useless to age meat that will be ground.

1. See the article *"Règles de base en microbiologie pour le gibier à poil et à plume"* (Basic microbiology rules for game animals and game birds) in the section *"Le coin du chasseur"* (The Hunter's Corner), Les Editions de l'Homme website, edhhomme.com/gibier.

The Effect of Cooking on Meat Tenderness

The method and amount of cooking undoubtedly affects the tenderness of meat. In fact, the tenderness of meat depends upon the balance between the conversion of the collagen into gelatin and the coagulation of the muscle fibers.

The Effect of Cooking on Muscle Fibers

While cooking, the proteins within the fibers "coagulate" or tighten up. In this process, the proteins expel the water they contain. It is as though the meat is a sponge saturated with water, with the heat of cooking exerting pressure on the sponge. The higher the temperature of the meat, the greater the pressure on the fibers, and the more the juices will come out of the meat.

Research has shown that the meat starts to lose its juices at an internal temperature of about 130°F (55°C), while the meat is still very rare. The start of this loss of juices is caused by the shrinkage (or thermal contraction) of the endomysium, the collagen that surrounds each muscle fiber. When the meat reaches an internal temperature of about 160°F (70°C), the loss of juices is accentuated. This is because the perimysium (the collagen coating the muscle bundles) contracts in turn and exerts additional pressure on the cells. A piece of meat that reaches an internal temperature of 175°F (80°C) will have lost as much as 30 to 35 percent of its water.

The Effect of Cooking on Collagen

The chemical bonds that hold the collagen molecules together come undone in the heat and humidity, which causes the collagen molecules to "solubilize" or transform into gelatin that is easy to chew. But there is a hitch: this transformation requires a much longer cooking time at a low temperature and a moist cooking environment. The conversion of collagen into gelatin occurs very slowly, starting at 122 to 140°F (50 to 60°C), but much more quickly starting at 175°F (80°C).

We understand why tender pieces of meat, which contain less connective tissue, can be cooked quickly (grilled, sautéed) and served rare: under these cooking conditions, the collagen does not have time to soften up. Conversely, tougher pieces of meat that have more connective tissue require a longer and slower cooking time for the chemical reactions that will transform the collagen into gelatin to take place. We use these pieces of meat for stews, braised dishes and pots-au-feu.

Effects of Heat on Meat

	Effects on muscle fibers	Effects on collagen*
Around 100°F (40°C)	The proteins begin to alter or to unwind. The water normally stored in the proteins is released and collects within the cells (muscle fibers). The meat is soft to the touch. The proteolytic enzymes** are activated and tenderize the muscle fibers.	No effect.
Between 120° and 130°F (50 and 55°C)	The proteins, which are now unwound, begin to bind or coagulate. More and more water is released from the proteins and collects in the cells. The proteolytic enzymes are inactivated starting at 120°F (55°C).	Beginning of the shrinkage or "thermal contraction" of the endomysium, the collagen coating the muscle fibers.
Around 140°F (60°C)	Coagulation continues and the meat becomes firmer to the touch. The water is expelled from the muscle cells under the pressure exerted by the collagen in the endomysium.	Thermal contraction of the collagen in the endomysium continues and exerts pressure on the muscle fibers.
Around 160°F (70°C)	Almost all of the water is drained from the cells under the additional pressure exerted by the collagen in the endomysium.	Beginning of the shrinkage or thermal contraction of the perimysium, the collagen coating the muscle bundles. The collagen begins to solubilize and transform into gelatin.
Over 175°F (80°C)	The muscle cells have lost almost all their water and have dried up. The meat is very firm to the touch.	The collagen transforms more quickly into gelatin.

*The temperatures at which collagen tightens, dissolves and transforms into gelatin are a few degrees higher in older animals.

**The role of the proteolytic enzymes in the tenderizing process of meat during cooking is not unanimously agreed upon among researchers. The most certain tenderizing mechanism remains that of the transformation of collagen into gelatin.

Selecting the Right Cooking Method

The cooking method should be adapted to the collagen content of meat in order to bring out its tenderness.

Tough Cuts

Oven-roasting at low temperature

- This cooking method suits large cuts of meat, for example, roasts weighing over 6½ lbs (3.2 kg). Usually, the roasts are cooked in the oven at temperatures between 325 and 350°F (between 160 and 180°C). However, more and more specialists in meat cooking are now recommending a lower temperature, between 225 and 250°F (between 110 and 120°C). At these temperatures, heat is transmitted very slowly from the outside to the inside of the roast. The coagulation of the muscle fibers occurs slowly and less water is expelled from the meat, provided the roast is not overcooked.[1] During this time, the collagen is in contact with the meat's natural moisture and it slowly transforms into gelatin.

- To be effective, low-temperature cooking should last several hours, which is not always practical! The result, however, is more even cooking and meat that is tender and juicy.

Braised dishes, pots-au-feu, stews

These popular cooking methods work well with tougher pieces of meat. The same method is used for cooking in a slow cooker.

When meat is cooked in a liquid, the heat is transmitted rapidly into the meat, which then easily reaches the temperature favoring the rapid transformation of collagen into gelatin (175°F/80°C and higher). There are several options:

- Simmer for 2 or 3 hours, covered, on low heat, or in the oven at a low temperature (275°F/140°C or lower);

- Cook for 6 to 8 hours at a low temperature in a slow cooker;

- Cook for 30 to 40 minutes in a pressure cooker (the transformation of collagen into gelatin occurs rapidly at the temperature reached in a pressure cooker).

Once the collagen is transformed into gelatin, the muscle fibers separate and the meat comes apart easily with a fork. However, because the muscle fibers lose almost all their moisture, it is important to serve the meat in its cooking juice so that it can re-absorb some of this moisture.

Tender Cuts

Grilling, frying, oven-roasting, sautéing

Cuts coming from the loin and rib area are naturally tender. The objective of cooking is to preserve this tenderness and minimize the loss of juices. The meat can be roasted, grilled, sautéed or fried. It will be tender and succulent if it is not overcooked, because, as we recall, the higher the internal temperature, the greater the loss of cooking juices due to the pressure exerted on the muscle fibers by the collagen bundles that contract in the heat[1]. Using a good meat thermometer is the key to success. This is why the majority of the recipes in this book list an internal cooking temperature that should be checked with a thermometer.

Are Marinades Effective?

Research shows that an effective marinade must be high in acid content: lemon juice, wine, wine vinegar, yogurt—the choices are endless. Acids partly break down the bonds holding the collagen molecules together in such a way that, during the cooking

---

1. See the chart of suggested cooking temperatures suggested by various organizations, page 25.

process, the molecules are more easily transformed into gelatin. Unfortunately, marinades only work on the surface (they only penetrate the meat a fraction of an inch/a few millimeters), so they have a limited effect, especially on thick cuts of meat. To maximize the tenderizing effect of a marinade, one needs a large quantity of an acidic ingredient, a sufficiently long period for the marinade to do its work (24 to 48 hours), and for the meat not to be too thick.

Safe Internal Temperatures

Internal temperatures suggested for cooking meat can vary. Both MAPAQ (Quebec Department of Agriculture, Fisheries and Food), in its booklet called *Votre guide du consommateur*[1] (Your Consumer's Guide) and the USDA* suggest higher cooking temperatures than those suggested in the book *Technologie culinaire à la carte*[2] (Culinary Technology à La Carte) that is used by chefs and by students in cooking schools in Europe. The cooking temperatures used in this book are close to those suggested in *Technologie culinaire à la carte*, but if you are more comfortable following other guidelines, feel free to do so.

From the USDA: "Cooked muscle meats can be pink even when the meat has reached a safe internal temperature. If fresh game has reached 160°F (71°C) throughout, even though it may still be pink in the center, it should be safe. The pink color can be due to the cooking method, smoking, or added ingredients such as marinades. Cook ground meats and other cuts of game meat such as chops, steaks and roasts to 160°F (71°C) to ensure destruction of foodborne bacteria and parasites. For tenderness, tough meats should be held at 160°F (71°C) longer or even cooked to higher temperatures. This will melt the tough connective tissue (collagen) producing fork-tender meats."

MAPAQ suggested temperatures		*Culinary Technology à La Carte* suggested temperatures	
Beef, veal, lamb			
Rare	145°F (63°C)	Rare	113 to 122°F (45 to 50°C)
Medium	158°F (70°C)	Medium	131 to 140°F (55 to 60°C)
Well done	170°F (77°C)	Well done	Above 140°F (60°C)
		White meat	158 to 176°F (70 to 80°C)
Farm-raised game	158°F (70°C)		
Wild game	170°F (77°C)		
USDA suggested temperatures			
Cooked ground game meat		160°F (71°C)	
Game meat chops, steaks or roasts		160°F (71°C)	

1. MAPAQ (Quebec Department of Agriculture, Fisheries and Food), *Votre guide du consommateur*.

2. Jean-Marc Wolff, Jean-Pierre Lebland and Nicole Soleihac, Technologie culinaire à la carte, *Paris, Delagrave, 2002*.

* United States Department of Agriculture

Comparative Table of the Nutritive Elements in Game Birds and Poultry

	Calories (Kcal)	Proteins (g)	Lipids (fat) (g)	Cholesterol (mg)	Iron (mg)
Game Birds					
Wild duck, cooked	170	30.0	4.4	N/A	9.9
Canada goose, flesh only, roasted	200	30.8	7.6	96	9.9
Woodcock	115	25.0	1.5	N/A	N/A
Ptarmigan, flesh, cooked	154	30.0	2.9	89	8.7
Grouse	106	22.0	2.0	N/A	N/A
Thrush	120	22.0	3.5	N/A	N/A
Plover	115	25.0	1.5	N/A	N/A
Lapwing	115	25.0	1.5	N/A	N/A
Pigeon	175	37.0	3.0	N/A	N/A
Poultry					
Roasting chicken, flesh only, roasted	167	25.0	6.6	75	1.2
Domestic duck, flesh only, roasted	201	23.5	11.2	89	2.7
Pheasant, edible portion, cooked	247	32.4	12.1	89	1.4
Quail, edible portion, cooked	234	25.1	14.1	86	4.4
Turkey, all categories, flesh only, roasted	170	29.3	4.5	76	1.8

Nutritional information is presented in 100-gram portions

Comparative Table of the Nutritive Elements in Game Meat and Livestock

	Calories (Kcal)	Proteins (g)	Lipids (fat) (g)	Cholesterol (mg)	Iron (mg)
Moose, roasted	161	35.0	1.3	78	5.0
Caribou (reindeer), meat, cooked	163	32.0	3.0	109	5.7
Deer (filet), lean, roasted, cooked, grilled	149	29.9	2.4	88	4.3
Caribou (reindeer) tongue, cooked	326	20.0	27.0	N/A	3.3
Caribou (reindeer), heart, boiled	145	28.0	3.5	N/A	8.9
Wild boar, roasted	160	28.3	4.4	77	1.1
Bison, roasted	143	28.4	2.4	82	3.4
Muskox	N/A	N/A	N/A	N/A	N/A
Beaver, roasted	127	27.0	1.5	117	4.9
Beaver, tail, roasted	437	11.0	43.0	N/A	0.7
Bear, stewed	259	32.4	13.4	98	10.7
Hare, cooked	140	29.0	2.1	123	5.8
Ringed seal, boiled	165	32.5	3.1	90	27.6
Beef, various cuts, steak, lean, cooked	234	35.5	8.9	86	3.4
Milk calf, shoulder roast, whole, lean, roasted	154	28.9	3.0	92	1.8
Horse, roasted	175	28.1	6.0	68	5.0
Pork, fresh, shoulder, picnic, lean, roasted	228	26.7	12.6	95	1.4
Rabbit, domestic, assorted cuts, roasted	197	29.1	8.1	82	2.3
Calf's liver, braised	192	28.4	6.5	511	5.1

Nutritional information is presented in 100-gram portions

Game Meat

Livestock

Game Birds

Duck	Pigeon
Goose	Pheasant
Woodcock	Quail
Sandpiper	Turkey
Ptarmigan	Thrush
Grouse	Lark
Guinea Fowl	Lapwing
Partridge	Plover
Northern Bobwhite	

Advice on the Preparation and Cooking of Game Birds

The preparation of game birds is the subject of much controversy. According to the French chef and author Auguste Escoffier, birds such as partridge, bobwhites, woodcocks and snipes benefit from being hung for some time—that is to say, preserved for several days in a well-ventilated area and left unplucked. This process of decomposition imparts a special aroma to the meat and greatly improves its quality.

While fresh meat is dry and flavorless, if properly hung and aged it is tender, succulent and cannot be matched for flavor.

Game birds are usually gutted immediately after they are killed. They are stored in a cold area for a few days, preferably hung by the beak, and then plucked.

Traditionally, birds such as pheasant and partridge were also pricked. This practice must be resolutely avoided. It can only damage the fine quality of the meat if the bird is young, and if old, it cannot restore the qualities that have been lost. A single slice of pork fatback wrapped around the bird is much more effective than pricking to protect it from the heat of cooking, and it does not alter the flavor at all.

Other than this, an old bird must never be served as is. It should instead be used to make stuffing or stock. Except for partridges, bobwhites, woodcocks and snipes, all birds must be consumed fresh.

At the risk of contradicting Escoffier, let's conclude by saying that, thanks to modern refrigeration techniques, it is better to age game birds some time in a cold room with ventilation at about 45°F (7°C).

The Different Species of Game Birds

Ducks

There are many species of ducks and aquatic birds, generally of average size, that can be distinguished from geese by their shorter neck and more flattened body. In general, there are marked differences in plumage between an adult male and an adult female. Duck's feet are located farther back on their body than geese, which makes walking more ungainly. Perching ducks (including the wood duck) are some of the most beautiful ducks in the world.

Dabbling ducks are not accustomed to diving; they feed off the surface of the water or on dry land. Diving ducks, which spend their lives in fresh water and salt water, look for food under the surface. It should be noted that it is mainly farm-raised or domestic ducks that grace our tables and that have delighted gourmets for so long.

Diving ducks

Canvasback, redhead, ring-necked duck, tufted duck, greater scaup, lesser scaup.

Sea ducks and mergansers (fish-eating ducks)

Common eider, king eider, harlequin duck, long-tailed duck, common scoter, surf scoter, velvet scoter, common goldeneye, Barrow's goldeneye, bufflehead, smew, hooded merganser, common merganser.

Dabbling ducks

Eurasian or common teal, American black duck, mallard, northern pintail, garganey, blue-winged teal, cinnamon teal, northern shoveler, gadwall, American wigeon.

Domestic ducks

Pekin (Long Island or Brome Lake) duck, Muscovy duck, Rouen duck, Khaki-Campbell duck, mule duck, Duclair duck, Indian runner duck.

Duck in Gastronomy

- Duck foie gras is mainly derived from the fattened mule duck. Enjoyed since ancient times, it is a dish fit for a king.

- Fattened duck breast is referred to as "magret."

- Some ducks have a very large breast (Muscovy), while others have a much smaller one (Pekin).

- In general, the breasts of young ducks are served *"à la goutte de sang"* (cooked to the drop of blood) (see Tips, page 68), whereas wild ducks, which have travelled a lot, should be braised.

- Wild duck has a much stronger flavor, as its diet is much more selective. It also lives at its own pace, making it a "happy" animal.

- Farm-raised duck is much more tender because it leads a sedentary life.

- Duck breast is usually roasted, sautéed or fried, while thighs are braised or made into confit.

- A duck that is shot suffers internal hemorrhaging; farm-raised duck, on the other hand, might be suffocated instead of bled, and so can be used in the famous "pressed duck" recipe.

AMERICAN BLACK DUCK
Anas rubripes

GREEN-WINGED TEAL (dabbling duck)
Anas crecca (Linnaeus)

HABITAT: The American black duck is the most common duck to be found in northeastern North America. It lives in relatively shallow fresh water and salt water.

SIZE AND COLOR: The lower and upper parts are dark brown. The top of the wings is white. Both the female and the male are large.

WEIGHT: From 1¾ to 3 lbs (875 g to 1.5 kg)

CHARACTERISTICS: The black duck is a favorite of hunters. It is also a bird much loved by gourmets for its generous size and refined flavor.

HABITAT: The green-winged teal nests in the northern areas of North America. It migrates to southern Canada, the United States, Mexico and the Caribbean.

It is distinguished from grouse, partridge and pheasant by its small size. Its characteristic call sounds like "bob-white."

SIZE AND COLOR: The female teal has brownish, spotted plumage. The whitish belly, however, is not clearly demarcated. The male is grayer, and its head is of a brownish-russet color with large metallic bands on the cheeks. Its average size is from 12 to 14 inches (30 to 35 cm) in length.

WEIGHT: 14 oz (400 g)

FOOD: It feeds on insects, snails, fry, tadpoles, aquatic plants and buds.

CHARACTERISTICS: This is North America's smallest dabbling duck. Its size distinguishes it from all the other species of duck commonly found in Canada.

BLUE-WINGED TEAL
Anas discors

MALLARD (dabbling duck)
Anas platyrhynchos (Linnaeus)

HABITAT: The blue-winged teal lives in shallow ponds and lakes, wetlands and along the grassy banks of slow-moving streams and rivers. It is rarely seen in salt water or brackish water. It is found in northeastern and central North America and migrates as far south as northern South America in the winter.

SIZE AND COLOR: Its size varies from 14 to 16 inches (35 to 40 cm). The head and top of the neck are dark gray with a touch of violet. There is large white crescent in front of its eyes. The under or ventral part of the head is blackish; the back, rump and tail are dark brown. The anterior feathers are blue and separated from the bright-green speculum by a thin white stripe. The breast, belly and sides are brown.

WEIGHT: Male, 14 oz (400 g); female, 12 oz (375 g)

CHARACTERISTICS: These small ducks, which feed on insects, snails, fry, tadpoles, aquatic plants and buds, are of high gastronomic quality.

HABITAT: The mallard is found in the wild in nearly every temperate zone in the Northern Hemisphere.

SIZE AND COLOR: As with nearly all ducks, the color and size distinguish the male from the female. With the male, the coat and scapulars are marked with fine, irregular or wavy gray and black lines. The metallic-green neck is trimmed with a thin white collar. The female has chestnut feathers ringed in dark brown; the head is a light fawn and the crown is dark with green reflections.

WEIGHT: Male, from 2½ to 3½ lbs (1.25 to 1.75 kg); female, from 2 to 2½ lbs (1 to 1.25 kg)

FOOD: It feeds on fleshy aquatic plants, seeds, insects and small aquatic animals. It is very fond of grain, wild rice and corn.

CHARACTERISTICS: The mallard is probably the best-known duck in the world.

BLACK SCOTER (sea duck)
Melanitta (nigra) americana (Linnaeus)

MUSCOVY DUCK
Cairina moschata

HABITAT: The black scoter (also known as the American scoter) is a large sea duck. It breeds mainly around Hudson Bay and James Bay, and in the southern part of the Hudson Strait and Ungava Bay as well as in Alaska. It winters along the Atlantic or Pacific coast.

SIZE AND COLOR: From 17 to 18 inches (43 to 45 cm). The adult male is the only scoter that does not have white patches on the head and wings. The female has uniformly pale cheeks, whereas the females of other scoter species have a lighter patch on each side of the head. It has a brown cap that stands out from the rest of its head, which is pale. The female has a white patch on its wings.

WEIGHT: $2\frac{1}{2}$ lbs (1.25 kg)

FOOD: It feeds mainly on fish, which gives it its culinary distinctiveness.

CHARACTERISTICS: The scoter lives in coastal salt waters (usually near the shore). It is rarely found on dry land except when nesting.

HABITAT: Farm.

SIZE AND COLOR: This duck has a very wide and shallow body. The male is black and white; the female is white. Its featherless face is red. The Muscovy duck has wattles that join to form a roll of flesh at the base of the beak.

WEIGHT: Male, 9 lbs (4.5 kg); female $6\frac{1}{2}$ lbs (3.25 kg)

CHARACTERISTICS: The Muscovy duck is a very particular species, different from *Anas platyrhynchos*, of which several sub-species are known.

Living in the wild in Argentina and Brazil, it was originally domesticated in Peru and imported to Europe by Christopher Columbus. In a culinary context, this duck is also known as the "Barbary duck."

This perching duck flies more easily than all other ducks derived from the mallard. Its external appearance is very different from that of other ducks. It has red wattles around the eyes, and the males are much larger than the females.

PEKIN DUCK (Also known as Long Island or Brome Lake Duck)
Anas platyrhynchos domestica

ROUEN DUCK

HABITAT: Farm.

SIZE AND COLOR: The Pekin duck has a wide body and a very developed breast. Its color is usually yellow, although there is a variety that turns pure white in the fall.

WEIGHT: Male, 7 lbs (3.5 kg); female, 6 lbs (3 kg)

CHARACTERISTICS: As the name indicates, the Pekin duck is native to China. It was introduced to the United States in 1873. It has been extensively improved and adapted to produce meat, which is of excellent quality. The Pekin duck reaches its market weight in eight weeks, but has a tendency to be very fatty.

In the United States, it has been crossbred with the Aylesbury duck, creating two varieties: the German Pekin and the American Pekin.

HABITAT: Farm.

SIZE AND COLOR: The Rouen duck has an elongated body that slopes downward toward to the back. Its coloring is similar to that of the mallard. Its head and neck are green, with a thin white border. The color of the female duck ranges from light beige to fawn.

WEIGHT: Male, from $7\frac{1}{2}$ to 9 lbs (3.75 to 4.5 kg); female, from $5\frac{1}{2}$ to $6\frac{1}{2}$ lbs (2.75 to 3.25 kg)

CHARACTERISTICS: The Rouen duck is native to France. The first colonists brought it from France to America. It is distinguished by the green eggs it produces.

Known for the beauty of its plumage. The plumage of both the male and the female are identical to that of the mallard male and female. The Rouen duck takes longer to grow to adult size, but its meat has the most distinctive flavor of all of the duck species.

MULE DUCK (domestic duck)

CHALLANS DUCK

HABITAT: Farm.

SIZE AND COLOR: This duck, a cross between the female Pekin duck and the male Muscovy duck, has been developed specifically for fattening. As a result of genetic selection, the plumage of the mule duck is primarily black and white, with a predominance of white. Earlier breeds of this duck have kept their multicolored plumage.

WEIGHT: It is the heaviest of all ducks. Male, about 9 lbs (4.5 kg); female, from $7\frac{1}{2}$ to 8 lbs (3.75 to 4 kg)

CHARACTERISTICS: This duck is one of the most suitable for the production of foie gras. After 13 weeks, it is fattened with 50 percent corn and 50 percent other food. The last 25 meals (2 per day) consist of 98 percent corn mixed with 2 percent lactic ferment and minerals. The breast of the fattened mule duck is referred to as "magret."

HABITAT: Farm.

SIZE AND COLOR: Its long and narrow head is well rounded. Its forehead is flat. The head and neck are brown and the legs are yellow. The female is slightly different from the male.

WEIGHT: Male, 5 to $5\frac{1}{2}$ lbs (2.5 to 2.75 kg); female, from 4 to 5 lbs (2 to 2.5 kg)

CHARACTERISTICS: Better known by the name Nantais duck, or occasionally Challandais duck, the Challans duck standard was created in 1934. It achieved "red label" status in France in 1947.

WOOD DUCK
Aix sponsa

ORPINGTON DUCK

HABITAT: The wood duck lives in lakes, ponds and streams in wooded areas. It is particularly fond of swamp-like environments. It can be found throughout the year in large parts of the U.S. and southern Canada, and winters further south, as far away as central Mexico.

SIZE AND COLOR: The white patches on the face are characteristic of the male. The small white area around the eye is particular to the female. The female's crest is shorter than that of the male. It has a brownish-gray head with a greenish luster. The head of the male in its nuptial plumage is iridescent green and intense blue with violet-green reflections. The size of the adult male wing: from 9 to 10 inches (23 to 25 cm); that of the adult female: from 8 to 9 inches (20 to 23 cm).

CHARACTERISTICS: According to my hunter friend Serge Yelle, this perching duck is the most delicious of the wild ducks. This species includes 14 breeds.

CHARACTERISTICS: The Orpington duck appeared in 1899 in Kent. The female—which yields an excellent clutch—is sometimes used for crossbreeding with Muscovy ducks. Their crossbreeding produces "mulards," which are a little smaller than Muscovy ducks.

AYLESBURY DUCK (Farm)

DUCLAIR DUCK (Farm)

WHITE-BACKED DUCK
Thalassornis leuconotus

MOTTLED DUCK
Anas fulvigula

NORTHERN SHOVELER
(dabbling duck)
Anas clypeata

HABITAT: The northern shoveler lives primarily in freshwater environments— marshes and ponds that are rich in vegetation. It is found in wetlands across large parts of North America.

SIZE AND COLOR: Its size varies from 17 to 21 inches (43 to 53 cm). It is easily recognizable by its enormous, flattened beak. When the male is in its nuptial attire, its bright-green head contrasts with its white breast and russet flanks. Its yellow irises differentiate it from all the other dabbling ducks. Both males and females have pale-blue patches at the front of the wings and a green speculum. The legs are orange.

CHARACTERISTICS: With its glossy green head and spoon-shaped bill in appearance, the northern shoveler is the most distinctive of the dabbling ducks.

NORTHERN PINTAIL
(dabbling duck)
Anas acuta (Linnaeus)

HABITAT: The northern pintail nests from Alaska and northern Canada and as far south as the Canadian prairies and the American Great Plains. It can be found in open areas of shallow fresh water and in large or small marshes. Outside of nesting season, it also lives in salt water or brackish waters on both coasts of North America.

SIZE AND COLOR: From 26 to 30 inches (66 to 76 cm). The adult male is easy to identify irrespective of its plumage: it has a long thin neck, a pointed tail and a fine but very visible white stripe along the back of its extended wings. Its head and neck are brown with a white stripe along both sides of the neck, except in the fall. The female has a long graceful neck.

WEIGHT: From $1\frac{1}{4}$ to 2 lbs (625 g to 1 kg)

CHARACTERISTICS: These magnificent ducks are very sociable. They generally form small flocks and often live in seclusion in the middle of an open area.

Geese

The goose was domesticated in Europe and Asia thousands of years ago. Naturally, the first colonists brought some with them to America. In fact, nearly all colonists kept some on their farms, as its yield was superior to that of other domesticated animals. It grazed and also served as a "guard dog." It provided farmers with meat, feathers for beds and pillows, fat for cooking, dusters for cleaning and quills for writing.

Raising geese is less widespread today, as it is difficult to prepare them after slaughtering to meet current consumption standards. Raising geese is costly, as egg production and hatching can be difficult; it is also a species that does not lay many eggs compared to other poultry. It can take as long as five years for geese to start reproducing adequately.

CANADA GOOSE
Branta canadensis (Linnaeus)

BRANT
Branta bernicla (Linnaeus)

HABITAT: Depending on the season, the Canada goose can be found as far north as the Arctic and as far south as Northern Mexico and the Gulf coast of the United States. In late winter/early spring it returns home to nest.

SIZE AND COLOR: From 22 to 43 inches (56 to 109 cm)

WEIGHT: From $2^{1}/_{2}$ to 11 lbs (1.25 to 5.5 kg)

FOOD: In the north, the Canada goose feeds on wild fruits, especially blueberries and black crowberries. In the south, it is fond of grain.

CHARACTERISTICS: Bird lovers and casual observers alike agree that seeing these birds flying high in the sky in a V-formation during their spring and fall migrations is a captivating and moving sight.

Sub-species: *Branta canadensis interior:* large, darker and browner.

HABITAT: The brant is a small goose that nests in the Arctic regions of North America and Eurasia. In North America, it winters along the Atlantic coast, from Massachusetts down to North Carolina.

SIZE AND COLOR: From 23 to 30 inches (58 to 76 cm)

WEIGHT: From 3 to $3^{1}/_{2}$ lbs (1.5 to 1.75 kg)

FOOD: The brant delays its northward migration until the beginning of June in order to continue feeding in the south; during its migration, it eats eelgrasses that appear at low tide or that it can pluck by ducking underwater.

CHARACTERISTICS: This small goose, which mainly lives in saltwater environments, is a favorite of hunters. It is a close relative of the Canada goose. Unlike the Canada goose, however, it does not fly in a V-formation, but in an asymmetrical formation or long wavy line. The brant is gregarious and lives in small flocks.

SNOW GOOSE
Chen caerulescens (Linnaeus)

SNOW GOOSE
(blue-morph snow goose)
Chen caerulescens

HABITAT: Snow geese are one of the most populous species of waterfowl in North America. They breed in the tundra in Alaska and northern Canada and migrate to coastal areas further south.

SIZE AND COLOR: From 25 to 30 inches (63 to 76 cm)

WEIGHT: From 6 to 7 lbs (3 to 3.5 kg)

CHARACTERISTICS: The snow goose has two color phases (or morphs): the first is blue, when it can be mistaken for the emperor goose; in the latter phase, however, the throat is black. The legs are orangey. During its white color phase, it is either white or grayish-white, with black at the tip of the wings. This small goose is exceptionally delicious.

HABITAT: The blue-morph snow goose lives in the wild, summering in northern Canada, Alaska and Greenland and traveling as far south as northern Mexico in the winter.

SIZE AND COLOR: The blue morph is a snow goose in its dark phase ("blue phase"). The adult has a white head and neck (often tinged with red), but the back part of the neck is often more or less mottled with blackish-brown. The top part of its back and the scapulars are dark brown. Its feathers are pale brown at the ends, and the legs are pinkish. The upper covert feathers are gray-blue. The immature goose has a different coloring: the head, neck, back and lower parts are slate gray.

WEIGHT: The adult ganders of the greater snow goose can weigh up to 7 lbs (3.5 kg); the females weigh a little less. Lesser snow geese weigh from $4\frac{1}{2}$ to $5\frac{1}{2}$ lbs (2.25 to 2.75 kg)

CHARACTERISTICS: *Chen caerulescens atlanticus* (or greater snow goose) is the largest snow goose, with no blue phase, whereas the *Chen caerulescens caerulescens* goose (or lesser snow goose) is smaller and goes through both coloration phases.

BEAN GOOSE
Anser fabalis (Latham)

BARNACLE GOOSE
Branta leucopsis (Bechstein)

HABITAT: This goose nests in eastern Greenland, in Iceland and occasionally in northern Canada. It is also found in the Scandinavian countries and northern Russia. Its presence is incidental in most parts of North America.

SIZE AND COLOR: Its size varies from 28 to 35 inches (71 to 89 cm). This goose has a brown neck. The back and wings are grayish-brown. The forehead and a small area at the base of the beak are white. The tail is dark brown and whitish at the end. The beak is pinkish and the legs and feet are orangey.

WEIGHT: From $3\frac{1}{2}$ to 12 lbs (1.75 to 6 kg)

CHARACTERISTICS: This goose is part of the tribe Anserini, along with the pink-footed goose (*Anser brachyrhynchus*) and Ross's goose (*Anser rossii [Cassin]*).

HABITAT: The barnacle goose lives in the wild. Like the bean goose, it nests primarily in eastern Greenland; a few specimens have been spotted in north-eastern Canada.

SIZE AND COLOR: Its head is mostly white, with a black band extending from the eye to the base of the black beak. The back of the head, neck and breast are black. Its back is bluish-gray. The beak, legs and feet are black.

WEIGHT: From $5\frac{1}{2}$ to 7 lbs (2.75 to 3.5 kg)

CHARACTERISTICS: This species resembles a small Canada goose, but is distinguished from the latter by its white forehead.

Other Wild Geese
ROSS'S GOOSE
Anser rossii or *Chen rossii*

GREATER WHITE FRONTED-GOOSE
Anser albifrons

GUINEA GOOSE

GRAY LANDES GOOSE

HABITAT: Farm.

SIZE AND COLOR: There are generally two varieties of Guinea goose: one is gray with a brownish sheen, the other is white with blue eyes. It has a long, slender head crowned with a wattle that is almost black with a white border. Its beak is small and black. Its body is elongated with strong, flat thighs.

WEIGHT: Gander, 8 to 10 lbs (4 to 5 kg); goose, 6 to 8 lbs (3 to 4 kg)

CHARACTERISTICS: This goose, which may have originated in Asia, is also known as the Chinese goose. The Guinea goose is not a descendant of the wild Greylag goose.

HABITAT: Farm.

SIZE AND COLOR: This goose is a mixture of light and dark gray, with a white abdomen and belly. The Gray Landes goose is smaller than the Toulouse goose. Its beak is orange with a pink tip.

WEIGHT: Gander, 12 to 14 lbs (6 to 7 kg); goose, 10 to 12 lbs (5 to 6 kg)

CHARACTERISTICS: This goose is a crossbreed, selected from the Production Toulouse goose. The Gray Landes goose is lighter. It produces foie gras of a higher quality and its meat is much more flavorful.

SEBASTOPOL GOOSE

TOULOUSE GOOSE

Production Toulouse (without flap)
Standard Dewlap Toulouse (with flap)

HABITAT: Accredited breeding establishment.

SIZE AND COLOR: This small, perfectly white goose has a round head and a short orange beak. Its breast is also rounded and its back has curly feathers that measure up to 16 inches (40 cm) in length. The curliness of its feathers is due to the lack of rigidity in the fine quills, measuring 1¼ to 1½ inches (3 to 4 cm) in length, which causes the feathers to ripple.

WEIGHT: Gander, 10 to 12 lbs (5 to 6 kg); goose, 8 to 10 lbs (4 to 5 kg)

CHARACTERISTICS: This accredited breed requires a large area of pastureland as it needs to roam freely. It also needs a source of water to help it maintain its white plumage.

HABITAT: Farm.

SIZE AND COLOR: The Standard Dewlap Toulouse has a large frame, broad back and dewlap. (The Production Toulouse does not have a dewlap.) Its head, back, wings and tail are dark gray, with a lighter-colored breast and thighs.

WEIGHT: Standard Dewlap Toulouse ganders, 20 to 24 lbs (10 to 12 kg); Production Toulouse ganders, 16 to 20 lbs (8 to 10 kg); goose, 14 to 18 lbs (7 to 9 kg)

CHARACTERISTICS: The Toulouse is descended from the wild goose (Graylag) and has star status among farm-raised geese.

Woodcocks, Sandpipers, Ptarmigans, Grouse and Guinea Fowl

The woodcock remains the favorite game bird in gastronomy. Saint-Just, in his epistle to Abbot of Herville, asserted the following: "The woodcock—when it is plump—is excellent game; it is always best during frosts; it is never gutted. By crushing woodcocks in a mortar, a delicious purée is produced, a rare and no less precious dish; if to this purée is added wings of pricked partridge, we obtain the highest result of culinary science. Once upon a time, when the gods descended on earth, they dined on nothing else."

This tribe or large family of shorebirds is found all over the world. Each species differs greatly in terms of size and coloring. The beak of the woodcock is usually straight, but it sometimes curves downwards or is slightly turned up; it is thinner than that of plovers; it is also soft and rather flexible along its entire length, and the tip is not distinctly hooked as with plovers. Its legs are thin, long or of average length, and their feet usually have a hind toe. Most woodcocks are gregarious and socialize in flight or in flocks on the shore, on moist ground and in salt and fresh water marshes.

The ptarmigan is a marvelous bird for gourmets! This circumpolar species lives in extremely cold environments. Its meat is of a very fine quality.

Grouse have fully or partially feathered legs. Spruce grouse live in conifer forests. The female spruce grouse resembles the ruffed grouse, but it is darker and the terminal band on its tail is blackish-brown. It also lacks a ruff on the sides of its neck.

AMERICAN WOODCOCK
Scolopax minor (Linnaeus)

COMMON SNIPE
Gallinago gallinago (Linnaeus)

HABITAT: The American woodcock nests in forests across eastern North America.

SIZE AND COLOR: From 10 to 12 inches (25 to 30 cm). It is cinnamon-colored, with a very long beak, large eyes set high on the head, and a short tail and neck.

WEIGHT: From 10 to 14 oz (300 to 400 g)

FOOD: The American woodcock feeds on worms, insects, snails and larvae.

CHARACTERISTICS: In gastronomic circles, it is considered the best of the game birds. Its cousin is the Eurasian woodcock (*Scolopax rusticola [Linnaeus]*).

HABITAT: The common snipe resides on marshy banks and shores from Alaska to the central U.S. In the winter it travels as far south as northern South America.

SIZE AND COLOR: This bird measures from 10 to 12 inches (25 to 30 cm) and displays different shades of brown and fawn. The upper parts are a mixture of yellow ochre and blackish feathers. The lower back has fawn-colored stripes. The head has a light fawn or whitish median stripe.

WEIGHT: From 7 to 10 oz (210 to 300 g)

FOOD: It feeds on worms, insects, slugs and mollusks.

CHARACTERISTICS: In spring, while flying over the lowlands, the common snipe frequently produces a low "hoo-hoo, hoo-hoo" sound. This is one of its courtship displays. The sound is produced during flight by the passage of air through the covert feathers on its tail.

SHORT-BILLED DOWITCHER
Limnodromus griseus

SOLITARY SANDPIPER
Tringa solitaria

HABITAT: The short-billed dowitcher, a member of the sandpiper family, breeds in marshy areas in the far north and depending upon where it makes its home winters on the east or west coast of North American and as far south as Brazil.

SIZE AND COLOR: From 10 to 12 inches (25 to 30 cm). It is one of the largest sandpipers in its family. Like the American woodcock and the common snipe, it has a long beak. It is cinnamon-colored and the bottom of its back is white.

WEIGHT: From 6 to 12 oz (175 to 375 g)

CHARACTERISTICS: This large Scolopacidae family is made up of many species including sandpipers, red knot, curlews, godwits, turnstones, snipes and woodcocks. In Europe, hunting is permitted for the Eurasian curlew, the black-tailed godwit, the red knot and the common snipe.

HABITAT: Unlike other sandpipers, the solitary sandpiper prefers to live in calm ponds and small lakes in wooded areas. It can, however, be found in more open areas, on muddy banks and next to small rivers.

SIZE AND COLOR: Its size varies from 7 to 9 inches (18 to 23 cm). The upper parts, including the rump, are very dark brown with a slightly green reflection, and white speckles. The legs are dark olive-green. The axillary feathers are marked by wide black and white stripes.

WEIGHT: From 6 to 10 oz (175 to 300 g)

CHARACTERISTICS: It migrates in the spring and fall. Its beak, which is soft and rather flexible along its whole length, is thinner than that of plovers. In Europe, hunting is permitted for the common redshank (*Trianga totanus*), the common greenshank (*Tringa nebularia*) and the green sandpiper (*Trianga ochropus*). In Quebec, the solitary sandpiper is a protected species, so it is forbidden to hunt it.

WILLOW PTARMIGAN
Lagopus lagopus (Linnaeus)

ROCK PTARMIGAN
Lagopus muta (Montin)

HABITAT: This large bird resides on the Arctic tundra. It lives permanently in the areas where it nests, although it does sometimes migrate.

SIZE AND COLOR: From 14 to 17 inches (from 35 to 43 cm). Larger than the rock ptarmigan, the willow ptarmigan changes plumage three times a year. Unlike the rock ptarmigan, its white winter plumage does not feature a black stripe on both sides of the eye. Ptarmigans are easily recognizable by their feathered toes.

WEIGHT: From 14 oz to $1\frac{1}{2}$ lbs (400 to 750 g)

FOOD: Willow buds.

CHARACTERISTICS: It lives in extremely cold environments on a selective diet, and its meat is highly prized in gastronomic circles.

HABITAT: The rock ptarmigan lives farther north than the other ptarmigans. During nesting season, the rock ptarmigan prefers barer, drier and more elevated terrain than the willow ptarmigan. In winter and during migrations, both species often share the same habitat.

SIZE AND COLOR: This magnificent bird of 13 to 16 inches (33 to 40 cm) in length has the particular characteristic of changing its plumage with the season, allowing it to blend in with its environment. In summer, the back, breast and flanks of the male are russet-brown spotted with black. Note the presence of a red wattle above the eye. The wings and the belly are white in all seasons. In the fall, the plumage turns gray, spotted with black. In winter, both the male and female are white with a black tail.

WEIGHT: From 10 oz to $1\frac{1}{4}$ lbs (300 to 625 g)

FOOD: It feeds on small berries on the tundra and the buds of shrubs.

CHARACTERISTICS: The rock ptarmigan lives in extremely cold environments and has a selective diet. Its meat is highly prized in gastronomic circles.

RUFFED GROUSE
Bonasa umbellus (Linnaeus)

SPRUCE GROUSE
Dendragapus canadensis (Linnaeus)

HABITAT: The ruffed grouse lives in the forests and along the shores of streams in large parts of North America. This species is particularly fond of forests with deciduous regrowth, mixed forests and the banks of rivers bordered with alder and willows.

SIZE AND COLOR: From 16 to 19 inches (40 to 48 cm). The ruffed grouse has a small crest on its head, a black or reddish-brown neck ruff and several stripes on its tail.

FOOD: The ruffed grouse feeds on berries, buds (particularly fir), leaves, flowers and grass tips.

CHARACTERISTICS: The ruffed grouse is also known as "drummer" or "thunder" chicken. There are nine sub-species known in Canada alone.

HABITAT: The spruce grouse lives year-round in northern conifer forests up to the tree line, and across Canada and part of the northern United States.

SIZE AND COLOR: The spruce grouse, which measures from 15 to 17 inches (38 to 43 cm), is much smaller than the wood grouse. The male, with its black breast, is easy to identify. The females more or less resemble the ruffed grouse, but they have bands on their backs and their shorter tails lack a subterminal band. They also do not have neck ruffs.

WEIGHT: From 3 to $5\frac{1}{2}$ lbs (1.5 to 2.75 kg)

FOOD: It feeds mainly on conifer needles and buds, particularly in winter. In summer, it enjoys wild berries.

CHARACTERISTICS: The spruce grouse is not a suspicious bird; unlike the ruffed grouse, it has never learned to fear humans. Its lack of timidity means that it can often be killed with a stick or a stone.

WOOD GROUSE or COMMON CAPERCAILLIE
Tetrao urogallus

GUINEA FOWL

HABITAT: Formerly widespread in red maple forests, this grouse is now found in conifer and mixed forests, peat bogs, on the edges of forests and in clearings.

SIZE AND COLOR: Imposing in size (from 34 to 40 inches/85 to 100 cm), it is the largest of the gallinaceans. Its plumage is dark and its breast is midnight blue with green reflections. The tail fans out in a semicircle. The wood grouse has red wattles above the eyes and a dark bristly beard.

WEIGHT: Males, about 7 lbs (3.5 kg); females, from 5 to 6 lbs (2.5 to 3 kg)

CHARACTERISTICS: The wood grouse is solitary and sedentary. Extremely timid, it fears humans and hates being disturbed.

HABITAT: Farm.

SIZE AND COLOR: The guinea fowl is gray, with silver pearls all over its stocky, compact body. It has red barbs on its short, wide head. Its featherless face is a bluish-white.

WEIGHT: From $2\frac{1}{2}$ to 4 lbs (1.25 to 2 kg)

CHARACTERISTICS: The guinea fowl was brought over from Africa by the Portuguese, and was then introduced to North America. It once lived in the wild, but has since been domesticated. Along the centuries it has borne several names, including "original fowl" and "guinea hen."

Partridges, Northern Bobwhites, Pigeons, Pheasant, Quail and Turkey

Partridge, pheasant and turkey bear similarities to hens in terms of the shape of their legs, their toes and their featherless nostrils. A few species have leg spurs, while others have a featherless patch on their head of varying sizes. The tail may be short or long, and can also be quite intricate. This extensive group includes some of the most beautiful birds. The gray or Hungarian partridge, which is very robust, was imported to North America as game. It is found along the length of the border between the U.S. and Canada. The rock partridge is often selected to be farm-raised. The sub-family Tetraonidae includes the ruffed grouse, which may be gray or red. It has thin stripes on its tail with a black terminal band.

Pigeon, introduced as a dish in North America only a few years ago, is highly prized in Europe. The rock dove (domestic pigeon) is just starting to appear in markets, but one must use caution when purchasing it, as its meat has a tendency to be firm and tough. Many different species of pigeon can be found living wild in tropical regions.

Native to Eurasia, most of the pheasant in North America are farm-raised. Pheasant meat is relatively dry, but when properly prepared it is delicious.

GRAY PARTRIDGE
Perdix perdix (Linnaeus)

RED-LEGGED PARTRIDGE
Alectoris rufa

HABITAT: The gray partridge is a species of foreign origin. It is found along the U.S./Canada border in flat farmland.

SIZE AND COLOR: The gray partridge has a plump body (12 inches/30 cm in length). It is recognizable by its russet head, throat and tail. The grayish feathers are striped with russet, the breast is gray, and the grayish-brown back is striped with yellow. In the male, the scapular and median covert feathers of the wing only bear one well-marked longitudinal stripe.

WEIGHT: From 12 oz to 1 lb (375 to 500 g)

FOOD: The gray partridge feeds on insects, larvae, worms and seeds.

CHARACTERISTICS: This bird, which is very hard to approach, takes flight in a clatter of wings while making clucking sounds. It flies and glides quite rapidly while remaining at a low altitude. In flight, its reddish tail is highly visible.

HABITAT: The red-legged partridge can be found in Europe, where it lives on hilly, dry and rocky terrain. Pastures bordered by forests are its favorite habitat. A varied landscape of hedges, crops, prairies, vineyards, fallow land and brush is particularly favorable. The presence of water is also essential. This partridge is not found in North America.

SIZE AND COLOR: From 14 to 15 inches (35 to 38 cm). This partridge is recognizable by its red beak and legs, as well as its flanks of bright and contrasting colors striped with russet, white and black. The top of its body is russet-brown, and the top of its head is gray.

WEIGHT: From 12 oz to 1¼ lbs (375 to 625 g)

CHARACTERISTICS: The red-legged partridge happily perches in trees and shrubs or on low walls.

ROCK PARTRIDGE
Alectoris graeca

NORTHERN BOBWHITE
Colinus virginianus (Linnaeus)

HABITAT: In Europe, this bird lives in the wild. In North America, the Rock Partridge can be found in the wild and on farms. It can be found at high elevations, on rocky and sunny mountainsides and in stony ravines.

SIZE AND COLOR: From 13 to 14 inches (33 to 35 cm). It resembles the red-legged partridge, but is distinguished by a large white dewlap under the throat, clearly outlined by a black collar. The feathers on its sides have vertical black stripes. Its underbody is brown with a grayish, not reddish-brown, sheen.

WEIGHT: From 10 to 15 oz (300 to 450 g)

FOOD: In summer, the rock partridge feeds on berries, tender leaves, crop seeds, spiders, insects and larvae. In winter it eats juniper berries.

CHARACTERISTICS: The meat of the farm-raised partridge does not have the same flavor as wild rock partridge, even if farms try to replicate its natural diet as closely as possible.

HABITAT: It is native to Mexico, the Caribbean and North America. It feeds on grain crops and corn.

SIZE AND COLOR: From 10 to 11 inches (25 to 28 cm). The male has a white throat and brow stripe bordered in black. On the female, the light areas are buff rather than white, and the darker areas are a reddish-brown. Scalloped stripes are visible on the flanks. The reddish upper parts distinguish the northern bobwhite from other bobwhites.

WEIGHT: From $5\frac{1}{4}$ to $8\frac{1}{2}$ oz (160 to 270 g)

CHARACTERISTICS: The northern bobwhite differs from other bobwhites in its distinctive facial markings and the reddish coloring of its upper part. Its small size distinguishes it from grouse, partridge and pheasant.

ROCK DOVE
(domestic pigeon)
Columbia livia

RING-NECKED PHEASANT
Phasianus colchicus (Linnaeus)

HABITAT: The Rock Dove likes trees and lives in fir and other coniferous forests. Introduced to North America some 400 years ago, when it was imported as a domestic breed, it has returned to its wild state in urban areas. It can also be found on farms along with other families of pigeon, including the Texan pioneer, the French mondain, the Roman and the king pigeon.

SIZE AND COLOR: Measuring 11 to 14 inches (28 to 35 cm) in length, the rock dove has two dark bands on its wings, reddish feet and a dark beak. It is easily recognized in flight by its white rump patch. It is smaller than its European cousin, the wood pigeon, which can measure up to 17 inches (43 cm) in length.

WEIGHT: From 14 oz to 1½ lbs (400 to 750 g)

CHARACTERISTICS: In the wild, the rock dove eats the seeds of fir trees and other conifers as well as acorns. It has also been known to eat snails and earthworms. When selecting a farm-raised pigeon for the table, choose only the squab. A squab is a pigeon that has not yet left the nest. After this stage, its meat becomes very tough.

HABITAT: These magnificent birds are native to Asia but are rarely spotted in the wild in North America.

SIZE AND COLOR: They measure 22 to 34 inches (55 to 85 cm) in height. The pheasant is one of the most colorful birds. It has a brilliant green head with red wattles around its eyes and usually a white band around its neck. It has a rust- and fawn-colored body with many feathers that have a golden sheen. The female is smaller and duller in color than the male.

WEIGHT: From 2 to 3 lbs (1 to 1.5 kg)

CHARACTERISTICS: The individual pheasants that were introduced in North America belonged to a number of different subspecies. The population seen today is hybrid and varied: it is preferable not to attempt to classify the North American population beyond the species (*Phasianus colchicus*).

QUAIL
Coturnix coturnix (Linnaeus)

WILD TURKEY
Meleagris gallopavo (Linnaeus)

HABITAT: Quail were introduced to North America in the late 1800s. Today, most are farm-raised and also live in the wild. It should be noted, however, that the flavor of these small birds in the wild is incomparable.

SIZE AND COLOR: The Japanese quail (*Coturnix japonica*) weighs about 4 oz (125 g). The American quail (*Coturnix coturnix*), however, is heavier at about 7 oz (210 g). The quail looks like a miniature partridge. It is brown on top, with russet-yellow stripes running down and across; the head is darker than its back. It has a russet throat and yellowish-white belly. The sides of the belly and breast are russet. The irises are a light brownish-red, the beak is gray and the legs are red or pale yellow.

WEIGHT: From 4 to 7 oz (125 to 210 g)

FOOD: Seeds, leaf tips, buds and insects.

CHARACTERISTICS: Its diet in a farm environment is obviously different than in the wild so it is important to recognize this when preparing the bird.

HABITAT: The wild turkey was once almost extinct in North America but in recent years the species has flourished. This turkey is also raised domestically.

SIZE AND COLOR: From 36 to 49 inches (91 to 124 cm). Of a coppery-bronze color spotted with white. Its head is large and bare, set on a body with grayish-blue wattles. The breast is large.

WEIGHT: Depending on age and sex, its weight can vary from 10 to 40 lbs (5 to 20 kg)

CHARACTERISTICS: The wild breed greatly resembles the domestic breed. The domestic turkey originates from a Mexican sub-species and can be distinguished from the wild turkey by the whitish or buff part of its feathers.

RED ARDENNES TURKEY

BRONZE TURKEY

HABITAT: Farm.

SIZE AND COLOR: This species of turkey has a full breast and a humped back. Its plumage is of a tawny red color with lighter areas. Its head and neck are bare. Its grayish-blue wattles can turn red when the animal is upset.

WEIGHT: Male, from 18 to 20 lbs (9 to 10 kg) (at times up to 40 lbs/20 kg); female, from 10 to 18 lbs (5 to 9 kg)

CHARACTERISTICS: Tawny orange (lighter for the female) with a russet back and copper reflections. The color becomes increasingly lighter descending toward the tail. The wings are white and pale russet. This representative of the French turkey family appeared on the markets of Ardennes towards the middle of the century. It was once considered a member of the French turkey family in the same way as the albino turkey. It acquired its name around 1850. Although its meat is succulent, this turkey has been somewhat supplanted by the white Beltsville turkey.

HABITAT: Farm.

COLOR: Bright copper-bronze with coppery-green reflections.

WEIGHT: Male, from 20 to 30 lbs (10 to 15 kg); female, from 12 to 16 lbs (6 to 8 kg)

CHARACTERISTICS: Once hunted in America, this species of turkey made its first appearance in Europe via Spain around 1530. The French and the English took an interest in it three centuries later. In America, the domestication of this wild animal dates back to the 16th century.

BELTSVILLE TURKEY
More than 70 percent of Christmas turkeys belong to this species.

Thrushes, Larks, Lapwings and Plovers

The thrush is a migratory bird. Its meat is very flavorful, particularly in the fall during the wine-harvesting season. Its plumage is gray, white and brown.

The lark is a migratory bird of great delicacy that greets the dawn in the countryside. It is particularly succulent come crop and wine harvesting season. It is recognizable by its gray plumage, darker on the belly, and its pointed beak. The lark flies very fast and at high altitudes, perpendicular to the ground. Although the lark may be consumed in other parts of the world, it is generally not used in North American cuisine.

The plover and the lapwing are wading birds that are generally found in ponds and marshes near the ocean. The plover can be recognized by its short black beak. Its black wings are spotted with greenish-yellow and its breast is dotted with green and yellow patches. The lapwing has thick black plumage on its back and a crest on its head. Its thighs and belly are white.

FIELDFARE
Turdus pilaris

REDWING
Turdus iliacus

HABITAT: This member of the thrush family is rarely found in North America, but it is widespread in Europe from Iceland to the Middle East.

SIZE AND COLOR: It has contrasting plumage. Slate-gray head and rump; brownish back; russet throat and breast. It measures approximately 11 inches (28 cm) in length with a wingspan of up to 18 inches (46 cm). The folded wing measures 6 inches (15 cm), and the tail just over 4 inches (10 cm).

CHARACTERISTICS: The fieldfare is the largest thrush. In spite of its reputation as fine gastronomical fare, this little bird rarely features in today's cuisine, and is often banned from being hunted.

HABITAT: Thrushes and robins that are part of the family Turdidae prefer diversified habitats that are a combination of hedges rich in berries, groves and cultivated areas. The redwing seeks out mistletoe trees.

SIZE AND COLOR: The redwing is recognizable by its distinct white eyebrows, which differentiate it from the song thrush. The anterior part of its wings is russet. It measures from 7 to 9 inches (18 to 23 cm) in length.

CHARACTERISTICS: This small thrush is native to Europe. Its presence is incidental in North America. The hunting of redwing thrush is permitted in Europe.

HORNED LARK
Eremophila alpestris (Linnaeus)

NORTHERN LAPWING
Vanellus vanellus (Linnaeus)

HABITAT: The horned lark is a land bird that lives in open terrain—Arctic tundra, coasts and in cultivated fields when bare.

SIZE AND COLOR: This land bird is larger than a sparrow, with a brown back and a thin beak. The horned lark is recognizable by its black throat and the sickle-shaped black stripe that stretches from the beak to just under the eyes. The tiny black ear tufts on the crown are often difficult to see. From 7 to 8 inches (18 to 20 cm) in length.

WEIGHT: From 1 to 1$\frac{1}{2}$ oz (30 to 45 g)

FOOD: This species looks for food on the ground, eating mainly insects, grass tips and seeds.

CHARACTERISTICS: The hunting of horned lark is currently forbidden in most countries. The hunting of skylark is permitted in Europe.

HABITAT: The northern lapwing mainly nests in Eurasia, from the British Isles to the Faroe Islands, in northern Sweden, in Russia up to a latitude of 62°N and in Siberia up to a latitude of 57°N.

SIZE AND COLOR: Measuring 11 to 12 inches (28 to 30 cm) in length, the northern lapwing is characterized by a long black crest on its head. The neck and the breast contrast with the white belly. The top of the body is dark with green reflections. The white tail is tipped with a black barb.

WEIGHT: From 5 to 10 oz (150 to 300 g)

FOOD: It feeds on insects, worms, small slugs and larvae.

CHARACTERISTICS: The northern lapwing is a fairly large plover that bears a long ragged crest. From a distance, it appears black and white, but up close, a green shimmer on the upper body can be discerned. It has a large black band across its breast. Hunting northern lapwing is permitted in Europe.

GASTRONOMIC VALUE: Its meat is best towards the month of November. The northern lapwing's eggs are highly prized, but these are protected.

AMERICAN GOLDEN PLOVER
Pluvialis dominica

AMERICAN COOT
Fulica americana

HABITAT: The golden plover is a typical tundra bird that migrates from Alaska and northern Canada to South America.

SIZE AND COLOR: In the summer, the golden plover is recognizable by its plumage that is finely speckled with gold on top. It has a large head with a short beak, a black belly, throat, cheeks and neck. It measures from 10 to 11 inches (25 to 28 cm) in length.

WEIGHT: From 5 to 7 oz (150 to 210 g)

FOOD: It feeds on insects, worms, larvae, beetles and snails.

CHARACTERISTICS: Hunting golden plover (*Pluvialis apricaria*) is permitted in Europe.

GASTRONOMIC VALUE: A bird with an especially delicate flavor that is best eaten roasted.

HABITAT: The American coot is a water bird that mainly lives in freshwater marshes and ponds, lakes, slow-running streams and on marshy ground.

SIZE AND COLOR: The common moorhen and the American coot are marsh birds of a dark gray color (that often looks black). They are the size of small ducks, but their beak resembles that of the domestic hen and their head is much slimmer than that of ducks. The white beak of the coot, as well as the absence of a white stripe along its flanks, distinguishes it from the common moorhen. It measures about 12 to 16 inches (30 to 40 cm) in length.

CHARACTERISTICS: The American coot is part of the family Rallidae, which includes cranes, rails and gallinules. This bird lacks strength for flapping its wings and is rather slow; it prefers to thread its way through the dense vegetation of marshes.

Duck recipes

Mallard Duck Breasts in Brioche with Apricots

Serves 4

Tip

To thicken stock, use 3 tsp (15 mL) cornstarch mixed with 6 tsp (30 mL) cold water.

Serving Tip

Serve extra-fine green beans on the side.

Variations

Instead of mallard duck, try Muscovy duck, mule duck, Khaki Campbell duck, Pekin (Long Island or Brome Lake) duck or northern pintail duck.

Brioche Dough

3¼ cups	all-purpose flour	800 mL
1 oz	fresh baker's yeast (approx.)	30 g
⅔ cup	warm water	150 mL
2 tbsp	granulated sugar	30 mL
2 tsp	salt	10 mL
1 cup	unsalted butter, at room temperature	250 mL
4	eggs	4
2	egg yolks	2

Mallard Duck

4	breasts (each 8 to 10 oz/250 to 300 g)	4
	Salt and freshly ground black pepper	
⅓ cup	vegetable oil	75 mL
¼ cup	butter	60 mL
12	dried apricots	12
2	egg yolks	2
	Milk	
1⅓ cups	thickened brown duck stock or store-bought equivalent (see Tip, left)	325 mL
	Armagnac	

1. *Brioche Dough:* Twelve hours before you plan to make the duck, make the dough. Place flour in a bowl. Make a well in center and add yeast and warm water. Add sugar, salt, butter, 4 whole eggs and 2 egg yolks. Mix, then knead dough. Cover with plastic wrap. Let rise in refrigerator for 12 hours. It should double in volume. Knead dough again. Set aside.

2. *Mallard Duck:* Preheat oven to 450°F (230°C). Season duck breasts with salt and pepper. Heat oil and butter in a heavy-bottomed skillet over medium heat. Add duck breasts and sear both sides, starting with fatty side. Remove from heat and let cool to room temperature for 5 minutes.

3. Divide dough into four balls and flatten with a rolling pin. Lay 3 dried apricots lengthwise on each flattened piece of dough. Place a duck breast on each piece of dough, then wrap in dough. Place on a tray, taking care to leave space between each breast. Cover with a dishcloth or foil, then let brioche pastry "expand" by placing on top of the stove for no more than 25 minutes. The heat emanating from the oven will be sufficient to make the dough rise.

4. Meanwhile, prepare egg wash by beating egg yolks with a little milk. Once dough has risen, baste generously with egg wash using a brush and place in 450°F (230°C) oven, 15 to 20 minutes.

5. Serve with thickened brown duck stock. Add Armagnac to flavor.

Roasted American Black Duck with Root Vegetables

Serves 4

Tips

Before cooking, remove the thighs for this recipe and use them for another that calls for thighs. In this recipe, the breasts are cooked to *à la goutte de sang*, a French cooking term that refers to a level of medium-rare doneness, which is determined by pricking meat with a skewer to see if a drop of fat appears with a pink dot in the center. The thighs would not be cooked in this time so need to be removed before cooking and used in another recipe.

A *mirepoix* is a mixture of equal amounts of chopped celery, onions and carrots. Raw, roasted or sautéed with butter or olive oil, it is the flavor base for a wide variety of dishes, such as stocks, soups, stews and sauces.

Variations

Use Pekin (Long Island or Brome Lake) duck, Muscovy duck, mule duck, mallard duck or Northern pintail duck instead of American black duck.

● Preheat oven to 450°F (230°C)

2	American Black ducks (preferably female) (each 1¾ to 2 lbs/875 g to 1 kg), thighs and legs removed (see Tips, left)	2
	Salt and freshly ground black pepper	
1½ cups	finely diced onions, carrots and celery, cooked and cooled (see Tips, left)	375 mL
2	bay leaves	2
2	sprigs thyme	2
8	juniper berries	8
2	thin slices pork fatback (4 by 2 inches/10 by 5 cm)	2
	Salt and freshly ground black pepper	
¼ cup	unsalted butter	60 mL
¼ cup	oil	60 mL
4	small parsnips	4
4	small carrots with tops	4
4	small parsley roots	4
1	Spanish onion, cut into 4 pieces, or any other root vegetable	1
⅓ cup	shallots, minced	75 mL
¾ cup	dry white wine	175 mL
1¼ cups	unthickened brown duck stock or store-bought equivalent	300 mL
2½ tbsp	butter, at room temperature	37 mL

1. Season ducks on inside with salt and black pepper. Stuff ducks with finely diced vegetable mirepoix, bay leaves, thyme and juniper berries.

2. Truss ducks, then wrap in fatback (see page 366). Generously season with salt and black pepper on outside. Heat butter and oil in an ovenproof skillet, preferably cast-iron. Add ducks and sear in preheated oven for 10 minutes. Remove pork fatback.

3. Reduce oven temperature to 400°F (200°C) and return ducks to oven for 25 minutes per pound (g). Breasts are cooked when pierced with a skewer and a droplet of fat appears with a tiny spot of pink in the center. This is what is known as *cuisson à la goutte de sang* (cooked to the drop of blood) (see Tips, page 68). Note that the thighs will not yet be cooked and why they must be removed first.

4. Meanwhile, cook parsnips, carrots, parsley roots and onion in salted water. Drain thoroughly, then place in the cooking juice for a few minutes. Adjust seasoning.

5. Remove ducks from oven and cover with foil. Keep warm on the stove. Remove excess cooking fat from pot, add shallots and white wine. Reduce, then add brown duck stock. Cook for a few minutes, then whisk in butter.

Duck à l'Orange

Serves 4

Tips

If you prefer, cook the poultry to the USDA recommendations (165°F/74°C).

Blanched orange zest can be substituted for orange segments.

Variations

Instead of the Pekin duck breasts, use goose, guinea fowl or all species of duck and chicken.

Flambé

Flambé is a French term meaning "flamed" or "flaming," a cooking procedure in which dishes have been doused in liquor and set aflame. If an alcohol hasn't been suggested, use an 80-proof liquor/liqueur or 40% alcohol by volume for flambéing. Choose liquors or liqueurs that are complementary to the food being cooked, such as fruit-flavored brandies for fruits and desserts and whiskey or cognac for meats.

- Meat thermometer

2	seedless oranges	2
2½ tbsp	Cognac	37 mL
2½ tbsp	Grand Marnier	37 mL
4	Pekin (Long Island or Brome Lake) duck breasts	4
	Salt and freshly ground black pepper	
¼ cup	butter	60 mL
¼ cup	oil	60 mL
1⅓ cups	Orange Sauce (page 359)	325 mL

1. Peel oranges and remove white skin. Separate oranges into segments. Combine Cognac and Grand Marnier in a medium bowl. Add orange segments and soak. Set aside.

2. Season duck breasts with salt and black pepper. Heat butter and oil in a skillet over medium heat. Cook duck breasts, starting on fatty side, until a thermometer inserted into the center registers 136°F (58°C) (see Tips, left).

3. Remove excess fat from skillet. Flambé breasts (see left) with the spirits used for soaking the orange segments. Remove duck breasts and set aside. Pour Orange Sauce into skillet and heat. Adjust seasoning. A few minutes before serving, add orange segments to sauce and heat.

Braised Duck with Olives

Tips

For the duck, use Rouen, mule or Muscovy duck.

Why peanut oil? Peanut oil has a very high smoke point so it is ideal for cooking at higher temperatures. The smoke point is the measurement of how much heat an oil can sustain before breaking down, spoiling the quality of its flavor and smell. The higher the smoke point, the better it is for frying.

Variations

Instead of duck, use goose, guinea fowl or chicken.

Bouquet Garni
This aromatic seasoning consists of parsley stems, a sprig of thyme and one or two bay leaves. They are tied together with string to facilitate handling.

• Ovenproof casserole dish

1	duck (3¼ lbs/1.625 kg) (see Tips, left)	1
1	carrot, finely diced	1
1	Spanish onion, finely diced	1
1	celery stalk, finely diced	1
1	bouquet garni	1
30	green or black olives, pitted	30
1⅔ cups	white wine	400 mL
⅓ cup	peanut oil (see Tips, left)	75 mL
2 cups	unthickened brown duck stock or store-bought equivalent	500 mL
10 oz	potatoes, diced	300 g
	Salt and freshly ground black pepper	

1. Cut duck into 8 pieces, leaving the bones. Place duck pieces in a large container and add carrot, onion, celery, bouquet garni, olives and white wine. Let stand at room temperature for 25 minutes. This will help the duck soak up more of the alcohol in the wine.

2. Preheat oven to 200°F (100°C). Heat peanut oil in a skillet and fry duck pieces until golden brown, 3 minutes per side. Place duck pieces in an ovenproof casserole dish with all of its aromatic elements. Add duck stock and cook slowly in preheated oven for 4 hours. The longer the cooking time, the tastier the dish will be. Halfway through the cooking, add diced potatoes to the sauce and finish cooking.

3. Remove duck pieces, olives and potatoes and place on a serving platter. Pour sauce through a sieve. Adjust seasoning as well as consistency, if necessary. Serve duck with sauce, olives and potatoes.

Duck with Rougemont Cider

Serves 4

Tips

Thicken stock with 3 tsp (15 mL) cornstarch and 6 tsp (30 mL) water.

A white roux is an equal mixture of butter and flour. Heat $\frac{1}{3}$ cup (75 mL) butter in a medium pot and add $\frac{1}{3}$ cup (75 mL) all-purpose flour and cook for a further few minutes

Variations

You could also use the thighs of goose, guinea fowl, turkey or chicken.

Cinnamon

Bark of the cinnamon tree, stripped of its epidermis, cinnamon is found in the form of small tubes or ground. Its flavor is strong and it should be used sparingly.

4	Pekin (Long Island or Brome Lake) duck thighs	4
1	bottle (12 oz/341 mL) dry (hard) apple cider, such as Rougemont	1
8	cooking apples, such Russet or Honey Crisp, peeled and finely diced	8
8	medium-size whole shallots	8
1	small piece cinnamon or $\frac{1}{2}$ tsp (2 mL) ground cinnamon	1
4	cloves garlic	4
	Salt and freshly ground black pepper	
$\frac{1}{3}$ cup	peanut or vegetable oil, divided	75 mL
$\frac{1}{3}$ cup	Calvados	75 mL
$1\frac{1}{4}$ cups	thickened brown duck stock or store-bought equivalent (see Tips, left)	300 mL
	White Roux, optional (see Tips, left)	

1. Place duck thighs in a large container. Add cider, apples, shallots, cinnamon and garlic. Season with salt and pepper. Pour 4 tsp (20 mL) of the oil over top. Let stand at room temperature for 25 minutes.

2. Heat remaining peanut oil in a skillet over medium-high heat. Add duck thighs and brown until golden brown, 5 minutes per side.

3. Remove duck thighs and place in a deep skillet or a large, shallow pot over medium heat on stovetop. (This is to allow some moisture to evaporate.) Flambé with Calvados (see page 68). Add duck stock then all soaking ingredients except diced apple, which will be set aside. Reduce heat to low to continue cooking process.

4. At end of cooking, remove pieces of duck and shallots. Pour sauce through fine-mesh strainer. Thicken sauce with a little white roux, if necessary. Pour through fine-mesh strainer again, then place back in skillet with pieces of duck, shallots and diced apple. Simmer for 2 to 3 minutes. Serve hot.

Mule Duck with Maple

In memory of a great chef, Renaud Cyr

Serves 4

Tips

Fresh bay leaves, which are quite fragrant, have been used throughout these recipes. If you have dry bay leaves double the amount called for in the recipes.

An *aiguillette* is a thin slice taken from the duck breast and cut in the direction of the fiber (lengthwise).

Serving Tip

You can accompany this dish with 1 cup (250 mL) thickened duck stock flavored with ½ cup (125 mL) maple syrup liqueur, such as Sortilège, and sautéed potatoes and extra-fine green beans.

Variations

Use goose, guinea fowl, all species of duck or chicken.

● Preheat oven to 450°F (230°C)

1	duck (3¾ to 4½ lbs/1.875 to 2.25 kg), thighs and legs removed (see Tips, page 66)	1
	Salt and freshly ground black pepper	
1	Spanish onion	1
2	cloves garlic	2
½	sprig thyme	½
¼	bay leaf (see Tips, left)	¼
¼ cup	peanut or vegetable oil	60 mL
¼ cup	unsalted butter	60 mL
⅓ cup	white wine	75 mL
½ cup	maple or apple cider vinegar	125 mL
5 oz	maple sugar	150 g
⅓ cup	maple syrup	75 mL

1. Season duck with salt and pepper. Stuff duck with onion, garlic, thyme and bay leaf. Truss duck (see page 365). Heat oil and butter in a baking dish. Place duck in dish and roast in preheated oven, basting regularly, 30 to 35 minutes.

2. Meanwhile, combine white wine, maple vinegar, maple sugar and maple syrup in a small saucepan over medium-high heat and cook until syrupy and the consistency that coats the back of a tablespoon.

3. Halfway through roasting, baste duck with maple mixture and cook until center of breast is done *à la goutte de sang* (see Tips, page 68). Breasts are cooked when pierced with a skewer and a droplet of fat appears with a tiny spot of pink in the center. Note that the thighs will not yet be cooked and why they must be removed first.

4. *To Serve:* Serve breasts as aiguillettes (see Tips, left) or in pieces.

Duck Thighs Confit

Serves 4

Tip
"Au piqué" means that meat is done when a knife tip can be easily inserted and removed.

Variations

Use the thighs from pheasant, guinea fowl, grouse, chicken or all species of duck.

***Duck Gizzard Confit:* Follow the method using 5 oz (150 g) of gizzards per person. Let stand in salt for 6 hours.**

Juniper berries
The juniper tree produces dark berries that are used in cooking, among other things. They are a prized ingredient in game and fowl recipes.

- Candy/deep-fry thermometer

4	Pekin (Long Island or Brome Lake) duck thighs	4
2 tbsp	chopped fresh or dried rosemary sprigs	30 mL
2 tbsp	dried thyme sprigs	30 mL
3	juniper berries, crushed	3
½	bay leaf or ¼ tsp (1 mL) bay leaf powder	½
4	cloves garlic, crushed	4
4 cups	coarse salt	1 L
4 cups	duck fat	1 L

1. Place duck thighs on a baking sheet. Rub with rosemary, thyme, juniper berries, bay leaf and garlic. Sprinkle coarse salt evenly over thighs and set aside, covered, in the refrigerator, 6 to 8 hours.

2. Heat duck fat to 195°F (90°C) in a large saucepan.

3. Thoroughly wash duck thighs, then pat dry to remove as much moisture as possible. Place duck thighs in fat and cook at 195°F (90°C) for 2 to 3 hours. It is very important not to exceed this temperature. To check doneness, stick a knife into the thickest part of the thigh; if it can be removed easily, the thighs are done. Preserve thighs in duck fat. Remove thighs and place in a large container, cover with duck fat and let cool in the refrigerator.

Duck Salmis

Tip

The success of a duck salmis recipe rests on two very important elements:

1. The duck must have been killed through strangulation for it to retain its blood.

2. To respect the cooking times, if using both the thighs and breasts, they must be cooked separately.

Variations

Instead of duck, use the breasts or thighs from pheasant, goose, pigeon (squab) or grouse.

Salmis

It is a type of stew made from different cooked meats that were cut up and used to make a sauce. An abbreviation of the French *salmigondis* (*sal*: salt and *condir*: to season), it suggests a highly seasoned preparation.

- Preheat oven to 400°F (200°C)

4	bone-in duck thighs or breasts (each 6 to 7 oz/175 to 210 g)	4
²⁄₃ cup	butter, divided	150 mL
8	shallots, minced	8
1¹⁄₃ cups	red wine	325 mL
²⁄₃ cup	unthickened brown duck stock or store-bought equivalent	150 mL
¹⁄₃ cup	Armagnac	75 mL
	Salt and freshly ground black pepper	

1. Roast duck thighs or breasts in preheated oven to *à la goutte de sang* doneness (see Tips, pages 66 and 68). Debone meat and roughly chop bones to collect blood and juice.

2. Heat half of the butter in a roasting tray over medium heat. Place deboned thighs or breasts in dish, then sprinkle with minced shallots. Add red wine, juice and blood. Simmer for 10 minutes, then remove pieces of duck. Set aside. Pour juice through fine-mesh strainer into a bowl.

3. Heat brown duck stock in a saucepan and add cooking juice. Finish sauce with Armagnac and remaining butter. Adjust seasoning with salt and pepper and pour juice over duck pieces.

Scoter Duck with Choucroute

Serves 4

To Mr. Sylvain Trapp, choucroute producer in the Gaspé region, winner of the 2008 Renaud Cyr award for his contributions to Quebec gastronomy

Serving Tip

Serve hot, accompanied by steamed potatoes.

Variations

Use goose, grouse, turkey or chicken instead of duck.

Choucroute

Choucroute or sauerkraut consists of finely shredded cabbage fermented in brine. It can be bought in jars or in bulk. It is prized in Eastern Europe. Some countries have made it their national dish.

- Preheat oven to 350°F (180°C)
- Large ovenproof pot

⅓ cup	duck fat or lard	75 mL
2	Spanish onions, peeled and finely diced	2
2	Russet apples, pears or quinces, peeled and finely diced	2
1¾ lbs	blanched drained rinsed sauerkraut (choucroute) (see left)	875 g
2	whole cloves garlic	2
½	bay leaf	½
½	sprig thyme	½
6	juniper berries	6
2	bottles (each 12 oz/341 mL) blonde (pale) ale	2
1	Scoter duck	1
	Salt and freshly ground black pepper	
⅔ cup	oil	150 mL

1. Heat duck fat in large ovenproof pot over medium heat. Add diced onions and apples and sweat, 2 to 3 minutes. Add sauerkraut, garlic cloves, bay leaf, thyme, juniper berries and ale. Cover and cook slowly in preheated oven for 30 minutes.

2. Meanwhile, cut duck into 8 pieces. Season with salt and pepper. Heat oil in a large skillet over medium-high heat and brown each piece. Add pieces of duck to sauerkraut mixture and continue to cook for 30 to 40 minutes, depending on the size of the duck. Adjust seasoning.

Duck Aiguillettes "à la Goutte de Sang" with Sour Cherry Sauce

Variations

Use the breasts of goose, pigeon (squab) or all types of ducks.

Aiguillettes

An *aiguillette* is a thin slice taken from the duck breast and cut in the direction of the fiber (lengthwise).

Sour cherries

Sour cherries are small and red with soft flesh and are very tart. They can be substituted with small wild cherries. They are an ingredient in the classic dish, Duck Montmorency.

- Cast-iron or copper skillet

3 tbsp	peanut oil	45 mL
3½ tbsp	unsalted butter	52 mL
2	mule duck breasts (each 10 oz/300 g)	2
	Salt and freshly ground black pepper	
6 tbsp	Kirsch (approx.)	90 mL
3 tbsp	finely diced carrots	45 mL
3 tbsp	finely diced celery	45 mL
2½ tbsp	finely minced shallots	37 mL
1¼ cups	Sour Cherry Sauce (page 357)	300 mL
	Whole sour cherries, optional	

1. Heat oil and butter in a cast-iron or copper skillet over medium-high heat. Season breasts with salt and black pepper. Add to skillet and cook to *à la goutte de sang* (see Tips, pages 66 and 68) doneness, starting with the fatty side.

2. When breasts are cooked, remove excess fat and flambé with Kirsch. Add carrots, celery and shallots and braise for 1 minute. Add Sour Cherry Sauce and simmer for a few minutes.

3. *To Serve:* When ready to serve, thinly slice breasts cutting lengthwise (see Aiguillettes, left). Pour sauce into a serving dish, slice breasts and place on top of sauce. Heat a few sour cherries in the sauce, if desired.

Roasted Duck Magrets with Grape Foie Gras

Serves 4

Variations

Instead of Muscovy duck breasts, use the breasts of goose, pigeon (squab) or all types of ducks.

Magret

Only the breasts of duck that have been force-fed can bear the name "magret." They are very tender. Like the mule duck, the Muscovy duck may be force-fed.

Grapes

Joseph Favre, a noted pioneer in French cuisine, once said: "I don't know if the grape was one of the fruits of the Garden of Eden, but I do know that it has always been a food of gods and great men."

- Ovenproof skillet

14 oz	red grapes	420 g
¾ cup	Monbazillac, Sauterne or Samos (fortified wine), divided	175 mL
¼ cup	peanut oil	60 mL
⅓ cup	unsalted butter	75 mL
2	Muscovy duck magrets	2
8 oz	duck foie gras (4 slices)	250 g
	Sel de Guérande or sea salt and white pepper	
1 cup	thickened brown game bird stock or store-bought equivalent	250 mL

1. Remove skin and seeds from grapes. Cut in two. Combine ½ cup (125 mL) of the wine and grapes in a medium bowl and soak in the refrigerator for 3 hours.

2. Preheat oven to 400°F (200°C). Heat oil and butter in an ovenproof sauté pan or skillet over medium-high heat. Add duck breasts and brown for 3 minutes per side. Cook in preheated oven to *à la goutte de sang* doneness (see Tips, pages 66 and 68). While breasts are cooking, season foie gras with salt and white pepper. Cook in another skillet over high heat on both sides and set aside.

3. Remove breasts from oven. To make sauce, deglaze with remaining ¼ cup (60 mL) Monbazillac or other fortified wine, reduce and add game bird stock. Simmer for a few minutes, then add soaked grapes.

4. *To Serve:* Pour sauce into each dish, slice breasts, place on top of sauce, alternating with foie gras.

Duck Foie Gras with Figs

Serves 4

Variation

Use goose foie gras instead of duck.

Figs

The fig tree rarely exceeds 16 feet (5 m) in height. Each broad fleshy leaf, measuring 4 to 8 inches (10 to 20 cm) across, is dark green on top, pale green underneath and has five to six deeply indented lobes. It is the only plant that produces its fruits inside a closed structure. The fig is therefore not a fruit in the true sense of the word, but a complete inflorescence or flower cluster. Each female flower produces an achene and it is this fertile part that makes up the pink, granular flesh inside the fig. Purple figs are used in cooking and pastry making, while white and green figs are generally dried.

4	fresh figs	4
1½ cups	apple ice cider or ice wine	375 mL
4	slices fresh (or frozen, thawed) duck foie gras (each 3 oz/90 g)	4
	Sel de Guérande or sea salt and freshly ground black pepper	
⅓ cup	duck stock reduction	75 mL

1. Cut figs into quarters. Combine apple ice cider and figs in a bowl and soak, about 20 minutes.

2. Twenty minutes before serving foie gras, cook figs and soaking liquid in a sauté pan or skillet over low heat until figs are soft, about 5 minutes. Strain, keeping cooking juices and setting figs aside. Reduce cooking juices by 90 percent.

3. Season slices of foie gras with salt and pepper. Fry foie gras slices in a nonstick skillet over high heat until pink, 2 to 3 minutes per side (according to their thickness). Remove from pan and keep warm. Deglaze skillet with cooking juice from figs and add duck stock reduction.

4. *To Serve:* Pour sauce into each dish, then add slices of foie gras. Place figs on each side.

Lacquered Szechuan-Style Duck

Serves 4

● Blender
● Skewer or trussing needle

Tip

To hang a duck in the refrigerator, let stand upright on a device such as a clean beer can or on a rack in a "nest" made of foil.

Variations

Instead of a female duck, you can use guinea fowl, grouse, chicken or any other duck.

Ginger

Herbaceous plant (Zingiberaceae) with fleshy rhizomes. It has a highly perfumed scent and pungent flavor. It is widely used in Asian cuisine. There are wild varieties of ginger that grow in varying parts of North America, but some may be protected or potentially toxic.

Rub

¼ cup	granulated sugar	60 mL
2 tbsp	salt	30 mL
2 tbsp	ground ginger	30 mL
3½ oz	fresh gingerroot, peeled and coarsely chopped	105 g
1	segment star anise	1
1 tsp	five-spice powder	5 mL
¼	bay leaf	¼
2	small female ducks (each about 1½ lbs/750 g)	2

Glaze

1 tsp	malt sugar, granulated sugar or brown sugar	5 mL
4 tsp	Chinese red vinegar	20 mL
1 tbsp	rice vinegar	15 mL
1 tbsp	red rice wine	15 mL

Sauce

⅓ cup	soy bean paste	75 mL
2 tbsp	granulated sugar	30 mL
2 tbsp	oyster sauce	30 mL
4 tsp	hoisin sauce	20 mL
4 tsp	sesame oil	20 mL
5 tbsp	vegetable oil, divided	75 mL

1. *Rub:* Combine sugar, salt, ground ginger, fresh ginger, star anise, five-spice powder and bay leaf in a blender and thoroughly blend. Stuff inside ducks. Let penetrate for about 20 minutes. Use a skewer or trussing needle to close the cavity. Immerse ducks in boiling water for 7 seconds, then quickly immerse in ice water to halt the cooking process. Let dry.

2. *Glaze:* Combine malt sugar, Chinese red vinegar, rice vinegar and rice wine in a medium bowl and blend together. Baste skin of ducks, which will give them a dazzling, dark reddish-brown color. Hang ducks for 6 hours in the refrigerator or a suitable cool location (see Tips, left) and let dry.

3. *Sauce:* In another medium bowl, combine soy bean paste, sugar, oyster sauce, hoisin sauce and sesame oil and blend together. Heat 3 tbsp (45 mL) of the vegetable oil in a skillet over medium heat. Pour in sauce mixture and bring to a boil. Simmer for 2 to 3 minutes. Let cool and set aside.

4. Preheat oven to 350°F (180°C). Place ducks on their backs on a rack and broil, 25 to 30 minutes. Turn and broil on their bellies for 15 minutes. At the end of the cooking process, heat 2 tbsp (30 mL) oil over medium-high heat and pour boiling oil over skin to crisp. Serve hot with sauce.

Goose recipes

Young Bernache Goose with Roasted Chestnut Stuffing and Cranberry Sauce

Tips

If you use frozen pre-cooked chestnuts, let them soak for a few minutes in the cooking juice of the shallots.

For fresh chestnuts: Heat 8 to 12 cups (2 to 3 L) water in a saucepan. Make an incision in outer skin of each chestnut then remove skin. Then soak three chestnuts at a time in boiling water for 1 minute. Remove from water and peel off inner skin immediately. Repeat procedure.

Non-sparkling alcoholic cider can be found at small hard cider producers and some liquor stores. If not available, increase the wine to 1 cup (250 mL) and add ¼ cup (60 mL) unsweetened cranberry juice as a substitute.

- Food processor
- Cheesecloth
- Meat thermometer

⅔ cup	unsalted butter	150 mL
½ cup	finely chopped shallots	125 mL
1 lb	fresh chestnuts with skin or frozen peeled chestnuts (see Tips, left)	500 g
¾ cup	Madeira wine	175 mL
¾ cup	white wine	175 mL
⅓ cup	non-sparkling cranberry-flavored apple cider (see Tips, left)	75 mL

Stuffing

4	slices bread	4
¾ cup	heavy or whipping (35%) cream	175 mL
4	sage leaves	4
2 to 3	egg whites	2 to 3
10 oz	minced goose thighs or minced pork butt	300 g
2 tbsp	chopped parsley	30 mL
6 cups	unthickened poultry, goose or duck stock or store-bought equivalent	1.5 L
1	young Bernache goose or snow goose (about 6 lbs/3 kg)	1
	Salt and freshly ground black pepper	
⅓ cup	vegetable oil	75 mL
	Cranberry Sauce (page 354)	

1. Heat butter in a saucepan over medium heat. Add shallots and sweat until golden, 3 to 5 minutes. Add chestnuts, Madeira wine, white wine and apple cider and cover and cook for about 10 minutes. Let cool.

2. *Stuffing:* Combine bread and cream in a large bowl and soak for 4 to 5 minutes. Add sage and 2 egg whites. If stuffing is too dry, add an additional egg white. Place mixture in food processor along with minced goose meat and chestnut mixture and thoroughly blend. Add salt and pepper to taste and parsley. Roll stuffing in cheesecloth to make a "foie gras torchon," a sausage shape narrow enough to fit inside the goose (see Tip, right).

3. Combine poultry broth and rolled stuffing in a large saucepan over medium heat and cook for 10 minutes. Let cool, then remove cheesecloth.

Tip

Foie gras torchon is a traditional form of terrine, *au torchon* ("in a towel"), where a whole lobe of foie is molded, wrapped in a towel and slow-cooked in a bain-marie.

Sage

It goes well with grilled tuna, eel, mutton, lamb, veal, pork chops, stuffing and certain vegetables. Sage also goes well with garlic and onions.

4. Season interior and exterior of goose with salt and pepper. Fill with stuffing. Sew up opening and truss goose carefully (see page 365).

5. Preheat oven to 450°F (230°C). Heat oil in a baking dish. Place goose in baking dish and roast in preheated oven, basting frequently, until golden brown, about 15 minutes. Cover with foil and reduce temperature to 350°F (180°F). Continue cooking until thermometer inserted into the thickest part of the thigh registers 185°F (85°C), about 20 minutes per pound (40 minutes per kg).

6. Heat Cranberry Sauce. *To Serve:* Spoon a portion of stuffing on each plate. Add a piece of goose and pour sauce on top.

Sautéed Snow Goose with Chanterelle Mushroom Fricassee and Cranberry Juice

Serves 4

Tips

If you prefer, cook the poultry to the USDA recommendations (165°F/74°C).

If you have a juicer use it to extract the cranberry juice. Still use 2½ cups (625 mL) cranberries.

A French cooking term, *à la goutte de sang*, refers to a level of medium-rare doneness, which is determined by pricking meat with a skewer to see if a drop of fat appears with a pink dot in the center.

You will have leftover cranberry butter. It will keep in the refrigerator for 3 days or in freezer for 12 days.

Variations

Instead of goose breasts, use the breast of duck, pheasant, pigeon (squab) or grouse.

- Preheat oven to 450°F (230°C)
- Ovenproof skillet

2½ cups	pure unsweetened cranberry juice (see Tips, left)	625 mL
4	shallots, minced, divided	4
1⅓ cups	unsalted butter, at room temperature, divided	325 mL
	Salt and freshly ground black pepper	
2 tbsp	dried cranberries, finely chopped	30 mL
¼ cup	peanut or sunflower oil	60 mL
4	small snow goose breasts (each 6 oz/175 g)	4
12 oz	chanterelle mushrooms	375 g
2 tbsp	finely chopped parsley	30 mL

1. Combine cranberry juice and half of the minced shallots in a saucepan and reduce by 90 percent. Let cool. Thoroughly mix reduction with 1 cup (250 mL) of the butter. Season with salt and black pepper and add chopped cranberries. Set aside.

2. Heat ¼ cup (60 mL) of butter and oil in an ovenproof skillet over medium heat. Add goose breasts and sear. Cook in preheated oven until breasts are cooked when pierced with a skewer and a droplet of fat appears with a tiny spot of pink in the center, about 16 minutes. This is what is known as *cuisson à la goutte de sang* (cooked to the drop of blood) (see Tips, left).

3. Meanwhile, heat remaining butter in a skillet over medium-high heat. Add chanterelle mushrooms and sauté until golden brown. Add salt and black pepper. At the end of cooking the mushrooms, add remaining shallots and parsley.

4. *To Serve:* Place goose breasts on serving plates and surround with fricassee of chanterelle mushrooms. Just before serving, pour 1 tsp (5 mL) of cranberry butter on each breast (see Tips, left). The butter will melt in the heat, coating the pieces of goose.

Slow-Cooked Goose Thighs

Tips

This recipe is based on the recipes of our ancestors, who let dishes simmer for long hours at low heat on the corner of the wood stove.

Sealing pastry is a fairly sticky dough that is used around the lid of a baking dish or slow cooker to seal it airtight and limit evaporation during a long cooking period.

Variations

Instead of goose thighs, use the bone-in thighs of duck, pheasant, guinea fowl, grouse, capon or chicken.

Quinces

This is a great dish to make when quinces are in season in the fall. The quince belongs to the rose family and is related to the apple and the pear. Native to the Middle East, it is found from Turkey to Iran. Quinces can be round- or pear-shaped, downy or smooth. The fruit turns from green to yellow as it ripens. All quinces have a fruity, pleasant aroma that goes well with game.

● Large ovenproof pot with tight-fitting lid, preferably cast-iron

1	6 to 7 oz (175 to 210 g) bone-in goose thigh per person	1
⅔ cup	peanut oil	150 mL
10 oz	savoy cabbage	300 g
8	cipollini onions	8
12	pieces (¾-inch/2 cm square) quince	12
12	chestnuts, skins removed (see Tips, page 88)	12
4	whole cloves	4
2	cloves garlic	2
1	sprig thyme	1
2	whole carrots	2
4	juniper berries	4
½	bay leaf	½
4 cups	unthickened brown duck or goose stock or store-bought equivalent	1 L
	Salt and freshly ground black pepper	

1. Season goose thighs with salt and pepper and coat in some of the peanut oil. Heat remaining peanut oil in a skillet over medium-high heat. Add goose and brown, 5 minutes per side. Drain fat and place goose in large cast-iron pot.

2. Blanch cabbage in a pot of boiling water. Cut into quarters. Add cabbage, onions, quince, chestnuts, cloves, garlic, thyme, whole carrots, juniper berries, bay leaf and duck stock to goose in pot.

3. Cover and insulate with a tight-fitting lid or heavy-duty foil and simmer over low heat, 8 to 9 hours. You could also use sealing pastry (see Tips, left).

Toulouse Goose Thighs with Kidney Beans

Serves 6 to 12

Tip

Fresh bay leaves, which are quite fragrant, have been used throughout these recipes. If you have dry bay leaves double the amount called for in the recipes.

Variations

Use the bone-in thighs of duck, pheasant, guinea fowl, grouse, capon or chicken instead of goose thighs.

- Large ovenproof pot with tight-fitting lid
- Meat thermometer

14 oz	dried red kidney beans	420 g
⅔ cup	duck or goose fat	150 mL
1	9 oz (270 g) bone-in goose thigh per person	1
2	whole onions	2
2	cloves garlic	2
2	whole carrots	2
½	bay leaf	½
1	sprig thyme	1
1	piece (7 oz/210 g) side bacon	1
½	smoked ham, butt portion (about 3 lbs/1.5 kg)	½
8 cups	unthickened brown duck or goose stock or store-bought equivalent	2 L
	Salt and freshly ground black pepper	

1. Soak kidney beans in a large bowl filled with cold water for 12 hours.

2. Heat duck fat in a heavy-bottomed skillet over medium-high heat. Add goose thighs and thoroughly brown, 5 minutes per side.

3. Preheat oven to 200°F (100°C). Combine goose thighs, onions, garlic, carrots, drained kidney beans, bay leaf, thyme, bacon and ham butt in a large ovenproof pot. Cover with brown stock. Do not add salt before cooking. Cover and cook in preheated oven until thermometer inserted into the thickest part of the thigh registers 185°F (85°C). Remove onion, cut carrots into large cubes and return to cooking pot. Season with salt and black pepper.

4. *To Serve:* Serve in a soup bowl, cutting bacon and ham butt in pieces to place alongside the goose.

Canada Goose Thighs Marinated in Cloudberry Juice

Serving Tip

Serve with cattail hearts or a rice pilaf.

Variations

Use the thighs of duck, pheasant, guinea fowl or grouse instead of goose.

Eastern teaberry

This small shrub in the heather family grows in bogs. Its young leaves, which are especially flavorful, are harvested to make tea. Look for it in health food and specialty stores.

- Large saucepan with tight-fitting lid
- Meat thermometer
- Ovenproof pot

4	goose thighs (each about 7 oz/210 g)	4
4 cups	cloudberry juice	1 L
2	Spanish onions, thinly sliced	2
2	carrots, sliced thinly into rounds	2
2¼ cups	brewed Labrador tea or eastern teaberry tea	550 mL
2	cloves garlic	2
1	bouquet garni	1
2 cups	unthickened brown duck or goose stock or store-bought equivalent	500 mL
	Salt and freshly ground black pepper	
	White Roux (page 351)	

1. Combine goose thighs, cloudberry juice, onions, carrots, tea, garlic and bouquet garni in a large saucepan with a tight-fitting lid. Cover and let sit in the refrigerator for at least 12 hours.

2. Preheat oven to 200°F (100°C). Transfer all ingredients to a large ovenproof pot. Add duck stock and season with salt and pepper. Cover and cook in preheated oven until thermometer inserted into the thickest part of the thigh registers 185°F (85°C), 4 to 5 hours.

3. Remove goose thighs from cooking juice and set aside in a warm place. Pour juice through fine-mesh strainer into a saucepan and thicken with white roux. Simmer over medium-low heat for 2 to 3 minutes. Adjust seasoning. Pour through fine-mesh strainer and add goose thighs.

Daube of Bernache Goose

Tip

If you are serving 8 people, then add 2 cups (500 mL) goose stock in Step 2 with goose thighs.

Variations

Use the bone-in thighs of duck, grouse, turkey, capon or chicken instead of goose thighs.

Daube

Daube, a type of stew, is a typical French Provençal recipe. What makes it special is that the meat is not browned. It is generally cooked with olives.

- Ovenproof saucepan with tight-fitting lid
- Meat thermometer

2	bone-in Bernache goose thighs per person (see Tip, left)	2
8	orange peels	8
2	cloves garlic	2
2	Spanish onions, coarsely diced	2
1	carrot, coarsely diced	1
2	stalks celery, diced	2
1	bay leaf	1
1	sprig thyme	1
4 cups	tannic red wine	1 L
⅔ cup	olive oil	150 mL
3	pitted black olives per person	3
	Salt and freshly ground black pepper	
7 oz	pork belly (uncured), chopped	210 g
4	medium-size potatoes	4

1. Place goose thighs, orange peels, garlic, onions, carrot, celery, bay leaf, thyme, red wine, olive oil, olives, salt and pepper in a container and let marinate in the refrigerator for 12 hours. Remove from refrigerator and drain, reserving thighs, vegetables and marinating liquid separately.

2. Preheat oven to 450°F (230°C). Lightly brown pork belly in a warm ovenproof saucepan. Soften vegetables, then brown thighs and add marinating liquid. Season with salt and pepper.

3. Reduce heat to 400°F (200°C). Make sure thighs are immersed completely in the braising liquid. Cover with tight-fitting lid and place in preheated oven. When half-cooked, add potatoes. Cook until thermometer inserted into the thickest part of the thigh registers 185°F (85°C).

Sautéed Goose Gizzards with Wild Mushrooms

Serves 4

Tip

Thicken stock with 3 tsp (15 mL) cornstarch mixed with 6 tsp (30 mL) cold water.

Serving Tip

Serve with potatoes boiled in salted water or cooked with gizzards.

Variations

Use the gizzards from duck, pheasant, guineas fowl, turkey or chicken instead of goose.

Marjoram

Marjoram is used in sauces to add more flavor to meats. It is also used as a condiment in marinades and in spice mixtures for stuffing, stews and sauces, especially tomato sauce. It is a very good accompaniment to salads, fish and vegetables. In recipes, it can easily be replaced by oregano.

- Cast-iron skillet

1¼ lbs	goose gizzards (approx.)	625 g
¾ cup	butter	175 mL
2	shallots, diced	2
2	cloves garlic, minced	2
1 tsp	marjoram	5 mL
⅓ cup	vegetable oil	75 mL
2½ tbsp	all-purpose flour	37 mL
1⅔ cups	thickened brown duck or goose stock or store-bought equivalent (see Tip, left)	400 mL
7 oz	chanterelle, porcini (cep) or hedgehog (pied de mouton) mushrooms	210 g
¼ cup	sunflower oil	60 mL
	Salt and freshly ground black pepper	
2 tbsp	minced chives	30 mL

1. Thoroughly degrease gizzards by removing the fat with a knife, cut into uniform cubes, blanch and set aside.

2. Heat butter in a skillet over medium heat. Add shallots and sweat until golden, 3 to 5 minutes. Add minced garlic and marjoram and sweat until softened, about 5 minutes.

3. Meanwhile, heat vegetable oil in a cast-iron skillet over medium-high heat. Add gizzards and brown until golden brown, about 3 minutes per side (or according to USDA recommendations, see Tips, page 106). Add flour and coat well. Continue to cook for 2 to 3 minutes.

4. Add gizzards to shallot mixture. Pour in duck stock and cook gizzards over low heat until tender, about 1 hour.

5. Meanwhile, thoroughly wash mushrooms and drain. Heat sunflower oil in a cast-iron skillet over high heat and sauté mushrooms until liquid is completely evaporated. Season with salt and pepper. A few minutes before serving, add mushrooms to gizzards. Sprinkle chives over top.

Goose Rillettes with Golden Raisins

Serves 15

Tip

The word *rillettes* comes from the old French word *rille*, which means a small piece of pork; for a purist this means that pork must be used in this type of recipe. Recipes vary according to their region: in some regions, rillettes contain only pork, in other regions, they may consist of pork and rabbit, or pork and goose.

Variations

Instead of goose meat, use duck, pheasant, guinea fowl or rabbit.

* Earthenware dish

2 cups	water	500 mL
1½ lbs	pork fat (leaf lard or kidney fat)	750 g
1½ lbs	pork shoulder blade	750 g
2½ lbs	boneless goose meat	1.25 kg
1	bouquet garni	1
	Salt and freshly ground black pepper	
½ cup	golden raisins	125 mL
¾ cup	Armagnac	175 mL
4 cups	unthickened duck or goose stock or store-bought equivalent	1 L
14 oz	boneless lean beef (outside round) or additional goose breast	420 g
1	leek, finely diced	1
7 oz	celeriac, finely diced	210 g
3	egg whites	3
3	packets (each ¼ oz/7 g) gelatin, soaked in ¼ cup (60 mL) cold water	3
2	sprigs tarragon	2
	Country-style bread	

1. Pour 2 cups (500 mL) water into a Dutch oven. Add pork fat and let melt slowly at very low heat.

2. Cut pork and goose meat into ¾-inch (2 cm) strips. Add to melted pork fat with bouquet garni and lightly simmer, stirring occasionally, over very low heat, 2 to 3 hours. Season with salt and pepper. At end of cooking time, remove excess fat and set aside. Adjust seasoning. Place rillettes in an earthenware dish and cover with cooking fat. Set aside. Let cool slightly, then refrigerate for at least 8 hours or until next day.

3. Soak raisins in Armagnac overnight.

4. Pour duck or goose stock into a saucepan and warm. Mince beef or goose meat with a knife. Add meat, leek and celeriac to saucepan. Whisk egg whites and pour over warm duck or goose stock, stirring slowly until mixture comes to a boil. Continue cooking at low heat, about 1 hour.

5. Gently filter mixture through fine-mesh sieve or cheesecloth. Add gelatin, tarragon and raisins expanded in Armagnac. Pour mixture into a dish measuring ¾ inch (2 cm) in height and refrigerate.

6. The next day, use spoons to serve 2 large "quenelles" (football-shaped scoops) of rillettes accompanied by 2 spoonfuls of duck or goose jelly with golden raisins and a few slices of country-style bread.

Goose with Gingerbread Crust, Hollandaise Sauce and Cranberries

Tip

The internal temperature of 165°F (74°C) is for health and safety standards. Restaurants often serve it at 128°F (53°C) which would explain pinker meat. If the food safety of rare-cooked poultry is a concern for you, cook to desired doneness or skip this recipe.

Variations

You could also use other kinds of goose, such as Toulouse, Guinea and barnacle.

Cranberries

Cranberries grow in bogs and are now cultivated commercially. The red berries are best if they are picked after several light frosts. They are made into jam or jelly to accompany poultry and are used in pies, cookies and cakes. They are also used to make a full-bodied rosé wine.

- Preheat oven to 200°F (100°C)
- Food processor
- Heavy-bottomed ovenproof skillet
- Meat thermometer

6	slices store-bought or homemade soft gingerbread loaf	6
2 to 4	goose breasts (depending on their thickness) (each about 7 oz/210 g)	2 to 4
	Fine sea salt and freshly ground black pepper	
⅓ cup	vegetable oil	75 mL
⅓ cup	unsalted butter	75 mL
⅓ cup	clover honey	75 mL
⅓ cup	apple cider vinegar	75 mL
⅓ cup	melted unsalted butter	75 mL
16	asparagus tips	16
¾ cup	dried cranberries or blueberries	175 mL
1¼ cups	Hollandaise Sauce (Classic Method, page 352)	300 mL

1. Place six slices of gingerbread loaf on a broiler pan tray and place in preheated oven. Leave in oven until thoroughly dry. Place in food processor and pulse until crushed. Set aside.

2. Increase oven temperature to 350°F (180°C). Generously season goose breasts with salt and pepper. Heat oil and butter in a heavy-bottomed ovenproof skillet. Cook breasts in preheated oven until a thermometer inserted into center of breast registers 118°F (48°C).

3. In a small bowl, combine honey and vinegar. Remove breasts from oven. Reduce oven temperature to 250°F (120°C). Baste breasts with clover honey and apple cider vinegar mixture. Coat breasts with gingerbread loaf crumbs. Place on broiler pan tray and continue to cook in oven, gently pouring a little melted butter on regularly. Remove from oven when meat thermometer inserted into center of breast registers 165°F (74°C) (see Tip, left). Let sit on top of stove, which will "relax" the meat fibers.

4. Cook asparagus until "al dente." Meanwhile, combine dried cranberries and Hollandaise Sauce in a large bowl.

5. *To Serve:* Arrange breasts on plates, add asparagus and pour sauce on top.

Woodcock, Grouse, Ptarmigan and Guinea Fowl recipes

⬤ ──────────────────────────────

Woodcocks
with Fine Champagne

Serves 4

- Preheat oven to 350°F (180°)
- Heavy-bottomed Dutch oven

Tips

There are several schools of thought if one should hang woodcocks or not. The choice is yours but, in any case, 24 hours in the refrigerator will not harm them.

As a chef, taste and texture considerations are paramount in my mind when I prepare food. However, organizations such as the USDA put food safety considerations at the forefront. With that in mind, they recommend all poultry livers and other giblets should be cooked to an internal temperature of 165°F (74°C).

Variations

Instead of woodcocks, use lark, thrush or wood pigeon.

4	woodcocks	4
	Salt and freshly ground black pepper	
4	small slices pork fatback	4
⅓ cup	duck fat	75 mL
⅓ cup	fine champagne	75 mL
⅔ cup	good-quality white wine	150 mL
¾ cup	unthickened brown game bird stock or store-bought equivalent	175 mL
⅔ cup	butter	150 mL
1½ tsp	chopped black truffles, optional	7 mL
4	slices four-grain bread or brioche	4

1. Pluck woodcocks and flambé (pass them over a flame to gently remove the down remaining on the skin). Remove insides and save all giblets except for gizzard. Season with salt and pepper and put giblets back inside woodcocks. (We usually leave the head and neck.) Truss woodcock (see page 365). Season with salt and pepper, then bard woodcocks with pork fatback (page 366).

2. Heat duck fat in a heavy-bottomed Dutch oven over medium heat. Add woodcocks and sear. Bake in preheated oven for 4 to 5 minutes. Reduce oven temperature to 325°F (160°C) and bake, about 10 minutes (or according to USDA recommendations, see Tips, left), depending on the size of the birds. Remove excess fat and flambé in fine champagne. Remove woodcocks and keep warm.

3. Add white wine to Dutch oven and reduce by half. Add game stock and whisk in butter. Adjust seasoning and mix in chopped truffles, if using.

4. Meanwhile, cut slices of bread or brioche into bird shapes and toast them. Collect all giblets that have cooked at the same time as the woodcocks. Strain through a sieve and spread with a spatula on bread or brioche slices.

5. *To Serve:* Place bread or brioche slices on plates or in serving bowls. Lay woodcocks on top, then pour sauce over top.

Roasted Woodcocks Flambéed in Marc de Gewürztraminer with Truffle Risotto

⊙

Serves 4

Tips

If you prefer, cook the poultry to the USDA recommendations (165°F/74°C).

Thicken stock with ¼ cup (60 mL) cornstarch and 6 tbsp (90 mL) water.

A French cooking term, *à la goutte de sang*, refers to a level of medium-rare doneness, which is determined by pricking meat with a skewer to see if a drop of fat appears with a pink dot in the center.

The woodcock is considered one of the most noble feathered birds in gastronomy. To give honor where honor is due, nothing less than truffles and Marc de Gewürztraminer should accompany it.

- Preheat oven to 300°F (150°C)
- Heavy-bottomed Dutch oven with lid

Woodcocks

4	large woodcocks or 8 small woodcocks	4
	Fine sea salt and freshly ground black pepper	
6 tbsp	unsalted butter	90 mL
⅓ cup	Marc de Gewürztraminer, Alsatian white eau-de-vie or other eau-de-vie	75 mL

Jus

¾ cup	unthickened brown game bird stock or store-bought equivalent	175 mL
⅓ cup	butter, at room temperature	75 mL
1½ oz	Périgord truffles, finely chopped	45 g

Truffle Risotto

⅓ cup	unsalted butter, divided	75 mL
⅓ cup	shallots, finely diced	75 mL
	Salt	
1⅔ cups	carnaroli or basmati rice	400 mL
6 cups	thickened light game bird stock or store-bought equivalent (see Tips, left)	1.5 L
¾ cup	grated Parmesan cheese	175 mL
1 oz	Périgord truffles, finely chopped	30 g
	Freshly ground black pepper	

1. *Woodcocks:* Pluck woodcocks gently to avoid damaging skin. Leave neck and head intact, which will help to gauge the quality of this dish. Sprinkle salt and pepper inside woodcocks, then truss them, taking care to arrange their heads (see photo, right).

2. Heat 6 tbsp (90 mL) unsalted butter in a heavy-bottomed Dutch oven with lid. Proceed to gently sear woodcocks over medium-high heat, starting with breasts and turning to sear other side, until golden brown. Cover and place in preheated oven. After 6 to 8 minutes, depending on the thickness of the meat, prick the backs of the thighs with a skewer. If a drop of fat appears with a pink dot in the center, remove woodcocks from Dutch oven (see Tips, left). Remove excess fat, then return woodcocks to Dutch oven and reheat on the stovetop. Pour Marc de Gewürztraminer over woodcocks and flambé. Remove woodcocks and place on a broiler pan tray. Cover with foil and keep warm in the oven with the heat turned off.

Variations

Instead of woodcock, you could use ptarmigan, quail, lark or pigeon.

3. *Jus:* Meanwhile, pour brown game bird stock into Dutch oven. Whisk in ⅓ cup (75 mL) butter and simmer for 2 to 3 minutes. Add finely chopped truffles. Adjust seasoning and set aside, keeping Dutch oven warm.

4. *Truffle Risotto:* Heat half of the butter in a skillet. Add shallots and sauté until transparent. Add salt to taste, then rice. Slowly pour light game bird stock on top until rice has absorbed all the liquid and is cooked, about 20 minutes. Remove from heat and add remaining butter, Parmesan cheese and finely chopped truffles. Season with pepper to taste. (The risotto should be cooked before the woodcocks and kept warm.)

5. *To Serve:* Spoon risotto onto individual plates and place a woodcock on top. Serve the jus whisked with butter in a gravy boat. Provide finger bowls and do not hesitate to use your fingers to savor this dish of kings.

Woodcock and Hare Pie

Tip

Four-spice mix (also known as *quatre épices*) is a spice blend containing ground pepper (white, black or both), cloves, nutmeg and ginger. Some variations of the mix use allspice instead of pepper or cinnamon in place of ginger.

Serving Tip

Serve pie hot with, for example, a truffle sauce.

Variations

Instead of woodcock, use lark, thrush or wood pigeon.

- Earthenware dish
- 9-inch (23 cm) pie plate
- Food processor

4	woodcocks	4
$\frac{1}{2}$ tsp	four-spice mix (see Tip, left)	2 mL
$\frac{1}{2}$ cup	Madeira wine, divided	125 mL
$\frac{1}{4}$ cup	Cognac	60 mL
5 oz	chicken liver	150 g
3 oz	fatty bacon, cut into cubes	90 g
$\frac{3}{4}$ cup	butter	175 mL
	Salt and freshly ground black pepper	
2	saddles of hare	2
2	hare thighs	2
1 lb	boneless pork neck, chopped	500 g
8	egg yolks	8
$1\frac{1}{2}$ oz	beef marrow	45 g
	Pastry for 9-inch (23 cm) double-crust pie	

1. Debone woodcocks and remove skin. Remove giblets and gizzard and set aside. Place birds in an earthenware dish with spices, half the Madeira wine and Cognac.

2. Chop giblets and combine with chicken liver and fatty bacon. Heat butter in a skillet over medium heat. Add giblet mixture and sear. Season with salt and pepper. Let cool. Pulse in a food processor, then strain through sieve. Set aside.

3. Debone saddles and thighs of hare and chop together with fresh pork. Season with salt and pepper. Add egg yolks and beef marrow, then mix with remaining Madeira wine.

4. Preheat oven to 300°F (150°C). Roll out half of the pastry dough and line a 9-inch (23 cm) pie plate. Place rabbit stuffing at bottom, then lay woodcocks in a circle on top with soaking liquid. In center, add half of the giblet stuffing and gizzards, then cover everything with the remaining giblet stuffing. Roll out the rest of the dough, form a circle and cover the pie. Make a small vent and bake in preheated oven until dough is golden brown, 40 to 45 minutes.

Woodcock Salmis à la Bernardine

Serves 4

This recipe was found in the library of the convent of Saint Bernard (1602). Source: Joseph Favre

Tip

Use aromatic herbs to your liking, such as marjoram, burdock, common locust or dog rose.

Variations

Instead of woodcock, use sandpiper, quail or ptarmigan.

- Preheat oven to 450°F (230°C)
- Heavy-bottomed ovenproof skillet
- Meat thermometer

8	woodcocks, depending on their size	8
	Salt and freshly ground black pepper	
⅔ cup	unsalted butter, divided	150 mL
¼ cup	vegetable oil, divided	60 mL
4	lemons	4
	Salt	
	Aromatic herbs (see Tip, left)	
½ cup	Dijon mustard	125 mL
⅔ cup	white wine	150 mL

1. Season woodcocks with salt and black pepper. Leave all giblets except gizzards inside the birds. Truss (see page 365).

2. Heat half the butter and oil in a heavy-bottomed ovenproof skillet over medium heat. Skewer the birds, if desired, and sear. Then place in preheated oven and cook for 2 to 3 minutes. Remove and cut up wings, thighs, breasts and rump in two. Set aside. Remove giblets and mash.

3. Zest one lemon and cut thinly. Juice lemons and add to giblets with zest. Add pieces of bird in the skillet. Season with a few pinches of salt and a pinch each of the chosen aromatic herbs. Add mustard and white wine. Place skillet on a warming try and stir so that each piece absorbs the seasoning and does not get attached to the other pieces. Cook, reducing the heat, and continue to stir for a few moments until thermometer inserted into the thickest part registers 165°F (74°C).

Spruce Grouse en Cocotte with Pied de Mouton Mushrooms and Lovage

Serves 4

Variations

Use duck, pigeon, guinea fowl or chicken instead of grouse.

Lovage

Lovage is a wild celery that has been cultivated in gardens since the 16th century. It is the ancestor of several varieties of vegetable, including garden celery and celeriac.

Pied de Mouton Mushrooms

Also known as hedgehog mushrooms. It is a high-quality mushroom when it is young, but turns bitter as it ages. It is most often found growing in circles in leafy or evergreen forests. Its flesh is white and brittle.

- Preheat oven to 350°F (180°C)
- Heavy-bottomed Dutch oven

8	cloves garlic	8
7 oz	lovage or celery	210 g
1	spruce grouse (4 lbs/2 kg)	1
1	slice pork fatback	1
	Salt and freshly ground black pepper	
4 oz	pork belly (uncured), cut into small cubes	125 g
1/3 cup	duck fat	75 mL
10 oz	pied de mouton mushrooms (see left)	300 g
2/3 cup	white wine	150 mL
3/4 cup	unthickened brown game bird stock or store-bought equivalent	175 mL

1. Blanch garlic cloves in a pot of boiling water. Cut lovage into sticks and cook in salted water. Rinse with cold water and set aside.

2. Remove insides of spruce grouse. Place liver and gizzard back inside. Truss and bard with pork fatback (see page 366). Season with salt and black pepper.

3. Fry pork belly in a heavy-bottomed Dutch oven over medium heat. Add grouse. Cook in preheated oven, basting often, 30 to 45 minutes.

4. Meanwhile, heat duck fat and sauté mushrooms. Season with salt and black pepper. When grouse is cooked remove from Dutch oven and set aside. Remove excess fat from Dutch oven and add white wine, brown game bird stock, garlic, mushrooms and lovage. Simmer for a few minutes. Cut up grouse, taking care to save the liver and gizzard, which you will cut into small cubes.

5. *To Serve:* Place a piece of grouse on a plate, add cubes of liver and gizzard and pour mushroom jus over top.

Grouse in Salt Crust

Tips

This is a great French classic using the *étouffée* cooking method, in which all the flavor is trapped inside the salt crust. It is a way of steaming the food trapped or "smothered" inside. It can be very enjoyable to prepare this for an evening with friends, because you can break the crust before your guests and serve them the grouse, as long as you carefully manage to cut up the poultry.

Thicken stock with 3 tsp (15 mL) cornstarch and 6 tsp (30 mL) water.

Variations

Use a large chicken, pheasant or guinea fowl instead of the grouse.

Salt crust

4¾ cups	all-purpose flour	1.175 mL
14 oz	coarse gray sea salt	420 g
3	egg whites, lightly beaten	3
	Warm water	

Grouse

1	grouse (2 to 2½ lbs/1 to 1.25 kg) or 2 small grouse	1
	Salt and freshly ground black pepper	
3	shallots	3
1	carrot, sliced into thin rounds	1
2	cloves garlic	2
1	sprig thyme	1
2	bay leaves	2
8	yellow pattypan squash	8
8	green pattypan squash	8
2 cups	unthickened light game bird stock or store-bought equivalent	500 mL
8	baby beets	8
8	fingerling potatoes	8
1¼ cups	thickened brown game bird stock or store-bought equivalent (see Tips, left)	300 mL
⅔ cup	port wine	150 mL
⅓ cup	Cognac	75 mL
⅓ cup	butter, at room temperature	75 mL

1. *Salt crust:* In a large bowl, combine flour and salt. Make a well in the center, then incorporate lightly beaten egg whites. Add warm water until a thick dough forms. Let stand for 30 minutes.

2. *Grouse:* Remove giblets and gizzards and discard. Season inside of grouse with salt and black pepper. Stuff with shallots, carrot, garlic, thyme and bay leaves. Truss grouse (see page 365).

3. Preheat oven to 350°F (180°C). Spread ½-inch (1 cm) layer of dough on parchment paper or foil. Lay grouse on paper or foil, then lay dough over top to envelope it. Cook in preheated oven until crust is seared, about 20 minutes. Reduce temperature to 325°F (160°C) and continue to cook, for 80 minutes.

4. Meanwhile, cook yellow and green pattypan squash and light stock in a large saucepan over medium heat for 5 minutes. Then add beets and potatoes and cook until tender, 12 to 15 minutes. The vegetables will take on a lovely pink color from the beets.

5. Heat brown stock in a saucepan over medium heat. Add port wine and Cognac. Whisk in butter. Adjust seasoning and keep warm.

6. *To Serve:* Serve on hot plates. Distribute vegetables, pour sauce over top, then lay pieces of grouse on top.

Spruce Grouse Aiguillettes with Blueberries

Recipe from Chef Pierre Higgins

Tips

Thicken stock with ½ tsp (2 mL) cornstarch and 1 tsp (5 mL) water.

An *aiguillette* is a thin slice taken from the grouse breast and cut in the direction of the fiber (lengthwise) into long thin slices.

Serving Tip

Serve with potatoes sautéed in butter and mixed diced vegetables.

Variations

Use any kind of grouse or guinea fowl.

4	spruce grouse	4
	Salt and freshly ground black pepper	
3½ tbsp	butter, divided	52 mL
Sauce		
¼ cup	blueberry vinegar	60 mL
¼ cup	blueberry liqueur	60 mL
⅓ cup	thickened duck or grouse stock or store-bought equivalent (see Tips, left)	75 mL
3 tbsp	heavy or whipping (35%) cream	45 mL
2 oz	fresh blueberries	60 g

1. Debone grouse breasts and cut into aiguillettes, thin filets that are cut in the direction of the fiber (see Tips, left). Season with salt and black pepper.

2. Heat half the butter in a skillet over medium-high heat. Add grouse aiguillettes and brown. Set aside and keep hot.

3. *Sauce:* Deglaze skillet with blueberry vinegar and reduce until almost dry. Add blueberry liqueur, duck stock and whipping cream and let reduce by half. Whisk in remaining butter and serve with a few fresh blueberries slightly reheated in the sauce.

Rock Ptarmigans with Locust Blossom Wine Sauce

In memory of my mentor, Chef Abel Benquet

Tips

Thicken stock with 1 tsp (5 mL) cornstarch and 2 tsp (10 mL) water.

Au piqué means that meat is done when a knife tip can be easily inserted and removed.

Variations

Use pigeon (squab), guinea fowl or chicken instead of rock ptarmigans.

- Preheat oven to 450°F (230°C)
- Heavy-bottomed ovenproof saucepan
- Meat thermometer

4	rock ptarmigans	4
	Salt and freshly ground black pepper	
1/3 cup	vegetable oil	75 mL
1 2/3 cups	locust blossom wine	400 mL
4	shallots, minced	4
24	white firm mushroom caps	24
1	carrot, finely diced	1
32	baby potatoes	32
2/3 cup	thickened brown game stock or store-bought equivalent (see Tips, left)	150 mL

1. Remove insides of ptarmigans, season interior with salt and pepper. Place livers back inside and truss birds (see page 365).

2. Heat oil in a heavy-bottomed ovenproof saucepan over medium heat. Add ptarmigans and sear on all sides. Cook in preheated oven until *au piqué*, or thermometer inserted into the center registers 165°F (74°C), for 10 minutes (see Tips, left). Remove ptarmigans and set aside.

3. Remove all fat from saucepan and deglaze with locust blossom wine and reduce by half. Add minced shallots, mushrooms, carrot, baby potatoes and thickened brown game stock. Simmer gently until ingredients are cooked through. Adjust seasoning. Debone ptarmigans and simmer in sauce, about 6 minutes. Serve on warm plates.

Rock Ptarmigans with Blueberries and Hazelnuts

To my son Joël, for his love of the Great North

Tip

Thicken stock with 1 tsp (5 mL) cornstarch and 2 tsp (10 mL) water.

Variations

Use pigeon (squab), guinea fowl or chicken instead of rock ptarmigans.

- Preheat oven to 400°F (200°C)
- Heavy-bottomed Dutch oven

⅔ cup	dry white wine	150 mL
6	American linden leaves (basswood), fresh or dried	6
4 oz	hazelnuts, finely chopped	125 g
1 cup	blueberries	250 mL
½ cup	thickened brown game stock or store-bought equivalent (see Tip, left)	125 mL
4	rock ptarmigans	4
	Salt and freshly ground black pepper	
½ cup	unsalted butter	125 mL
⅓ cup	vegetable oil	75 mL
¾ cup	water	175 mL

1. Combine white wine and linden leaves in a large saucepan over medium-high heat and reduce by half. Add hazelnuts and blueberries and cook, 4 to 5 minutes. Add brown stock and cook, 4 to 5 minutes. Set aside.

2. Season ptarmigans inside and out with salt and black pepper. Truss (see page 365). Heat butter and oil in a heavy-bottomed Dutch oven over medium heat. Add ptarmigans and sear. Transfer to preheated oven and cook for 12 to 15 minutes, depending on size.

3. Debone the breast of each ptarmigan and the first bones behind the thigh. Cut bones into small pieces, place bones back into Dutch oven with water. Reduce by half. Pour mixture through strainer. Add blueberry-hazelnut stock and simmer, 2 to 3 minutes.

4. *To Serve:* Pour blueberry-hazelnut stock on each plate and top with breasts and thighs.

Willow Ptarmigans en Cocotte with Fiddleheads and Wild Garlic

● (page marker)

Serves 4

Variations

Use lark, thrush, wood pigeon or plover instead of ptarmigans.

Ostrich Fern (Fiddlehead Fern)

The fiddleheads, the shoots of the fiddlehead fern, are edible. This plant should not be confused with the sensitive fern or the bracken fern, which are toxic. Fiddleheads are delicious. Their taste is somewhere between the artichoke and asparagus and they are a true springtime treat for their fans.

● Preheat oven to 350°F (180°C)
● Heavy-bottomed Dutch oven

4	ptarmigans	4
1½ cups	fresh fiddleheads	375 mL
¼ cup	vegetable oil	60 mL
¼ cup	butter	60 mL
	Salt and freshly ground black pepper	
½ cup	malt whiskey	125 mL
24	pearl onions	24
12	cloves wild garlic	12
7 oz	wild mushrooms, such as porcini (cep), chanterelle or hedgehog (pied de mouton)	210 g

1. Remove insides of birds and discard or keep giblets for another recipe. Truss birds (see page 365).

2. Cook fiddleheads in salted water until tender but firm. Rinse in cold water and drain.

3. Heat oil and butter in a heavy-bottomed Dutch oven over medium-high heat. Season ptarmigans with salt and pepper and slightly brown. Cook in preheated oven for 6 to 7 minutes.

4. Remove ptarmigans and keep warm. Remove excess fat from pot and flambé with whiskey (see page 68).

5. Cook onions and wild garlic in a skillet over low heat. When onions are half cooked, add wild mushrooms and cook for 2 to 3 minutes more. Five minutes before serving, add fiddleheads and place ptarmigans back in Dutch oven. Cover and reheat.

6. *To Serve:* Serve ptarmigans in a soup plate, surrounded by hot vegetables.

Roasted Willow Ptarmigans with Sarsaparilla

● Preheat oven to 350°F (180°C)
● Heavy-bottomed Dutch oven

Serves 4

4	willow ptarmigans	4
	Salt and freshly ground black pepper	
¼ cup	vegetable oil	60 mL
¾ cup	butter, divided	175 mL
2 tbsp	gin	30 mL
⅔ cup	dry white wine	150 mL
1	red or Spanish onion, finely diced	1
5 oz	sarsaparilla	150 g
2	cloves garlic	2
⅔ cup	unthickened brown game stock or store-bought equivalent	150 mL
½ cup	heavy or whipping (35%) cream	125 mL
2¼ lbs	sweet potatoes	1.125 kg

Tip

A French cooking term, *à la goutte de sang*, refers to a level of medium-rare doneness, which is determined by pricking meat with a skewer to see if a drop of fat appears with a pink dot in the center.

Variations

Instead of willow ptarmigans, use pigeon (squab), guinea fowl or chicken.

Sarsaparilla

Perennial forest plant found in abundance in forests of maples. The small, blue-black berries are edible and their flavor is reminiscent of juniper berries. The berries are harvested and traditionally eaten raw by Canada's aboriginal people.

Source: Jean-Claude Vigor, Cuisine amérindienne.

1. Season willow ptarmigans inside and out with salt and black pepper, then truss (see page 365). Heat oil and 4½ tbsp (67 mL) of the butter in a heavy-bottomed Dutch oven over medium heat. Sear ptarmigans. Cook in preheated oven for 10 minutes.

2. Remove some of cooking fat and add gin and white wine. Let alcohol evaporate, then add diced onion, sarsaparilla and garlic cloves. Continue cooking until ptarmigans have reached à *la goutte de sang* doneness (see Tip, left and page 140), 6 to 8 minutes. Remove ptarmigans from Dutch oven as well as cloves of garlic.

3. To make sauce, add game stock to Dutch oven and reduce by 20 percent. Add 4½ tbsp (67 mL) of butter. Return ptarmigans to Dutch oven. Cover and reheat.

4. Meanwhile, warm cream. Cook sweet potatoes in boiling salted water until softened. Mash in a vegetable mill or by hand with a potato masher. Add remaining butter and warmed cream. Adjust seasoning.

5. *To Serve:* Place ptarmigans on plate, pour cooking juice with sarsaparilla over top and serve with sweet potatoes.

Fried Guinea Fowl Liver Mousse with Apple Compote and Caramel Sablés

Serves 4

Recipe by Chef Martin Boucher

Variations

Use the livers of duck, wild turkey, pheasant or chicken instead of guinea fowl livers.

12 oz	guinea fowl livers	375 g
	Salt and freshly ground black pepper	
2½ tbsp	butter	37 mL
3 tbsp	port wine	45 mL
⅓ cup	brown poultry stock reduction (demi-glace) (Variations, page 347)	75 mL

Apple Compote

2	apples, such as Golden Delicious, finely diced	2
½	onion, finely diced	½
Pinch	four-spice mix (see Tip, page 110)	Pinch
	Salt and freshly ground black pepper	
2½ tbsp	butter	37 mL

Caramel Sablés

¾ cup	granulated sugar	175 mL
⅓ cup	butter	75 mL
⅓ cup	heavy or whipping (35%) cream	75 mL
3	egg yolks	3
1¼ cups	all-purpose flour	300 mL

1. Season livers with salt and pepper. Heat butter in a skillet over medium-high heat. Add livers and sear until pink, 1 minute per side (or according to USDA recommendations, see Tips, page 106). Remove and set aside.

2. To make sauce, deglaze skillet with port wine and poultry stock and reduce slightly. Adjust seasoning.

3. *Apple Compote:* Combine finely dice apples and onion. Add four-spice mix. Season with salt and black pepper. Heat butter in a skillet over medium heat. Add apples and sweat mixture until lightly browned. Set aside.

4. *Caramel Sablés:* Preheat oven to 400°F (200°C). In a large bowl, combine sugar, butter, cream, egg yolks and flour. Roll out dough to a thin layer. Cut into 12 rectangles. Reduce oven temperature to 350°F (180°C). Place rectangles on a baking sheet and bake in preheated oven for 10 minutes.

5. *To Serve:* Place 3 triangles on a plate per person. Top each with apple compote and then liver. Add sauce.

Asian-Flavored Guinea Fowl Suprêmes

Serves 4

Recipe by Chef Danielle Neault

Serving Tip

Accompany with small sautéed mushrooms or extra-fine green beans.

Variations

Use the breasts of duck, grouse or chicken instead of guinea fowl.

- Preheat oven to 400°F (200°C)
- Ovenproof skillet
- Meat thermometer

1 tbsp	butter	15 mL
1	shallot, minced	1
2 tbsp	granulated sugar	30 mL
2 tbsp	white wine vinegar	30 mL
2 cups	unthickened brown poultry stock or store-bought equivalent	500 mL
2 tbsp	hoisin sauce	30 mL
½ tsp	hot sauce	2 mL
2 tbsp	peanut butter	30 mL
	Salt and freshly ground black pepper	
4	guinea fowl breasts, deboned, skin removed	4

1. Heat butter in a skillet over medium heat. Add shallots and sweat. Add sugar and caramelize, stirring often, until golden brown, 3 to 4 minutes.

2. Deglaze skillet with wine vinegar. Add poultry stock, hoisin sauce, hot sauce and peanut butter and reduce by half. Season with salt and black pepper. Pour sauce through a fine-mesh strainer. Set aside in a warm place.

3. In an ovenproof skillet, sear guinea fowl breasts over medium heat. Cook in preheated oven until a thermometer inserted in center of breast registers 175°F (80°C), 10 to 12 minutes.

4. *To Serve:* Pour sauce onto individual serving plates and lay breasts on top.

Parmentier of Guinea Fowl Thighs with Leeks and Celeriac Purée

Variations

Use the thighs of pheasant, chicken, turkey or grouse instead of guinea fowl.

- 3-inch (7.5 cm) diameter deep cookie cutter with 2-inch (5 cm) sides, or empty food can with both ends removed
- Meat thermometer

6 cups	Court-Bouillon (page 348)	1.5 L
1 cup	white vermouth, such as Noilly Prat	250 mL
4	guinea fowl thighs	4
⅔ cup	brown guinea fowl, poultry or equivalent stock reduction (demi-glace) (Variations, page 347)	150 mL
½ cup	brown poultry stock reduction	125 mL
	Salt and freshly ground white pepper	
⅔ cup	milk or heavy or whipping (35%) cream	150 mL
5 cups	diced celeriac	1.25 L
8 oz	potatoes, diced	250 g
½ cup	unsalted butter, at room temperature, divided	125 mL
2	leek whites, thinly sliced	2

1. Heat court-bouillon over medium heat. Add vermouth and guinea fowl thighs and cook until a thermometer inserted into the thickest part of the thighs registers 165°F (74°C). Let thighs sit in the cooking liquid until cooled a little.

2. Remove thighs from court-bouillon. Remove skin, debone and shred meat. Place skin and bones in court bouillon over medium heat and let simmer for 15 minutes. Pour bouillon through a colander, return to saucepan and reduce by 90 percent. Add brown stock reduction and shredded guinea fowl meat. Season with salt and pepper, then set aside and keep warm.

3. Meanwhile, to make vegetables, season milk or cream with salt and black pepper in a large saucepan. Add diced celeriac and potatoes and bring to a boil over medium heat, stirring frequently.

4. Heat 2 tbsp (30 mL) of the unsalted butter in a skillet over medium heat. Add leeks and gently sweat until golden, 3 to 5 minutes. Season with salt and black pepper. Set aside and keep warm.

5. When potatoes and celeriac are cooked, drain and mash. Add remaining butter. Season with salt and black pepper and add a little milk or cream as needed.

6. *To Serve:* Place cookie cutter on a dish. Add a layer of guinea fowl, followed by a layer of leek and then a layer of vegetable purée. Remove cookie cutter and serve.

Breast of Ruffed Grouse
with Endives and Maple Syrup

Serves 4

Variations

You can use duck, pigeon (squab), guinea fowl or chicken in place of the grouse.

- Preheat oven to 425°F (220°C)
- Meat thermometer

4	ruffed grouse	4
4 cups	water	1 L
4	endives (each 2 to 3 oz/60 to 90 g)	4
⅔ cup	unsalted butter, divided	150 mL
	Salt and freshly ground black pepper	
⅓ cup	vegetable oil	75 mL
⅓ cup	maple syrup	75 mL

1. Debone grouse breasts. Roughly chop bones and brown in preheated oven until uniformly golden. Add water and cook, for 30 minutes. Strain liquid and set aside.

2. Peel endives, removing bitter part (base and heart). Place in a skillet, pour liquid over top, then add 2 tbsp (30 mL) of the butter. Add salt and black pepper, cover and cook over medium heat, about 12 minutes. Endives should be completely cooked. Let chill in their liquid. (Endives can be cooked the day before.) When endives are cold, press thoroughly to remove cooking liquid.

3. Reduce oven temperature to 350°F (180°C). In a skillet, heat ⅓ cup (75 mL) of the butter and vegetable oil. Season deboned grouse breasts and thighs with salt and black pepper. Add to skillet and sear over high heat. Place in preheated oven and finish cooking until thermometer inserted into the center of the thickest part of the thigh registers 170°F (77°C).

4. Heat remaining butter in a nonstick skillet over medium heat and slowly cook endives until golden. Add maple syrup and continue cooking, tossing carefully and frequently, until maple syrup is almost gone and endives are caramelized and golden brown on each side.

5. *To Serve:* Serve each person one endive and one roasted breast or thigh.

Roasted Ruffed Grouse with Black Trumpet Mushrooms and Caraway

Serves 4

Variations

Use pigeon (squab), guinea fowl or chicken instead of grouse.

Black Trumpet or Horn of Plenty Mushroom

This high-quality mushroom is available in the autumn. It has a strong fruity mirabelle plum scent.

- Preheat oven to 350°F (180°C)
- Ovenproof skillet

8 oz	black trumpet mushrooms	250 g
⅓ cup	olive oil	75 mL
4	shallots, minced	4
	Salt and freshly ground black pepper	
4	medium-size ruffed grouse	4
⅓ cup	peanut oil	75 mL
⅓ cup	white vermouth, such as Noilly Prat	75 mL
⅓ cup	port wine	75 mL
1 tsp	caraway powder	5 mL
3	caraway seeds, chopped	3
⅔ cup	butter	150 mL
4	slices country-style bread	4

1. Thoroughly clean black trumpet mushrooms. Heat olive oil in a skillet over high heat and sauté mushrooms and shallots. Season with salt and pepper and set aside.

2. Remove insides of ruffed grouse. Season with salt and black pepper inside and out. Place cleaned liver and gizzard back inside and truss (see page 365).

3. Heat peanut oil in a heavy-bottomed ovenproof skillet over medium heat. Add grouse and sear. Place skillet in preheated oven and continue cooking for 8 to 15 minutes (or according to USDA recommendations, see Tips, page 106), depending on their size. Remove grouse and keep warm.

4. To make sauce, remove excess fat from skillet. Add vermouth, port wine and caraway powder and seeds. Season with salt and black pepper. Simmer for a few minutes, then pour through fine-mesh strainer. Remove trussing strings. Place grouse in skillet and surround with mushrooms and cook over medium heat. Add cooking juice from vermouth and port wine and a few dabs of butter. Simmer for a few minutes.

5. *To Serve:* Toast bread. Remove cooked gizzards and livers from grouse. Mince quickly, then spread on slices of toasted bread. Debone grouse, lay on bread, then pour sauce on top. Serve with black trumpet mushrooms.

Braised Wood Grouse with Capiteux Blackcurrant Wine Sauce

Serves 4 to 8

Recipe dedicated to Monna et filles of l'Île d'Orléans

Tips

Thicken stock with 3½ tsp (17 mL) cornstarch and 7 tsp (35 mL) water.

Fresh bay leaves, which are quite fragrant, have been used throughout these recipes. If you have dry bay leaves double the amount called for in the recipes.

Serving Tip

Serve with potatoes cooked in salt water.

Variations

Use duck, pigeon (squab), guinea fowl or chicken instead of grouse.

1	wood grouse	1
1⅓ cups	red or Spanish onion, finely diced	325 mL
2	carrots, finely diced	2
3 cups	black currant fortified wine, such as Monna et filles Capiteux	750 mL
2	cloves garlic	2
2 oz	parsley root	60 g
6	black peppercorns	6
Pinch	four-spice mix (see Tip, page 110)	Pinch
½	bay leaf	½
1 cup	unthickened brown game bird stock or store-bought equivalent	250 mL
2½ tbsp	olive oil	37 mL
⅓ cup	lard	75 mL
	All-purpose flour	
1⅔ cups	demi-glace sauce or brown game bird stock, thickened (see Tip, left)	400 mL
	Salt and freshly ground black pepper	
10 oz	fresh or frozen blackcurrants	300 g

1. Cut wood grouse into equal portions of 4 oz (125 g) each. Place pieces in a large bowl. Add onions, carrots, black currant wine, garlic, parsley root, peppercorns, four-spice mix, bay leaf and 1 cup (250 mL) brown game bird stock. Add olive oil. Cover and let marinate overnight in the refrigerator.

2. The next day, remove grouse from marinade (reserving marinade) and pat dry. Heat lard in skillet over medium heat. Coat pieces of grouse in flour and sauté each piece until golden brown, about 5 minutes per side.

3. Preheat oven to 170°F (80°C). Place grouse and marinade in a Dutch oven. Add demi-glace sauce or brown game bird stock. Cook in preheated oven, 2 to 3 hours, depending on the age of the bird (which the supplier can tell you). Remove pieces of grouse, pour sauce through fine-mesh strainer. Adjust seasoning and add blackcurrants. Simmer.

Pairing Wines with Game

As with the art of creating a culinary dish, the urge to discover, analyze and sample all the wines the world has to offer is a pursuit driven by passion. If, for some, cooking is a labor of love, for others, the "addiction" of yearning to collect wines and start a cellar borders on the obsessive. You start off with a couple dozen bottles in a small corner of your abode, only to end up daydreaming of a temperature-controlled cellar where you can come and admire your collection every day.

A cellar constitutes a large investment, as does game cuisine. They are both suited to special occasions, since we do not have venison and a Clos Vougeot to grace our tables every day. Nothing, however, prevents us from more modestly taking advantage of the liquor store's wine list, which offers a first-rate selection along with suggestions from its very competent advisors to help us make our choice, whether for everyday wine or special occasions, and with a price tag to suit every budget.

I will nevertheless touch on wines for special occasions so as to pair them harmoniously with the game that you have hunted or have had the good fortune to receive as a gift.

First, we must determine whether the dish is to be accompanied by a wine to highlight it, if it is the dish that is to enhance a vintage wine or if the two are meant to be wed in blissful harmony.

For example: you have a Château d'Yquem 1947 in your possession. What culinary delight is worthy of it? It is a wine fit for a special occasion, which should be complemented by cuisine that can only further enhance it—the proverbial cherry on top. Aromas of honey, acacia and quince will grace this memorable tasting and the wine will reign supreme!

At other times, it will be the cuisine under the spotlight. The wine will play a supporting role; it will have to be subtler than the flavors of the sauce or the game.

At this point, reflection and research are important. If I've prepared several partridges and I decide to take advantage of the occasion to enjoy them with wine-loving friends, how do I pair the two?

First, I would ask myself what the partridges that I hunted fed on: berries, wild cherries, currants or cranberries, or simply foliage? This is because the source of nutrition will always have an impact on the flesh of the game. Second, I would select the cooking method for my partridges: they will be roasted and accompanied by a sauce of berries—either wild or cultivated. Since partridge meat is delicate and very subtle, my wine will also need to be fine and subtle, with berry aromas. All things considered, I would pair my partridges with a Volnay that ticks all the boxes and offers a whiff of violet. Wine and cuisine in perfect harmony!

Can you use the same wine if you cook venison in the same sauce? The answer is no. Why? Simply because venison has a much stronger flavor and aroma, especially if it has been marinated. I would therefore settle on a much more tannic and full-bodied wine. I would choose a Bordeaux wine, a Pauillac, the quality of which reads as follows: "Medium dark ruby, a touch of blue, aroma of ripe fruit, tart, with herbaceous scents, and an unusual confit quality, reminiscent of geranium.[1]" The complexity of this wine as well as its body will complement my roast haunch of venison perfectly, along with a sauce of berries from our forests.

While this may sound complicated, it really isn't. All you need is a few moments of planning to make your dinner party a resounding success. As a cook first and foremost, I will leave it to the wine experts to advise you. If, on the other hand, it is a wine that I want to introduce to you, the paired dish will in turn need to enhance it. But that's a whole other story!

1. Jean Lenoir, *Le Nez du Vin (Wine Aromas)*, Carnoux, Éditions Jean Lenoir, 1998.

Partridge, Pigeon, Northern Bobwhite, Pheasant, Quail and Turkey recipes

Gray Partridge Braised with Cabbage

Serves 4

Tip

Blanch bacon in a pot of boiling water for a few minutes to remove some of the salt. Drain and let cool.

Variations

Instead of partridge, use ptarmigan, guinea fowl, pigeon (squab), chicken or ruffed grouse.

Bay Leaf

This spicy leaf with a balsamic scent has a warm, bitter flavor that has earned it well-deserved recognition. An essential ingredient in a bouquet garni and many spice blends, it adds flavor at the start of cooking to braised dishes and highly seasoned soups, as well as to pickles, vegetables, mushrooms, cured meats and vinegars.

- Preheat oven to 350°F (180°C)
- Meat thermometer
- Large Dutch oven

2	fairly large partridge (each about 12 oz/375 g)	2
1	head green cabbage	1
1/3 cup	duck fat	75 mL
2	Spanish or red onions, sliced thinly	2
2	cloves garlic, minced	2
2	carrots, thinly sliced	2
5 oz	blanched bacon (see Tip, left)	150 g
1	Toulouse sausage or other pork sausage such as Italian sausage, cut into 1/2-inch (2 cm) thick slices	1
1/2	bay leaf	1/2
1 1/4 cups	game bird fumet (concentrated stock)	300 mL

1. Remove insides of partridge. (Use giblets for another recipe.) Truss (see page 365).

2. Cut green cabbage in half and remove leaves. Blanch in a large quantity of water to soften.

3. Heat duck fat in a large Dutch oven over medium-high heat. Add partridge and brown on all sides. Remove from pot. Add onions, garlic and thinly sliced carrots and braise. Remove all ingredients from pot to prepare for assembly.

4. Line bottom of Dutch oven with one-third of the blanched cabbage leaves, then lay partridge on top. Spread a layer of one-third of the cabbage leaves, then onions and carrots, then blanched bacon, then Toulouse sausage, bay leaf and game stock. Finish with remaining cabbage leaves. Cook in preheated oven very slowly until a thermometer inserted into center of the thickest part of the thigh registers 185°F (85°C) for at least 2 hours. Remove trussing strings and serve.

Partridge Cooked in Clay

In memory of Roger Jeannin, a great chef and a specialist in game.

Tips

This is the *"étouffée"* cooking method, similar to cooking in salt crust (page 114), or with a casserole dish sealed with pastry dough.

Clay is available from artist or craft supply stores.

You can even prepare this recipe in a conventional oven. In this case you place the partridge in a 300°F (150°C) oven for 3 to 4 hours, depending on its size.

Variations

Use snow goose, chicken, lamb or duck instead of partridge or grouse.

In homage to North American Indian culinary tradition. The late Bernard Assiniwi, in his book *Recettes typiques des Indiens* [Typical Recipes of the Indians] (Leméac, 1972), used this method to cook a moose head.

4	partridge or grouse	4
	Salt and freshly ground black pepper	
²⁄₃ cup	coarsely chopped celery	150 mL
1¼ cups	wild berries	300 mL
	Clay (see Tips, left)	
	Full-bodied game sauce	

1. This recipe can only be prepared under very special circumstances. You first make a wood fire that will produce a lot of embers. While the fire crackles, select the stones that will serve as the casing and place them in the embers to get very hot. At the same time, dig a hole large enough for the stones, embers and partridge to easily fit inside. Prepare partridge with or without the feathers. You can also make this in a conventional oven (see Tips, left).

2. *With feathers:* Remove insides of partridge. Season interior with salt and pepper. Stuff with celery and wild berries and envelope in a thick layer of clay.

3. *Without feathers:* Pluck partridge, wrap in foil, then coat in clay, leaving a small hole as a vent.

4. *Both methods:* Place embers in the hole, then line with burning-hot stones. Place partridge in hole and cover with embers. Place a small stick, such as a garden stake, in the vent and cover with earth. Let cook for 4 to 8 hours. Remove partridge. The clay will be baked and solidified. Break the mold and serve immediately.

5. *To Serve:* Cut partridge into pieces and serve with a full-bodied game sauce.

Young Partridge en Cocotte with Elderflower

Serves 4

Tip

If you prefer, cook the poultry to the USDA recommendations (165°F/74°C).

Variations

Instead of partridge, use ruffed grouse, baby grouse, Cornish hen or baby guinea fowl.

Elderflower

The elderflower is a "health tree." All of its parts can be used, including the bark. The dried flowers give off a very pleasant scent and are delicious. They can be found in natural food stores. If you are picking wild elder yourself, make sure you have correctly identified it. Raw elderberries can make some people sick. Buy from a reputable dealer.

- Preheat oven to 350°F (180°C)
- Large heavy-bottomed Dutch oven
- Meat thermometer

12	cipollini onions	12
1¼ cups	unthickened brown game bird stock or store-bought equivalent	300 mL
4	morel mushrooms, fresh or rehydrated	4
12 oz	crosnes (chorogi or Chinese artichoke)	375 g
4	large partridge	4
	Salt and freshly ground black pepper	
⅓ cup	hazelnut oil	75 mL
⅓ cup	pomace brandy (marc) or preferred spirits, such as Cognac or Armagnac	75 mL
1 cup	white wine, such as Chablis or other	250 mL
3 cups	brown poultry stock reduction (demi-glace) (Variations, page 347)	750 mL
⅓ cup	unsalted butter	75 mL
1 tbsp	powdered elderflower (see left)	15 mL

1. Braise onions in brown game stock in a skillet over medium heat. When onions are half-cooked, in about 10 minutes, add morel mushrooms. Simmer until onions are completely cooked. Set aside to keep warm.

2. Cook crosnes in salted water until crunchy, about 6 minutes. Drain and set aside.

3. Remove insides of partridge. Season partridge inside and out with salt and pepper. Truss (see page 365). Heat hazelnut oil over medium heat in a heavy-bottomed Dutch oven large enough to hold the partridge without squeezing together. Add partridge and sear, starting with breasts, then back. Cook in preheated oven until thermometer inserted into the thickest part of the thigh registers 150°F (66°C).

4. Remove trussing strings, then remove cooking fat from Dutch oven. Flambé with pomace brandy and add white wine. Reduce by 90 percent. Then add brown poultry stock reduction. Arrange cipollini onions, morel mushrooms and crosnes around partridge. Add butter and season with salt and pepper. Reduce oven temperature to 150°F (66°C) (see Tip, left) and cook, about 15 minutes more.

5. Sprinkle with dried elderflowers, then serve from Dutch oven immediately. As the pot is very hot, you can start by serving the thighs with the vegetables and the sauce, followed by the breasts.

Roasted Pigeon, Braised Figs and Pine Nuts, Truffle Juice with Foie Gras

Serves 4

Tip

A French cooking term, *à la goutte de sang*, refers to a level of medium-rare doneness, which is determined by pricking meat with a skewer to see if a drop of fat appears with a pink dot in the center.

Variations

Use partridge, quail, lark, thrush or small chicken.

Black Truffle
To some people, this subterranean tuber is the king of mushrooms. Its aromas and flavors are worthy of a holiday feast. It is highly prized but also very expensive. French epicure Jean Anthelme Brillat-Savarin called black truffle "the diamond of the kitchen."

- Dutch oven
- 4 skewers
- Meat thermometer

8	fresh figs	8
2/3 cup	white wine	150 mL
2/3 cup	port wine	150 mL
3	shallots, minced	3
2/3 cup	toasted pine nuts	150 mL
	Salt and freshly ground black pepper	
4	pigeons (squabs) (see Tips, page 144)	4
1/3 cup	truffle juice	75 mL
2/3 cup	fresh duck foie gras, diced	150 mL

1. The day before the meal, soak figs in white wine, port wine, shallots and toasted pine nuts. Cover and let stand on the counter or in the refrigerator for about 12 hours.

2. When you are ready to cook, preheat oven to 350°F (180°C). Arrange figs tightly packed together in a Dutch oven. Add soaking ingredients and season with salt and pepper. Cover and cook slowly in preheated oven, about 20 minutes. To check if figs are cooked, insert a needle in center; if needle comes out warm, the figs are cooked. Taste liquid, adjust seasoning and set aside.

3. Remove insides of pigeons and discard. Season pigeons inside and out with salt and pepper. Truss (see page 365) and place pigeons on skewers. Increase oven temperature to 400°F (200°C) and cook, basting off. Reduce temperature to 350°F (180°C) and continue cooking for about 20 minutes. Breasts are cooked when pierced with a skewer and a droplet of fat appears with a tiny spot of pink in the center. This is what is known as *cuisson à la goutte de sang* (cooked to the drop of blood) (see Tips, left and page 140). Note that the breasts will be cooked before the thighs (see Step 5).

4. Meanwhile, combine truffle juice and foie gras in a large bowl. Season with salt and pepper. Add to cooking juice of figs.

5. When pigeons are cooked, remove trussing strings. Debone breasts and place on a dish. Pour juice overtop and garnish with warm figs. During meal, continue to cook thighs until a thermometer inserted into the thickest part of the thigh registers 170°F (77°C), about 10 minutes. Serve as the next course.

Pigeon with Garlic Flowers

Preheat oven to 475°F (240°C)
Ovenproof skillet
Meat thermometer

Tips

When selecting a farm-raised pigeon for the table, choose only the squab. A squab is a pigeon that has not yet left the nest. After this stage, its meat becomes very tough.

This internal temperature of 165°F (74°C) is for health and safety standards. Restaurants often serve it at 136°F (58°C), which results in a pinker meat. If the food safety of rare-cooked poultry is a concern for you, cook to desired doneness or skip this recipe.

4	pigeons (squabs) (see Tips, left)	4
	Salt and freshly ground black pepper	
4	whole shallots	4
4	cloves garlic	4
¼ cup	vegetable oil	60 mL
7 oz	pine bolete mushrooms or porcini, diced	210 g
2½ cups	diced mixed vegetables such as celery, carrots, shallots (see Tips, page 66)	625 mL
½ cup	white vermouth, such as Noilly Prat	125 mL
½ cup	chopped garlic flowers	125 mL
⅓ cup	unsalted butter	75 mL

1. Remove insides of pigeons and discard. Season insides with salt and pepper. Cut shallots lengthwise. Place inside pigeons with garlic cloves. Truss (see page 365). Season on outside with salt and pepper.

2. Heat oil in an ovenproof skillet over medium heat. Arrange pigeons in a ring and sear in preheated oven for 5 to 6 minutes. Reduce temperature to 325°F (160°C). Baste pigeons frequently. When pigeons are three-quarters cooked and thermometer registers 118°F (48°C) in the center of breasts, remove vegetable oil. Arrange diced vegetables around pigeons, then add white vermouth. Return to oven and continue cooking until thermometer inserted into the center of the breasts registers 165°F (74°C) (see Tips, left). Remove pigeons from skillet and set aside. Incorporate garlic flowers and then add butter.

3. *To Serve:* Remove trussing strings, then serve pigeons whole with the cooking juice and vegetables.

Farm-Style Pigeon en Cocotte with Artichoke Bottoms and Baby Peas

Variations

Use partridge, quail, guinea fowl or chicken instead of pigeon.

4	artichokes	4
10 oz	extra-fine green peas, fresh or frozen	300 g
1/3 cup	vegetable oil, divided	75 mL
7 oz	mushrooms	210 g
1	piece (5 oz/150 g) side bacon, cut into small cubes	1
3/4 cup	pearl onions	175 mL
4	pigeons (squabs) (see Tips, page 144)	4
	Salt and freshly ground black pepper	
1/2 cup	dry white wine	125 mL
3/4 cup	unthickened brown game bird stock or store-bought equivalent	175 mL
1/2 cup	unsalted butter	125 mL

1. Cook artichokes in a large quantity of salted water until tender. Rinse in cold water. Trim the stem and slice off the top of the artichoke so the heart is visible and scoop out the hairy choke. Set aside. Partially cook peas in salted water if they are fresh (or let them thaw). Drain and set aside.

2. Heat half of the oil in a skillet over medium heat. Sauté mushrooms until all liquid has evaporated, about 8 minutes. Set aside.

3. Blanch bacon and set aside. Place pearl onions in a small saucepan, cover with salted water and partially cook. Drain and set aside.

4. Preheat oven to 450°F (230°C). Remove insides from pigeons. Season with salt and pepper inside and out. Truss (see page 365). Heat remaining oil in a skillet, sear pigeons, then cook in preheated oven until partially cooked, about 8 minutes.

5. Remove excess fat, pour in white wine, then arrange bacon cubes, mushrooms and pearl onions around pigeons. Continue cooking in oven until breasts are cooked when pierced with a skewer and a droplet of fat appears with a tiny spot of pink in the center. This is what is known as *cuisson à la goutte de sang* (cooked to the drop of blood) (see Tips, pages 140 and 142). If the thighs are not sufficiently cooked at this time, leave in oven until a thermometer inserted into the center of the thighs registers 165°F (74°C), 8 minutes more.

6. Remove pigeons, remove trussing strings and set aside to keep warm. Add baby peas, artichoke bottoms and game stock to other vegetables. Simmer for a few minutes and finish with butter. Debone pigeons.

7. *To Serve:* Serve breasts first. Fill artichoke bottoms with baby peas, mushrooms, bacon cubes and pearl onions.

Roasted Northern Bobwhites with Rowanberry and Highbush Cranberry Compote

Tip

Thicken stock with 1½ tsp (7 mL) cornstarch and 3 tsp (15 mL) water.

Variations

Use pigeon (squab), guinea fowl or chicken instead of bobwhites.

Highbush Cranberry

This shrub (also known as squashberry) measures 10 to 13 inches (25 to 32 cm) in height. It is often found growing on the edges of rivers and in maple forests. Its small red berries are harvested after the first frosts. A North American Indian tradition consists of pouring highbush cranberry syrup on a bed of clean snow and eating it like maple taffy.

- Preheat oven to 400°F (200°C)
- Dutch oven
- Meat thermometer

32	baby potatoes	32
4	northern bobwhites	4
	Salt and freshly ground black pepper	
⅓ cup	peanut oil	75 mL
½ cup	dry white wine	125 mL
½ cup	thickened brown game stock or store-bought equivalent (see Tip, left)	125 mL
4½ tbsp	unsalted butter	67 mL
Compote		
⅔ cup	rowanberries	150 mL
⅔ cup	highbush cranberries or regular cranberries	150 mL
¾ cup	minced shallots	175 mL
¾ cup	granulated sugar	175 mL
1 cup	toasted hazelnuts, finely chopped	250 mL
⅓ cup	water	75 mL
	Juice of 1 lemon	

1. Blanch potatoes, drain and set aside.

2. Truss northern bobwhite (see page 365). Season with salt and pepper. Heat oil in a Dutch oven over medium heat and roast bobwhites, for 2 minutes per side. Surround bobwhites with baby potatoes. Place Dutch oven in preheated oven and cook until a thermometer inserted into the thickest part of the thigh registers 155°F (68°C), 6 to 8 minutes (see Tips, page 140). Remove bobwhites and potatoes from Dutch oven.

3. To make sauce, remove cooking fat from Dutch oven and deglaze with white wine and brown game stock. Whisk in butter.

4. *Compote:* Place rowanberries, cranberries, minced shallots, sugar and chopped toasted hazelnuts in a saucepan over medium heat. Add water and cook for 15 to 30 minutes. At the end, add lemon juice. Set aside.

5. *To Serve:* Remove trussing strings. Cut up bobwhites and serve hot with potatoes. Serve rowanberry and cranberry compote and sauce on the side in gravy boats.

Northern Bobwhites with Oyster Mushrooms en Cocotte

Serves 4

Tip

Thicken stock
with 3 tsp (15 mL)
cornstarch and 6 tsp
(30 mL) water.

Variations

**Use pigeon (squab),
guinea fowl or
chicken instead
of bobwhites.**

- Heavy-bottomed Dutch oven
- Meat thermometer

4	northern bobwhites	4
Marinade		
2	Spanish onions, finely diced	2
2	carrots, finely diced	2
2	stalks celery, finely diced	2
1	bouquet garni	1
3	cloves garlic	3
3	juniper berries	3
1	whole clove	1
3 cups	dry white wine	750 mL
3 tbsp	white wine vinegar	45 mL
1/4 cup	olive oil	60 mL
	Salt and freshly ground black pepper	
1 1/4 cups	thickened game bird stock or store-bought equivalent (see Tip, left)	300 mL
14 oz	oyster mushrooms	420 g
2/3 cup	butter	150 mL
2/3 cup	peanut oil	150 mL
	Chopped chives	

1. *Marinade:* Place bobwhites in a large bowl. Add onions, carrots, celery, bouquet garni, garlic, juniper berries, clove, white wine, vinegar, olive oil, salt and black pepper. Cover and marinate in the refrigerator for at least 12 hours. Remove bobwhites from marinade, reserving marinade. Set bobwhites aside in the refrigerator.

2. To make sauce, reduce marinade by 90 percent. Pour through a fine-mesh strainer and add brown game bird stock. Simmer for 30 minutes. Set aside.

3. Clean oyster mushrooms thoroughly. Heat butter in a heavy-bottomed skillet over high heat and sauté mushroom. Season with salt and pepper and set aside.

4. Preheat oven to 350°F (180°C). Heat peanut oil in a heavy-bottomed Dutch oven over medium-high heat. Season bobwhite with salt and black pepper. Brown birds thoroughly, then place in preheated oven and cook until a thermometer inserted into the thickest part of the thigh registers 160°F (71°C), 15 to 25 minutes (see Tips, page 140). Remove excess cooking fat and add sauce. Simmer for a few minutes.

5. *To Serve:* Serve as is or deboned on a bed of oyster mushrooms. Sprinkle with chopped chives.

Pheasant in the Style of Monsieur Garcin

Serves 4

In homage to a great Montreal restaurateur, Monsieur Pierre Garcin

Tips

Thicken stock with 3 tsp (15 mL) cornstarch and 6 tsp (30 mL) water.

This recipe is particularly suited to an older pheasant, whose muscles are firmer. If you wish, you can leave all the aromatic ingredients in the sauce, except the garlic clove and bouquet garni.

Serving Tip

A potato purée makes a nice side dish.

Variations

Instead of pheasant, use guinea fowl or chicken.

- Meat thermometer

2	male pheasant	2
24	whole shallots, minced	24
1	piece (7 oz/210 g) smoked side bacon, cut into ½ inch (1 cm) thick strips	1
10 oz	mushrooms, diced	300 g
1	bouquet garni	1
4	cloves garlic	4
4 cups	red wine	1 L
⅔ cup	grapeseed oil	150 mL
¼ cup	red wine vinegar	60 mL
1 cup	butter, divided	250 mL
⅓ cup	peanut oil	75 mL
	Salt and freshly ground black pepper	
1 cup	thickened brown game stock or store-bought equivalent (see Tips, left)	250 mL
	Toasted pine nuts	

1. The day before or even two days before, place pheasant in a bowl. Arrange shallots, bacon, mushrooms, bouquet garni and garlic around pheasant. Add red wine, grapeseed oil and wine vinegar. Cover with plastic wrap and let stand in the refrigerator for 2 to 3 days. (The action of the alcohol content in the wine and the vinegar will have a tenderizing effect on the flesh of the pheasant.)

2. Remove pheasant and pat dry with paper towel. Pour marinade through a colander and set liquid and aromatic ingredients aside separately.

3. Add ⅓ cup (75 mL) of the butter to a saucepan over medium heat, sweat aromatic ingredients, then pour in marinade. Cook for 30 minutes. Pour through fine-mesh strainer, reduce by three-quarters and set aside.

4. Preheat oven to 400°F (200°C). Place pheasant in a Dutch oven. (Do not pack together too closely.) Heat remaining butter and oil over medium heat. Season pheasant with salt and pepper. Sear pheasant, then cook in preheated oven, basting often using a spoon, until thermometer inserted in the thickest part of the thigh registers 170°F (77°C).

5. When pheasant is cooked, remove from oven and let rest. Remove excess fat from Dutch oven and add game stock and marinade. Season with salt and pepper, pour through fine-mesh strainer, add toasted pine nuts and set aside.

6. *To Serve:* Cut pheasant in four and remove drumsticks, as they are often stringy. Lay a thigh and wing on a plate, then pour sauce over top.

Roasted Baby Pheasant
with Madeira Wine Sauce

Tip

Thicken stock with
2$\frac{1}{2}$ tsp (12 mL)
cornstarch and 5 tsp
(25 mL) water.

Serving Tip

Serve with wild rice.

Variations

**Instead of pheasant
breasts, use the
breasts of guinea
fowl or chicken.**

- Food processor
- Meat thermometer

2	pheasant	2
3 oz	slivered almonds	90 g
$\frac{1}{2}$	slice white bread	$\frac{1}{2}$
4$\frac{1}{2}$ tbsp	dried unsweetened cranberries	67 mL
2	eggs	2
	Milk	
	All-purpose flour	
$\frac{2}{3}$ cup	unsalted butter, divided	150 mL

Madeira Wine Sauce

$\frac{3}{4}$ cup	Madeira wine	175 mL
3 tbsp	Cognac	45 mL
2	shallots, minced	2
$\frac{3}{4}$ cup	thickened brown game bird stock or store-bought equivalent (see Tip, left)	175 mL
	Salt and freshly ground black pepper	

1. For this recipe, we only use the breasts of the pheasant; the thighs can be prepared the same way as duck thighs (see recipe, page 70). Debone pheasant and set breasts aside in refrigerator. Place thighs in freezer or refrigerator and use within 2 days.

2. Toast almonds. Remove crust from bread. In a food processor, finely chop bread, toasted almonds and dried cranberries and blend together until a bread crumb mixture. Set aside. Beat eggs with a little milk. Place flour, eggs and bread crumb mixture in three separate bowls.

3. Heat $\frac{1}{3}$ cup (75 mL) of the butter in a heavy-bottomed skillet over medium heat. Dip pheasant breasts in flour, then eggs, then in bread crumb mixture. Add to skillet and cook slowly until golden brown and skin is crispy, 2 minutes per side. Reduce heat to low and finish cooking until thermometer inserted into the thickest part of the thighs registers 170°F (77°C).

4. *Madeira Wine Sauce:* Reduce Madeira wine and Cognac by 90 percent with shallots. Add brown game bird stock, thicken, then finish with the remaining butter. Adjust seasoning.

5. *To Serve:* Pour sauce onto plates, place whole breasts on top.

Rock Partridge with Cuvée de la Diable Honey Wine

Serves 4

To the winners of the 2008 Renaud Cyr Award: Anicet Desrochers-Dupuis and Anne Virginie Schmidt of API-Culture Hautes Laurentides Inc.

Serving Tip

Serve hot with puréed potatoes or cattail hearts.

Variations

Instead of rock partridge, use pigeon, guinea fowl or chicken.

Why do some birds require marinating or soaking?

It is obvious that young rock partridge, whose flesh is tender, do not require this procedure, but older rock partridge should be marinated or soaked in order to tenderize their flesh. On the other hand, farm-raised rock partridge, which do not have a lot of flavor, will acquire the taste of the ingredients in the marinade or soaking liquid that is used.

- Dutch oven
- Candy/deep-fry thermometer

6 oz	acacia flower honey	175 g
1/8 tsp	essential oil of acacia flower, optional	0.5 mL
3/4 cup	white wine vinegar	175 mL
3 cups	honey wine, such as La Cuvée de la Diable	750 mL
4	rock partridge	4
4	shallots, finely minced	4
1	stalk celery, finely minced	1
2	carrots, finely minced	2
1	bouquet garni	1
1/4	bay leaf	1/4
1/3 cup	sunflower oil	75 mL
	Salt and freshly ground black pepper	
	Cornstarch or white roux	
1/3 cup	butter	75 mL

1. Combine honey, acacia essential oil, if using, and white wine vinegar in a saucepan over medium heat and cook until caramelized. When mixture reaches desired color, immediately add honey wine. Let cool.

2. Place rock partridge in a bowl large enough so birds are not completely submerged. Add cooled honey wine and surround with shallots, celery, carrots, bouquet garni and bay leaf. Cover and steep for 1 or 2 days in the refrigerator, turning partridge two times a day.

3. Preheat oven to 400°F (200°C). Drain partridge and pat dry with paper towel. Set aside marinade. Heat oil in a Dutch oven over medium heat and sear partridge. Season with salt and pepper. Place Dutch oven in preheated oven and cook for 6 to 8 minutes. The rock partridge will be barely cooked (it will finish cooking in the stock in Step 5). Debone breasts and backs of thighs. Cover meat with a damp cloth and refrigerate for up to 1 hour while preparing sauce.

4. To make sauce, cut carcass into chunks and add to marinade. Cook all ingredients over medium heat, 30 to 35 minutes. Pour through fine-mesh strainer, pressing very firmly on the ingredients to extract as much flavor as possible. Reduce stock by half. Adjust seasoning, thicken with cornstarch or white roux and whisk in butter.

5. Place deboned rock partridge in sauce and simmer slowly until liquid registers 185°F (85°C) on thermometer. Do not let boil, as this would harden the flesh of the birds.

Rock Partridge Cooked in the Style of Renée and Jacques Bax

Serves 4

Tips

If you don't have a meat grinder, use a food processor. The meat will be finer.

Thicken stock with 1½ tsp (7 mL) cornstarch and 3 tsp (15 mL) water.

Renée and Jacques Bax were one of the first in Quebec to sell quail, foie gras and guinea fowl.

Serving Tip

You can serve crosnes or salsify and potato mousseline on the side.

Variations

Instead of partridge, use pigeon (squab), guinea fowl or chicken.

- Electric grinder (see Tips, left)
- Ovenproof skillet
- Meat thermometer

Stuffing

2	slices white bread	2
½ cup	heavy or whipping (35%) cream	125 mL
2	breasts or thighs of large partridge	2
3½ oz	veal meat	105 g
	Salt and freshly ground black pepper	
8 oz	fresh duck foie gras	250 g
⅓ cup	Armagnac	75 mL
1	egg white	1
4	small rock partridge	4
¾ cup	unsalted butter, divided	175 mL
⅓ cup	vegetable oil	75 mL
2	shallots, minced	2
¾ cup	port wine	175 mL
⅔ cup	thickened brown game stock or store-bought equivalent (see Tips, left)	150 mL
⅓ cup	julienned black truffle	75 mL

1. *Stuffing:* Soak slices of bread in cream. Run partridge breasts, soaked bread, cream and veal meat through a grinder. Season with salt and pepper and set aside in refrigerator. Remove nerve from foie gras and cut into small cubes. Soak for 15 minutes in Armagnac, then blend with stuffing in the refrigerator and egg white. Store in refrigerator.

2. Preheat oven to 400°F (200°C). Season rock partridge inside and out with salt and pepper, then stuff. Close up the openings, then truss birds (see page 365). Heat ⅓ cup (75 mL) of the butter and oil in an ovenproof skillet over medium heat. Sear rock partridge, then cook in preheated oven until thermometer inserted in the thickest part of the thigh registers 170°F (77°C). Add minced shallots and baste using a spoon, for 1 minute. Remove cooking fat, then add port wine and reduce by half. Remove rock partridge from oven and keep warm.

3. To make sauce, add game stock, adjust seasoning, then pour through fine-mesh strainer. Whisk in remaining butter and add julienned black truffle. Set aside.

4. *To Serve:* Remove trussing strings. Cut rock partridge in two and carefully retrieve the stuffing. Debone rock partridge. Immediately place pieces on top of stuffing and pour sauce over top.

Quail with Walnuts and Port Wine

Serves 4

Serving Tip

Serve with wild rice or puréed celery root.

Variations

Use guinea fowl, chicken or partridge instead of quail.

- Large ovenproof skillet

4	large or 8 small quail	4
	Salt and freshly ground black pepper	
²⁄₃ cup	port wine or Madeira wine	150 mL
1	star anise, crushed	1
²⁄₃ cup	chopped walnuts	150 mL
¼ cup	peanut oil	60 mL
²⁄₃ cup	unsalted butter, divided	150 mL
¼ cup	Cognac	60 mL
¹⁄₃ cup	brown game bird stock reduction (demi-glace) (Variations, page 347)	75 mL
8	shelled walnuts	8

1. Season quail inside and out with salt and pepper. Then truss (see page 365) and set aside.

2. Combine port wine with star anise and chopped walnuts in a large bowl. Let steep for a few hours.

3. Preheat oven to 350°F (180°C). Heat peanut oil and half of the butter in an ovenproof skillet over medium-high heat. Brown quail on each side, then remove excess fat. Cook in preheated oven for 2 to 3 minutes. Remove from oven and flambé with Cognac. Add soaking liquid, then return to oven and cook, basting with juice a few times, 4 to 8 minutes. Remove quail and reduce cooking juice by a third.

4. To make sauce, add brown game bird stock reduction to skillet. Whisk in remaining butter, then add walnuts. Adjust seasoning.

5. *To Serve:* Remove trussing strings and serve quail with sauce poured over top.

Quail with Dried Currants and Pomace Brandy

*Recipe by
Chef Marc Jobin*

Tips

You can use the Chicken and Veal Stuffing (page 158) for this recipe.

Ask your butcher to debone the quail or to debone quail yourself, split down the back and flatten. Carefully cut out breast and backbones with tip of sharp knife. Do not remove bones in wings or legs.

Variations

Instead of quail, use pigeon (squab), guinea fowl or chicken.

- Meat thermometer

¼ cup	dried currants	60 mL
¾ cup	pomace brandy, such as Marc de Bourgogne, divided	175 mL
9 oz	fine poultry stuffing (see Tips, left)	270 g
	Salt and freshly ground black pepper	
8	quail, deboned (see Tips, left)	8
6 oz	sweet red grapes	175 g
¼ cup	peanut oil	60 mL
⅔ cup	butter, divided	150 mL
⅓ cup	white wine	75 mL
2	shallots, minced	2
1 cup	unthickened brown game bird stock or store-bought equivalent	250 mL

1. Place dried currants and ⅓ cup (75 mL) of the pomace brandy in a small bowl. Cover and let soak overnight at room temperature. Then add to fine poultry stuffing. Season with salt and pepper. Stuff deboned quail and reassemble to make look like a boned quail. Then "truss" with foil. Cut a strip of foil ½ inch (1 cm) wide and long enough to wrap around the quail. (Traditional trussing with string would not work as no bones remain.)

2. Preheat oven to 350°F (180°C). Peel red grapes. Cut in two and remove seeds. Set aside. Heat peanut oil and ⅓ cup (75 mL) butter in a large ovenproof skillet over medium-high heat. Season quail with salt and pepper. Add to skillet and place in preheated oven to sear quail and to quickly brown the skin on top. (The skin will brown through the foil as it will conduct heat.) After 4 to 5 minutes of cooking, remove foil, remove three-quarters of the cooking fat and continue to cook until a thermometer inserted into the center of the quail registers 140°F (60°C), 8 to 14 minutes (see Tips, page 140).

3. To make sauce, remove quail and excess fat from skillet. Flambé skillet with remaining pomace brandy. Add white wine, peeled grapes and minced shallots. Simmer for 2 minutes, then add game stock. Adjust seasoning. Whisk in remaining butter.

4. *To Serve:* Serve each quail deboned with sauce poured on top.

Spit-Roasted Quail with Cedar Jelly Sauce

Tips

This recipe is mainly suited to spit roasting. If you don't have a barbecue with a rotisserie, you can thread the quail onto metal skewers and cook directly on the grill; turn the skewers often and watch carefully for flare-ups.

Cedar jelly is made from the leaves of the eastern white cedar. It is available in specialty stores and wild game suppliers.

Variations

Use lark, thrush, wood pigeon or plover instead of quail.

- Barbecue grill with rotisserie (see Tips, left)
- Meat thermometer

8	quail	8
	Salt and freshly ground black pepper	
¾ cup	toasted hazelnuts, finely ground	175 mL
2	slices pork fatback, cut into 8 pieces	2
¼ cup	hazelnut oil	60 mL
¼ cup	plum eau-de-vie	60 mL
⅓ cup	cedar jelly (see Tips, left)	75 mL

1. Remove insides of quail and, except for gizzard, set aside all giblets. Season interior of birds with salt and pepper. Place chopped toasted hazelnuts inside. Truss birds and bard with pork fatback (see page 366).

2. Place quail on rotisserie skewer over high heat and cook for 8 to 12 minutes. Have a baking sheet under the skewers to collect the cooking fat for basting the quail.

3. Remove pork fatback and baste quail with hazelnut oil and cooking fat. Cook until thermometer inserted into the thickest part of the thighs register 170°F (77°C). Remove quail and flambé with eau-de-vie.

4. *To Serve:* Serve immediately with cedar jelly on the side.

Stuffed Quail Wrapped in Vine Leaves and Bacon

Serves 4

Tips

It is possible to find quail sold commercially that is already deboned and stuffed. If this is unavailable, ask your butcher to debone them.

To debrine means to partially or completely eliminate the salt content in certain foods that have been preserved in brine. This is done by immersing the food in a bowl of cold water or by running cold tap water over it.

Variations

Use northern bobwhite, small Cornish hen or baby partridge instead of quail.

- Meat grinder
- Meat thermometer
- Heavy-bottomed Dutch oven

Chicken and Veal Stuffing

8 oz	skinless boneless chicken breast	250 g
4	slices bread	4
⅔ cup	heavy or whipping (35%) cream	150 mL
4 oz	minced veal (shoulder)	125 g
	Salt and freshly ground black pepper	
½ cup	dried cranberries or blueberries	125 mL
¼ cup	chopped chives	60 mL
1	egg white	1
1 tbsp	potato starch	15 mL

Quail

4	large quail	4
	Salt and freshly ground black pepper	
½ tsp	blueberry essential oil, optional	2 mL
4	slices bacon	4
¼ cup	almond oil	60 mL
4	vine leaves, debrined (see Tips, left)	4
1 cup	tannic red wine	250 mL
¾ cup	unthickened brown game bird stock or store-bought equivalent	175 mL

Red Wine Butter

1 cup	tannic red wine	250 mL
2½ tbsp	minced shallots	37 mL
¾ cup	butter, at room temperature	175 mL
8 oz	arugula leaves	250 g
20	yellow beet chips	20

1. *Chicken and Veal Stuffing:* Using a meat grinder with a medium-size screen, grind chicken breast. Soak bread in cream, then run through grinder. Thoroughly blend ground veal with chicken and bread. Season with salt and pepper. Add dried cranberries, chives, egg white and potato starch. Set aside.

2. *Quail:* Spread out quail (see Tips, left). Season with salt and pepper. Using your finger, baste lightly with blueberry essential oil, if using. Stuff quail with chicken and veal stuffing, then reassemble to look like a boned quail. Wrap quail with a slice of bacon. Set aside in refrigerator.

Recipe continues, page 160...

Stuffed Quail Wrapped in Vine Leaves and Bacon *(continued)*

3. One hour before serving, preheat oven to 400°F (200°C). Heat almond oil in a heavy-bottomed Dutch oven. Cover each quail carefully with a large debrined vine leaf. Place quail in Dutch oven and cook in preheated oven, basting regularly for 7 to 8 minutes.

4. Reduce temperature to 325°F (160°C) and continue cooking until thermometer inserted in the thickest part of the thigh registers 170°F (77°C).

5. *Red Wine Butter:* Pour red wine into a saucepan, add shallots and reduce by 90 percent. Let cool completely. Add butter. You will not need all the red wine butter. Refrigerate leftovers for up to 2 days.

6. Remove quail from Dutch oven and keep warm at the front of the oven. Remove excess fat from Dutch oven. Pour in 1 cup (250 mL) red wine and reduce by 90 percent. Add brown game stock. Whisk in ¼ cup (60 mL) of red wine butter. Return quail to Dutch oven. Set aside to keep warm.

7. *To Serve:* Arrange quail on plates. Serve with arugula leaves and yellow beet chips. Serve sauce separately.

Stuffed Turkey Poult with Corn and Herb Fumet

Serves 6 to 10

Tips

You can use the Chicken and Veal Stuffing (page 158) for this recipe.

Thicken stock with 2½ tsp (12 mL) cornstarch and 5 tsp (25 mL) water.

Serving Tip

Serve with puréed corn or lentils.

Variations

Use guinea fowl or chicken instead of turkey poult.

Tarragon
Its fresh, tender leaves are used to add flavor to many dishes and sauces. On the other hand, its slightly anise flavor is particular and not everyone likes it. It is an essential ingredient in béarnaise sauce and is used to make excellent vinegar.

- Preheat oven to 375°F (190°C)
- Dutch oven
- Meat thermometer

1½ cups	cooked corn kernels (about 9 oz/270 g)	375 mL
2½ tbsp	chopped chives	37 mL
⅓ cup	chopped tarragon	75 mL
⅓ cup	bourbon or other whisky	75 mL
1 lb	fine poultry stuffing (see Tips, left)	500 g
	Salt and freshly ground black pepper	
1	turkey poult (3½ to 5 lbs/1.75 to 2.5 kg)	1
1	slice pork fatback	1
½ cup	peanut oil	125 mL
1 cup	mixed diced vegetables, such as onions, carrots and celery	250 mL
2	cloves garlic	2
¾ cup	thickened brown poultry or game stock or store-bought equivalent (see Tips, left)	175 mL
2 tbsp	chopped marjoram	30 mL
⅓ cup	chopped parsley	75 mL
2 tbsp	chopped cilantro	30 mL

1. Combine corn, chives, tarragon and bourbon in a large bowl. Add fine poultry stuffing and blend well. Season with salt and black pepper to taste. Set aside.

2. Season turkey poult inside and out with salt and pepper. Fill with stuffing. Sew openings closed, then truss (see page 365). Bard with pork fatback so that the melting fat will go into the meat of the turkey poult.

3. Heat oil in a Dutch oven. Place turkey poult inside. Place immediately in preheated oven. Baste often with cooking fat. After about 40 minutes, insert thermometer in the thickest part of the thigh and, if the temperature registers 122°F (50°C), surround turkey poult with mixed diced vegetables and garlic. Remove pork fatback. Continue cooking until thermometer inserted into the thickest part of the thigh registers 176°F (80°C). Remove turkey poult and set aside to keep warm. Remove excess cooking fat, then add brown stock. Cook for about 15 minutes, then pour mixture through a fine-mesh strainer. Add marjoram, parsley and cilantro. Adjust seasoning and keep warm.

4. *To Serve:* Remove trussing strings. Cut turkey poult into equal portions. Remove stuffing and divide into equal portions, then serve stuffing on top of the pieces of turkey poult. Pour sauce over top.

Turkey Poult Stew with Wild Herbs

Tip

Wild spring herbs include wild carrots, wild chicory, burdock, coltsfoot, live-forever and young sorrel leaves, depending on availability. The wild herbs and vegetables can be replaced by cultivated varieties.

Serving Tip

Serve coarse salt and ox-eye daisy capers on the side.

Variations

Instead of turkey poult, use guinea fowl, young fowl, goose or snow goose.

- Large Dutch oven
- Meat thermometer

1	turkey poult (2 to 3 lbs/1 to 1.5 kg)	1
Pinch	each various wild spring herbs (see Tip, left)	Pinch
6	baby parsnips	6
2	Spanish onions	2
1	head garlic	1
1	sprig thyme	1
1	bay leaf	1
1	clove	1
4	potatoes	4

1. In a large Dutch oven over medium heat, "bathe" turkey poult in a lot of water, which it needs in order to cook. Start cooking in cold water, as the heating of the water will help to gradually coagulate the blood inside evenly. During this procedure, blanch all herbs.

2. When turkey poult starts to boil, skim, then add a large pinch of each herb, along with baby parsnips, onions, garlic, thyme, bay leaf and clove. Do not add salt, as the coltsfoot replaces the salt. Cook slowly over low heat until a thermometer inserted into the thickest part of the thigh registers 185°F (85°C). Cooking time will vary according to the size and age of the turkey poult.

3. Cut potatoes in two lengthwise and cook in the cooking juice. Meanwhile, assemble all the aromatic ingredients, chop and distribute in soup plates. Add potatoes and pieces of turkey poult over top. Pour a little bouillon on top.

Breast of Wild Turkey Poult with Garden Herbs and Daisy Capers

Serving Tip

A few green beans will complete the dish.

Variations

Instead of wild turkey poult breasts, use the breasts of turkey, a large chicken or veal.

Sorrel

This plant is very acidic due to its exposure to the sun. Sorrel goes very well with several kinds of fish and enhances its flavor. Sorrel must be cooked, then frozen or sterilized.

Herb Mix

1/4 cup	unsalted butter	60 mL
3 1/2 oz	sorrel leaves, chopped	105 g
3 1/2 oz	spinach leaves, chopped	105 g
	Sprigs fresh thyme, chopped	
1 1/2 oz	marjoram leaves, chopped	45 g
1 tbsp	sage leaves, chopped	15 mL
3 1/2 oz	beet leaves, chopped	105 g
1 1/3 cups	finely diced vegetables, such as celery, carrots, onions	325 mL
4 oz	mushrooms, chopped	125 g
	Salt and freshly ground black pepper	
1/2 cup	brown game bird stock reduction (demi-glace) or equivalent (Variations, page 347)	125 mL

Polenta

8 cups	water	2 L
	Salt	
1 1/4 cups	polenta	300 mL
2 1/4 cups	shredded Fontina or other cheese	550 mL
1 1/2 cups	shredded Tomme cheese	375 mL
3/4 cup	unsalted butter	175 mL
	Freshly ground black pepper	

Wild Turkey Poult

4	boneless wild turkey poult breasts (each 7 oz/210 g)	4
	Salt and freshly ground black pepper	
1/4 cup	walnut oil	60 mL
1/4 cup	unsalted butter	60 mL
1/2 cup	Madeira wine	125 mL
1/3 cup	Cognac	75 mL
1/2 cup	unthickened brown game bird stock or store-bought equivalent	125 mL
24	daisy capers	24

1. *Herb Mix:* Heat unsalted butter in a heavy-bottomed skillet over medium heat. Add sorrel, spinach, thyme, marjoram, sage, beet leaves, celery, carrots, onions and mushrooms and slowly braise until liquid is completely evaporated. Season with salt and pepper. Thicken with brown game bird stock reduction. Set aside.

2. *Polenta:* Bring water to a boil. Add salt. Slowly pour in polenta, stirring constantly. Add shredded Fontina and Tomme cheeses and cook for about 50 minutes. Stir regularly with a wooden spoon. Melt butter. Just before serving, gently incorporate butter. Season with black pepper and keep warm.

Thyme

Thyme is essential to a bouquet garni. It blends beautifully with lamb and marinades, and it is an important element in Mediterranean cuisine.

3. *Wild Turkey Poult:* Lay out turkey poult breasts. If they are too thick, place between two sheets of foil and hit uniformly with the flat side of a large knife in order to flatten. Season both sides with salt and black pepper, then coat with the herb mix. Set aside.

4. Heat walnut oil and butter in a skillet over medium heat. Sear wild turkey poult breasts on each side, then cook slowly, basting regularly for 4 or 5 minutes. Remove cooking fat and deglaze with Madeira wine and Cognac. Add brown game bird stock. Keep warm.

5. *To Serve:* Spoon polenta onto each plate, then turkey poult breast. Pour jus on top and sprinkle on daisy capers.

Thrush, Lark and Lapwing
recipes

Thrushes Sautéed in Walnut Oil with Wild Chanterelle Mushrooms

Serves 4

Tip

Thicken stock with 2½ tsp (12 mL) cornstarch and 5 tsp (25 mL) water.

Serving Tip

Accompany with a purée of chestnuts, to which you have added chopped walnuts.

To Decant

To transfer a murky liquid to another container after allowing it to stand long enough for the impurities suspended in it to sink to the bottom.

- Preheat oven to 350°F (180°C)
- Cast-iron skillet
- Meat thermometer

Walnut Wine

10	green (unripened) walnuts, scalded and crushed	10
Pinch	ground cinnamon	Pinch
Pinch	ground mace	Pinch
Pinch	ground cloves	Pinch
1¼ cups	40-proof alcohol	300 mL
12	thrushes	12
1	slice pork fatback	1
	Salt and freshly ground black pepper	
¾ cup	butter, divided	175 mL
8 oz	chanterelle mushrooms	250 g
⅓ cup	vegetable oil	75 mL
¼ cup	walnut oil	60 mL
⅔ cup	thickened brown game bird stock or store-bought equivalent (see Tip, left)	150 mL
4	shallots, minced	4
12	shelled walnuts, halved	12
⅔ cup	chopped chives	150 mL

1. *Walnut Wine:* Cover walnuts, cinnamon, mace and cloves with 40-proof alcohol. Let soak for a minimum of 4 days and a maximum of 9 days. Decant, then pour through a coffee filter. (If the liquid is still murky, clarify or "fine" it, see Tip, left, by adding 1 tsp/5 mL egg white. Shake well, then let stand for 24 hours. Decant and filter again.)

2. When ready to make recipe, remove insides of thrushes. Truss and bard with pork fatback (see pages 366). Season with salt and black pepper and set aside.

3. Heat 6 tbsp (90 mL) of the butter in a cast-iron skillet over high heat. Add mushrooms and sauté until golden brown, about 5 minutes. Season with salt and pepper. Set aside.

4. Heat vegetable and walnut oils in an ovenproof Dutch oven over medium heat. Arrange thrushes inside and cook in preheated oven until half cooked (when the thermometer inserted into the thickest part of the bird registers 130°F/54°C), about 10 minutes. Remove small slices of pork fatback and leave at the bottom of the Dutch oven. Continue cooking thrush until thermometer inserted into the thickest part of the bird registers 168°F (76°C), about 10 minutes more.

5. Once thrushes are cooked, remove excess cooking fat and flambé with some of the Walnut Wine. Add brown stock and shallots. Add walnut kernels and remaining butter to thicken sauce.

6. *To Serve:* Reheat chanterelle mushrooms, add chopped chives and adjust seasoning. Make a bed of chanterelle mushrooms on a serving plate. Lay thrushes on top of mushrooms and pour remaining Walnut Wine over them.

Larks with Wild Cherries

Serves 4

Tips
You can substitute farm-grown or preserved cherries for wild cherries.

Look for jars of cattail hearts in specialty stores.

Variations
Instead of larks, use thrush, wood pigeon or plover.

Wild Cherries
There are many varieties of cherries. Sweet, red and black heart cherries, and bigarreaux cherries, which have a pale, brittle flesh, are all descendants of the wild cherry. Other cherries are hybrids of the wild cherry and the morello, or sour cherry, whose tart and juicy fruit (Montmorency cherries), go well with game.

- Heavy-bottomed Dutch oven

1¼ cups	wild cherries (see Tips, left)	300 mL
⅓ cup	kirsch	75 mL
8	larks, depending on their size	8
¼ cup	vegetable oil	60 mL
	Salt and freshly ground black pepper	
3	shallots, finely chopped	3
⅔ cup	unthickened brown game stock or store-bought equivalent	150 mL
1	jar (9 oz/270 g) cattail hearts (see Tips, left)	1
¼ cup	butter	60 mL

1. The season for wild cherries is very short so dry them in order to preserve and use throughout the year. If fresh, remove pits and soak in kirsch for at least 12 hours. If dehydrated, soak in water for 1 or 2 minutes for them to become engorged with water, then perform the same procedure as for fresh cherries.

2. Preheat oven to 350°F (180°C). Remove insides of larks and truss well (page 365). Heat oil in a heavy-bottomed Dutch oven. Season larks with salt and pepper and sear at high heat. Cook in preheated oven for 5 to 6 minutes, depending on their size. Remove from oven and remove excess cooking fat.

3. Place soaked cherries in Dutch oven and flambé. Remove birds and set aside to keep warm. Add minced shallots, then brown game stock. Cook for 2 to 3 minutes. Add cattail hearts and butter and simmer, 2 to 3 minutes more. Adjust seasoning. Place larks on top of cherries and cattail hearts. Cover and keep warm until ready to serve.

Larks in Potato Nests

Tip

Non-sparkling cranberry-flavored alcoholic cider can be found at small hard cider producers and some liquor stores. If not available, increase the wine to 1 cup (250 mL) and add ¼ cup (60 mL) unsweetened cranberry juice as a substitute.

- Preheat oven to 450°F (230°C)
- Meat thermometer

8 oz	duck foie gras, cut into cubes	250 g
3 tbsp	freeze-dried cranberries	45 mL
2	shallots, minced	2
½ cup	non-sparkling cranberry-flavored apple cider, divided (see Tip, left)	125 mL
8 or 16	larks, deboned, depending on size	8 or 16
8	large potatoes	8
	Salt and freshly ground black pepper	
½ cup	unsalted butter	125 mL
¾ cup	unthickened brown game bird stock or store-bought equivalent	175 mL

1. Blend together foie gras, cranberries, shallots and ¼ cup (60 mL) of the cider in a small bowl. Open up larks and stuff with mixture. Reform the bird shape by "trussing" with foil. Cut a strip of foil ½ inch (1 cm) wide and long enough to wrap around the larks. (Traditional trussing with string would not work as no bones remain.) Set aside in the refrigerator.

2. Cook potatoes with skin on in water for 10 minutes. Rinse with cold water. Remove skin, then dig into each potato to form a "nest" for the larks to rest in. Season potatoes with salt and pepper. Place 2 larks in each potato. Place potatoes in an ovenproof dish. They should fit together tightly. Add a tiny dab of butter on each lark.

3. Bake in preheated oven for 3 minutes. Reduce temperature to 350°F (180°C) and continue cooking until thermometer inserted in the thickest part of the thigh registers 170°F (77°C). Heat brown stock and add remaining apple cider. Pour brown game stock mixture over larks.

Lark or Thrush Pie

⦿

Serves 6 to 8

Variations

Instead of lark, use woodcock, quail, bobwhite or thrush.

For Holiday Feasts

This recipe is a souvenir from my years as an apprentice. It is a meal of exceptional quality that requires an enormous amount of time to prepare, but it is worth it, for a special occasion.

- Meat thermometer
- Meat grinder

12 to 36	larks, depending on their size	12 to 36
	Salt and freshly ground black pepper	
Pinch	powdered thyme	Pinch
Pinch	powdered bay leaf	Pinch
Pinch	powdered nutmeg	Pinch
½ cup	fine Champagne	125 mL
3 tbsp	grapeseed oil	45 mL
Pie Filling		
5½ oz	veal shoulder, nerve removed	160 g
5½ oz	pork throat	160 g
2 oz	fatty bacon	60 g
	Salt and freshly ground pepper	
6 oz	cep or morel mushrooms, finely chopped	175 g
6	shallots, minced	6
4 tbsp	butter	60 mL
3 tbsp	vegetable oil	45 mL
Lark Stuffing		
48	quail livers	48
3½ oz	duck foie gras	105 g
½ cup	chopped truffles	125 mL
	Salt and freshly ground black pepper	
Pie		
1¾ lbs	puff pastry dough	875 g
1	slice pork fatback	1
2	egg yolks	2
⅓ cup	Madeira wine	75 mL

1. Pluck larks and flambé (pass them over a flame to gently remove the down remaining on the skin). Debone and save livers and intestines. Lay larks on a dish (skin on the outside). Season with salt, pepper, thyme, bay leaf and nutmeg. Sprinkle larks uniformly with fine champagne and grapeseed oil. Cover with plastic wrap and let marinate in the refrigerator, turning occasionally, 1 to 2 hours.

2. *Pie Filling:* Cut veal, pork and fatty bacon into small cubes. Season with salt and pepper, then use a meat grinder to finely grind the meat. Wash mushrooms, then chop finely with a knife, along with shallots. Heat butter and oil in a skillet over medium heat and sweat mushrooms and shallots until golden, 3 to 5 minutes. Add meat filling and cook over high heat, 2 to 3 minutes. Let cool on a tray at room temperature for no more than 30 minutes.

3. *Lark Stuffing:* Collect cooking fat from the pie filling. Heat a heavy-bottomed skillet over high heat and sear quail and lark livers (take care just to sear them, not cook them). Add intestines. Set aside. Cut foie gras into small cubes. In a small bowl, mix foie gras, truffles, quail and lark livers and intestines. Add 2 tbsp (30 mL) of pie filling. Mix gently, incorporating the marinade liquid of the larks. Season with salt and pepper.

4. *Pie:* Lay out larks. Place 1 tsp (5 mL) of stuffing on each one, then reform into bird shape. Roll out half of the puff pastry dough in a circle measuring 7 inches (18 cm) in diameter and $\frac{1}{3}$ inch (0.7 cm) in thickness. Cut up pork fatback and place on dough, leaving $\frac{3}{4}$ inch (2 cm) border around the edge.

5. Spread half of the stuffing over pork fatback, then lay stuffed larks around the circumference. Spread the other half of stuffing, taking care to completely cover larks. Mix egg yolks with a little water for egg wash and baste the edge of the lower layer of dough. Cover with remaining dough.

6. Place in refrigerator for at least 1 hour. Baste dough with egg wash, then draw patterns with the prongs of a fork. Make a $\frac{1}{4}$ inch (0.5 cm) hole in the center to allow steam to escape.

7. Preheat oven to 550°F (290°C). Place pie in preheated oven to brown dough. Reduce temperature to 350°F (180°C) and cover with foil. Place a thermometer in the vent. When thermometer registers 175°F (80°C), pour in the Madeira wine using a small funnel. Serve hot.

Lapwings en Cocotte with Carrot and Orange Juice

Serves 4

To Chef François Blais, chef and owner of Bistro B in Quebec City, winner of the 2008 Renaud Cyr Award, which recognizes artisanal contributions to Quebec's culinary culture

Variations

Instead of lapwings, use lark, partridge, quail or thrush.

- Preheat oven to 400°F (200°C)
- Ovenproof skillet

2	carrots	2
4	oranges	4
8 to 12	lapwings (2 to 3 per person, depending on their size)	8 to 12
	Salt and freshly ground black pepper	
⅓ cup	vegetable oil	75 mL
2 tbsp	Armagnac	30 mL
3	shallots, minced	3
⅓ cup	unsalted butter	75 mL
12	quail or lapwing eggs, poached	12
5 oz	cooked Chinese noodles	150 g

1. Extract carrot juice using an electric juicer or use ¾ cup (175 mL) carrot juice. Squeeze oranges. Set aside.

2. Season lapwings with salt and pepper inside and out. Truss carefully (see page 365). Pour oil in an ovenproof skillet and lay lapwings tightly together. Place, uncovered, in preheated oven, for 6 minutes.

3. Remove fat and flambé with Armagnac. Remove lapwings. Add minced shallots, carrot juice and orange juice to skillet and reduce by half. Whisk in butter. Adjust seasoning. Heat Chinese noodles.

4. *To Serve:* On each plate, form a nest with the Chinese noodles. Lay poached quail or lapwing eggs on top, then place lapwings on top of eggs. Pour sauce over top.

Game Animals

Moose

Caribou

Deer

Wild Boar

Bison

Muskox

Bear

Beaver

Hare and Rabbit

Squirrel

Seal

Tips on Using the Meat and Offal of Game Animals

by Laurier Therrien, venison specialist, and Marcel Bouchard, chef

In general, we tend to overlook the offal of game. It is true that toxic substances accumulate in the offal of certain animals and that parasites may be found there, but this is the exception. Here are some tips and specifications that will help you enjoy offal in complete safety.

The hunter can judge the health of the game he is pursuing, as observations made before killing provide important clues. You must avoid an animal that is exhibiting odd behavior, limping, holding its head low, has its tail between its legs or that shows bruises. After the kill, the animal must be eviscerated as quickly as possible while strictly observing the rules of hygiene. Wearing gloves is recommended and, if the animal must be quartered for transporting, the pieces of meat must be wrapped in cotton. Some of these fabrics have a protective coating that prevents flies from landing on the meat. You must avoid washing the game in water, so as not to contaminate the meat. The dried blood on the surface provides good protection. If the animal is soiled, wipe it with clean cloths or paper towels. Transport the animal with the skin on.

The Different Species of Game Animals

Moose

All the offal of the moose is edible and highly prized by connoisseurs, because these pieces are large and easy to prepare.

The heart: The heart can be served as a steak of $\frac{1}{2}$-inch (1 cm) thickness, cooked pink and rare, whole, stuffed and cooked in the oven at low heat, cut into cubes or cooked in milk and light game stock.

The liver: It is important to know that the color of the liver of the male moose is very different from that of the female. The liver of a female moose is red and has a rather sweet flavor. The liver of the male moose is pink and soft and has a rather acrid flavor, particularly during the rutting season. To prepare the liver, it is recommended that you remove the transparent membrane that covers it before you cook it, and let the liver sit in milk to soak, which will remove some of the bitterness.

The kidneys: The kidneys, which are often disdained by hunters, are nevertheless delicious. They must be removed immediately after the kill and kept cold. They must be wrapped separately if you intend to freeze them to use at a later date.

The tongue: Unlike the kidneys, the tongue is considered a choice morsel, highly prized by experienced hunters. It has a very delicate flavor and requires careful preparation. It is removed by making an incision under the lower jaw to extract the entire length of the tongue.

The thymus: The thymus glands, or sweetbreads, are found in immature moose, as they are in beef calves. Like the kidneys, the thymus glands must be removed immediately after the kill and then frozen. These sweetbreads are of high quality and are cooked like those of beef calves.

Caribou

When killed for commercial purposes, Agriculture Canada rejects all livers and kidneys, because many of these organs are contaminated by cadmium and different parasites. I therefore highly recommend that you do not consume these parts. On the other hand, the heart and the tongue are absolutely impeccable. They are the prime cuts of meat consumed by the Inuit and North American Indians. In many cases, these may be eaten raw. I have personally eaten them this way, but prefer them to be slightly cooked. The testicles (aka Rocky Mountain Oysters) are also considered a delicacy.

Deer

In this case, we are referring to white-tailed deer, although it is possible to find other varieties of deer in certain hunting areas. All of the offal has almost the same characteristics and are prepared in the same way, with a few exceptions:

The heart: The fatty part in the upper section of the heart as well as the bit of cartilage that may be found there must be removed.

The liver: It is dark and has a pronounced flavor. There is no difference in color or texture between the liver of the male and that of the female.

Wild Boar and Wild Boar Piglet

This animal that lives in the wild in Europe is highly prized. The food it prefers to eat imparts special flavors to its meat that are of a rare quality.

Bison and Muskox

The bison and muskox resemble beef cattle in anatomical terms. The offal can be consumed without any problem. The heart, liver and tongue can be cooked in the same way as for beef. Even the tail, jowls and testicles (aka Rocky Mountain Oysters) are a delicacy.

Black Bear

The meat of the bear wrongly has a bad reputation. This meat is delicious, especially in the springtime, when the animal comes out of hibernation. Its meat is less fatty than in the fall, and therefore tastier. Bear meat can be eaten without risk, but its offal must be consumed sparingly. It is worth noting that all of the preparations and recipes for wild boar can be used for bear.

Beaver

The meat of the beaver probably has the most distinct flavor because of its habitat and its food, which consists of leaves, specifically aspen. The green sap flavor that permeates its meat leaves no one indifferent. The aroma of beaver meat is accentuated by the fact that it cannot be bled, because only trapping is permitted. It is better to eat young specimens in the springtime, as their meat is more delicate and of a more pleasing texture than those of older beaver.

Snowshoe Hare and Arctic Hare

Hares are generally snared. Their meat is delicious, but often firm. This is why they are usually cooked in a sauce. Arctic hares are exceptionally flavorful. The offal of wild and farm-raised hares is edible.

Seal

This animal, whose nutritional qualities we know little about, has helped to ensure the survival of many people living in coastal regions. Its meat is very dark, almost black. Its offal is very popular and almost always kept by the residents of these regions for their personal consumption. It is thus very difficult to find, unless you know a trapper and have an agreement with him to supply you.

Other Animals That Are Hunted or Trapped

We hunt coyote, wolf, groundhog, raccoon, fox, red squirrel, gray squirrel, river otter, Canada lynx, bobcat, porcupine, American pine marten and muskrat. My North American Indian and Inuit friends have invited me to taste the meat of a number of these animals, and I must admit that, in general, I have been pleasantly surprised.

Other Animals Eaten Around the World

We eat kangaroo, chamois, antelope, mouflon (wild sheep), ostrich, and many other animals.

MOOSE
Alces alces

FAMILY: Cervidae

WEIGHT: Male, 660 to 1,320 lbs (300 to 600 kg); female, 485 to 880 lbs (220 to 400 kg)

LENGTH: Up to 8 feet (2.50 m)

HEIGHT: Up to 6 feet (1.8 m) at the shoulder

How does one explain why this magnificent cervid is not found on the tables of our restaurants? So much the better, in my opinion. Although the rules of the game give it a chance to survive during the hunting season, poaching would leave it powerless and defenseless. It is better that we respect the moose and accord it royal status for the table.

HABITAT: Leafy and evergreen forests.

FOOD: In winter, the moose feeds on the branches and bark of maples, birch, willow and aspen. In summer, it mostly eats aquatic plants such as horsetail, arrowhead and water lily. The food that it consumes affects the flavor of its meat.

CHARACTERISTICS: This large animal, similar in height to a horse, is a very important cervid in our forests. It is a revelation to witness the excitement of hunters when hunting season opens. The call of the female is a very special moment for them.

The moose has a cumbersome walk and exceptionally good hearing. Its eyesight, on the other hand, is poor. Unlike the caribou, the moose is solitary, except in winter and during the rutting season. It moves about in a well-defined area. The moose is an impressive animal. The male, with its majestic antlers, reigns over most of our forests up to the 55th parallel.

WOODLAND CARIBOU
Rangifer tarandus

FAMILY: Cervidae

WEIGHT: Male, 265 to 575 lbs
(120 to 260 kg); female, 198 to 364 lbs
(90 to 165 kg)

LENGTH: up to 8 feet (2.50 m)

HEIGHT: up to 5 feet (1.45 m)

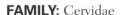

HABITAT: In summer, the caribou lives
on the Arctic tundra. In winter, it lives in
sub-Arctic regions where there is a lot of
lichen (taiga).

CHARACTERISTICS: The name caribou
comes from the Mi'kmaq word *xalibu,* which
means "the animal that digs." This large
animal has a shaggy muzzle and flattened
antlers. Caribou are nomadic and live in
herds of 10 to 15, except during the period
of migration when they congregate in the
hundreds. The caribou's diversified diet and
its habitat—north of the 44th parallel—
endow it with unique gastronomic qualities.

The herd in Quebec, where I live,
is large (800,000 to 900,000 head in the
territory, including Labrador). Every spring,
the herd leaves its winter habitat in the
spruce forests for calving grounds located
far away on the Arctic coastal tundra. It
is still not understood how these animals
know the migratory routes. They retreat to
their dens to calve in the months of April
and May. After the birth of the young, the
entire herd gathers over several square miles.
This gathering is one of the last great natural
wonders of Quebec, as impressive as the
gathering of bison, once upon a time.

This animal has great culinary qualities,
but in Canada only the Inuit have the right
to hunt caribou commercially. We are thus
dependent on the Inuit for introducing us to
this meat. Being city dwellers, alas, we only
cook the nobler parts of this animal. Only
sport hunters have the opportunity to taste
and have their family and friends discover
the delicious flavor of caribou offal, neck
and shanks.

WHITE-TAILED DEER
Odocoileus virginianus

NAME: Deer

FAMILY: Cervidae

WEIGHT: Male, 176 to 374 lbs (80 to 170 kg); female, 132 to 265 lbs (60 to 120 kg)

LENGTH: 63 to 85 inches (1.60 to 2.15 m)

HEIGHT: 35 to 39 inches (90 cm to 1.0 m)

Other Families
AMERICAN ELK
Cervus canadensis

There are five other sub-species of elk, including the famous Boileau deer (*Cervus elaphus elaphus*), currently enjoyed in fine restaurants, *Cervus elaphus canadensis* (Erxleben 1777), *Cervus canadensis manitobensis* (Millais, 1915), *Cervus elaphus* (Nelson V. Bailey, 1935) and *Cervus canadensis roosevelti* (Merriam, 1897).

SITKA DEER
Odocoileus hemionus sitkensis

MULE DEER
Odocoileus hemionus

EUROPEAN ROE DEER
Capreolus capreolus

The white-tailed deer has cousins: the black-tailed deer, the mule deer and the Sitka deer. Highly prized in gastronomy, all of its parts are delicious. Out of respect, it is considered a duty to use the entire animal.

HABITAT: The habitat of the deer is widespread. It can be found from Hudson's Bay to northern South America as well as Central America. It lives in fields, orchards and mixed forests.

FOOD: Deer feed on leaves, plants, trees and shrubs as well as fruits and mushrooms.

CHARACTERISTICS: This elegant cervid is solitary, except during the rutting season and in winter, when it joins its fellow deer to wreak havoc in an effort to protect itself against the intense cold.

This graceful, slender and big-eyed animal makes us want to pet it. It is distinguished by its tail measuring almost 12 inches (30 cm) in length. Like the cat and the dog, the deer express its moods with its tail, wagging it from left to right or raising it high to reveal the white tuft underneath.

NAME: Wild boar (adult)
Piglet (young animal)

FAMILY: Suidae

WEIGHT: 88 to 660 lbs (40 to 300 kg)

LENGTH: up to 70 inches (1.80 m)

HEIGHT: 35 inches (89 cm)

HABITAT: The wild boar is found in Europe, southern Russian and Scandinavia. In North America, the wild boar we find on our tables is generally farm-bred. The wild boar prefers damp and marshy regions and lives in herds.

FOOD: In nature, the wild boar lives on acorns, chestnuts, roots, potatoes and occasionally truffles.

CHARACTERISTICS: Wild boar meat has been highly prized since ancient times. The older the animal, however, the tougher the meat and the longer it needs to be marinated.

The boar is a violent, destructive and even dangerous animal. It bears a great resemblance to the pig.

The adult wild boar has black hair, while the young boar has gray hair with yellow stripes. Up to the age of 6 months, wild boar are called "piglets." At two years of age, the females are called "sows" and older males are called "solitary boars."

AMERICAN BISON or BUFFALO
Bison bison

FAMILY: Bovidae

WEIGHT: Male, 1,014 to 1,587 lbs (460 to 720 kg); female, 794 to 1,014 lbs (360 to 460 kg)

LENGTH: 10 to 13 feet (3 to 4 m)

HEIGHT: 5 to 6 feet (1.5 to 1.8 m)

HABITAT: This species lives in a wide variety of habits, from the arid plains to cultivated poplar stands, as well as on the prairie, in the fluvial valleys and even mixed pine woods.

FOOD: Bison mainly graze on grass, broadleaf plants and sedges. They eat rye, oats, bluegrass, hay, rushes, lichen and cranberries.

CHARACTERISTICS: The bison is the largest land mammal in North America. It is a gregarious animal that forms tight herds of 4 to 20 animals. Some say that these are family groups. These bands can in turn join together to form enormous herds counting thousands of head.

This animal is curious, but also wary and easily frightened. Bison turn in circles if they are attacked or flee in disarray if there is a general panic. The females and the young are more frolicsome than the males, outdoing one another to run and to butt heads.

These bovids spend a lot of time grooming themselves, which consists mainly of rolling in muddy holes, taking sand baths, goring bushes and rubbing against the trunks of trees.

The bison has a very fine sense of smell and excellent vision. It can detect certain odors up to 1 mile (1.6 km) away and spot a moving object more than half a mile (1 km) away. It is estimated that the population of bison in Canada before the arrival of Europeans was between 40 and 60 million. The populations in the East were exterminated in the 1800s and by 1875 the herds in the West were reduced to a handful of isolated groups. Luckily, people became aware of the threat of extinction in time and the balance is now in the process of being restored.

MUSKOX or MUSK OX
Ovibos moschatus

FAMILY: Bovidae

WEIGHT: Male, 573 to 772 lbs (260 to 350 kg); female, 353 to 518 lbs (160 to 235 kg)

LENGTH: 6 to 8 feet (1.8 to 2.4 m)

HEIGHT: 3 to 5 feet (90 cm to 1.5 m)

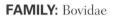

HABITAT: Native to Canada's boreal region, the muskox lives in the Arctic islands, northwestern Greenland and Alaska.

FOOD: In winter, it grazes on Labrador tea, cranberries, crowberries, dwarf birch and willow; in summer, it feeds on rushes, Canada bluegrass, fireweed and campion.

CHARACTERISTICS: Muskox are gregarious, normally forming herds of 3 to 100 head (15 on average). The males prefer to live alone or in small groups for most of the year. These animals apparently have very good vision and an excellent sense of hearing. They move about heavily and slowly. If threatened with danger, however, they run astonishingly quickly, in tight rows. They then regroup in a circle, and the oldest charge the enemy.

The population, quite limited at the start, was the subject of exploitation in the Canadian Arctic during the 19th century. The animals were killed for their meat as well as their skins, which were made into travel blankets. Between 1864 and 1916, more than 15,000 skins were harvested. In 1930, it was estimated that there were no more than 500 head of muskox on the continent.

BLACK BEAR
Ursus americanus

FAMILY: Ursidae

WEIGHT: Male, 220 to 606 lbs
(100 to 275 kg); female, 187 to 320 lbs
(85 to 145 kg)

LENGTH: 4 feet 6 inches to 6 feet 4 inches
(1.40 to 1.9 m)

HEIGHT: 2 feet 4 inches to 3 feet
(70 to 90 cm)

In a book published in 1855 by L. M. Lombard, *Le cuisinier et le médecin* (*The Cook and the Doctor*), it says: "Bear fat, once the particular odor that impregnates it has been removed, is excellent, sweet, and can easily replace butter in recipes. All one needs to do is melt it and then, while it is still hot, throw in a certain amount of salt and sprinkle water on it. A powerful explosion is produced, followed by thick smoke, which removes, as it wafts away, the bad odor of the fat.

Some people eat bear meat. In America, smoked and salted bear hams are a favorite; bear meat is imported throughout Europe, where it is just as highly esteemed, but it is a meal reserved for the tables of the wealthy. The feet of this animal constitute a very delicate food. The meat of the bear only suits hardy palates."

I had the good fortune to serve springtime bear to several great European chefs. I can assure you that they loved this fine meat.

HABITAT: The black bear can be found in all of the wooded regions of North America, as well as the mountainous regions of Mexico.

FOOD: In summer, the bear lives on small fruits—strawberries, raspberries, blackberries, cherries, cranberries, hazelnuts and serviceberries—as well as on honey. After its hibernation period, it lives on spruce needles, larvae and even dead animals.

CHARACTERISTICS: The black bear is solitary, except during the rutting season and while raising its young. It lives in dense leafy and evergreen forests, areas that have been deforested due to fire, scrub and sometimes even on the tundra. It can be found near streams and lakes or at the edges of swamps.

This animal is considered a choice large game animal loved by sport hunters for its delicious meat, especially when it is young.

NORTH AMERICAN BEAVER
Castor canadensis

FAMILY: Castoridae

WEIGHT: 33 to 77 lbs (15 to 35 kg)

LENGTH: 3 feet to 3 feet 6 inches
(0.90 cm to 1.1 m)

HABITAT: Once virtually extinct in
Europe, the beaver has been successfully
reintroduced to numerous northern countries.
In North America, its natural habitat is
Canada, large portions of the United States
and northern Mexico. The beaver lives on the
edges of streams, lakes and marshes bordered
by deciduous trees (aspen and poplar), where
it finds food in abundance.

FOOD: It feeds on the tender bark of some
trees, as well as leaves, twigs, buds and
aquatic plants.

CHARACTERISTICS: This mammal
belongs to the rodent family. It is a builder
of dams, and has been nicknamed "nature's
engineer." In fact, it is the only animal,
besides man, that modifies its habitat. It is
interesting to note that beaver that eat birch
taste better than beaver that eat aspen.

Beavers live in social groups on the edges
of streams and lakes. Their tails are flat
and covered in scales and their feet are
webbed. They put remarkable effort into
the construction of their two-story dens.

The lower level, which is underwater, is
a storage area for their food; they live on
the upper level during the winter. Beavers
gnaw through trees with their teeth and
cut wooden piles to build their dens. They
gather mud, using their tails as trowels to
pack the mud as they construct the den.

L. M. Lombard, in his book *Le cuisinier et
le médecin* (*The Cook and the Doctor*) wrote,
in 1855: "The meat of the beaver is tough,
malodorous and unpleasant-tasting. Hunters
prefer to eat the hindmost part, which is
tender and sweet, similar in taste to tuna
and eel. …The beaver provides "castoreum,"
a rich, oily and highly pungent substance
secreted in ovoid sacs that are located near
the reproductive organs."

The beaver meat that I have tasted was
delicious and delicate.

SNOWSHOE HARE, VARYING HARE

Lepus americanus

FAMILY: Leporidae

WEIGHT: 3 to 5 lbs (1.5 to 2.5 kg)

HABITAT: The snowshoe hare is found in forested areas throughout most of Canada, Alaska, and as far south as Tennessee, where it lives in cooler mountainous areas.

FOOD: The hare lives on grass and plants during the summer. It will occasionally eat a few mushrooms or the young shoots of shrubs. In winter, it settles for certain kinds of bark (maple, spruce, pin, cedar and willow), which gives its meat a particular flavor.

CHARACTERISTICS: The hare occupies a territory of 3 to 15 hectares of conifers, copse and undergrowth. It eats toward the end of the day and, when stalked, remains immobile to blend into the landscape. It can run 25 mph (40 km/h) and hop a distance of 13 to 20 feet (4 to 6 m) in a single bound. It is white in winter and grayish-brown in summer. Smaller than the hares found in Europe and the Arctic, it is distinguished by its brown tail in summer (the European hare has a black tail and the Arctic hare has a white tail).

Other Hares

MOUNTAIN HARE
Lepus timidus

BROWN HARE, EUROPEAN HARE
Lepus europaeus

ARCTIC HARE
Lepus arcticus

FAMILY: Leporidae

WEIGHT: 6 to 15 lbs (3 to 7.5 kg)

HABITAT: The Arctic hare lives in the tundra, which includes the northern regions of Greenland, the Canadian Arctic islands and Northern Canada as well as in Labrador and Newfoundland.

FOOD: In summer its diet consists of seaweed, sedges, birch, Arctic willow and crowberries. In winter it lives on twigs and the roots of willows and birches. This very particular diet gives its meat a special flavor.

CHARACTERISTICS: It is the largest hare in North America. It is most active at nightfall. The Arctic hare is all white, with black-tipped ears. During the short Arctic summer its back turns grayish brown. It is distinguished from the snowshoe hare by its much larger size and by its weight. The Arctic hare is gregarious for the most part, living in groups of 10 to 60 individuals.

DOMESTIC RABBIT

FAMILY: Leporidae

WEIGHT: 6 to 11 lbs (3 to 5.5 kg)

HABITAT: Farm.

FOOD: Farm-raised rabbits are not difficult to feed: vegetable peelings and grass gathered at the edges of ditches are a treat for them.

CHARACTERISTICS: There are countless breeds of rabbit. What we see in the photo is the Giant Papillon. All rabbits are descendants of the wild, or European, rabbit. The Romans were mad for rabbit meat.

Other Rabbits
Wild
EUROPEAN RABBIT
Oryctolagus cuniculus

Farm-raised
FLEMISH GIANT
BLANC DU BOUSCAT
RUSSIAN GIANT
REX
POLISH
FAUVE DE BOURGOGNE
NEW ZEALAND

AMERICAN RED SQUIRREL
Tamiasciurus hudsonicus

FAMILY: Sciuridae

WEIGHT: 7 to 8 oz (210 to 250 g)

HABITAT: The American red squirrel is a tree squirrel. It lives in forested and mountainous areas across North America. It prefers cool and coniferous forests, but can also be found near human habitations if there is forest nearby.

SIZE AND COLOR: The red squirrel is much smaller than the gray squirrel, typically measuring 11 to 15 inches (28 to 38 cm) in length, tail included. It has a reddish brown back and a white or cream underside. Its tail, which is smaller and flatter than the tail of other tree squirrels, may be yellowish-gray or rusty red with a black band. The American red squirrel is a different species from the Eurasian red squirrel (Sciurus vulgaris), which is protected in the UK and Europe.

FOOD: The red squirrel has a voracious appetite. Although it mainly eats seeds, nuts and conifer cones, it also feeds on fungi, flowers, bark, tree sap and insects, and has even been known to eat birds' eggs and baby mice. Its keen sense of smell helps it to locate its multiple caches of food, even under several feet (meters) of snow.

CHARACTERISTICS: This delicate looking creature is fearless and will aggressively defend its territory and food stores from intruders. Squirrel meat is considered a delicacy and is also a staple in traditional Appalachian cuisine.

Other Squirrels
GRAY or BLACK SQUIRREL
FOX SQUIRREL
NORTHERN FLYING SQUIRREL

SEAL
Phoca

FAMILY: Phocidae

WEIGHT: 287 to 408 lbs (130 to 185 kg)

LENGTH: up to 6 feet (1.8 m)

Seals can live up to 35 years of age, but the average lifespan is about 23 years.

Seal meat is highly nutritious. The seal has very powerful blood circulation; its meat retains a lot of blood, making it a challenge to prepare.

HABITAT: The seal can be found in many parts of the world, from the North Atlantic to Antarctica. Most live in locations where the water is cold, but there are some warm water species.

CHARACTERISTICS: Counting about 5.5 million, the seal population is significant. Seals are gregarious and migratory. One seal can eat 44 to 55 lbs (20 to 25 kg) of fish per day. Many culinary studies are currently underway with a view to commercializing seal meat.

Moose, Caribou and Deer
recipes

⊙ ─────────────────────────────────

Continued, next page

Filet of Virginia Deer on Gingerbread Loaf with Confit of Onions, Fava Beans and Chanterelles

Serves 4

Recipe by Chef Danielle Gordjin

Chanterelles
The chanterelle mushroom (Cantharellus) is a yellow mushroom with white flesh and slightly fruity flavor. Prized by gourmets, it is a wonderful accompaniment to game.

Confit

12	pearl onions	12
7 oz	fava beans	210 g
1½ tbsp	butter, divided	22 mL
1½ tbsp	granulated sugar	22 mL
2 cups	poultry or vegetable stock	500 mL
6 oz	chanterelles	175 g

Venison

4	venison filet medallions (each 5 oz/150 g)	4
	Salt and freshly ground black pepper	
1½ tbsp	butter, divided	22 mL
2 tbsp	vegetable oil	30 mL
¼ cup	thinly sliced onions	60 mL
3 tbsp	granulated sugar	45 mL
¼ cup	wine vinegar	60 mL
⅔ cup	Madeira wine or sherry	150 mL
⅓ cup	unthickened brown veal or game stock or store-bought equivalent	75 mL
6	slices homemade or store-bought gingerbread loaf, ½-inch (1 cm) thick, divided	6
	Thin slices cold butter to whisk into sauce, optional	
11 oz	duck foie gras	330 g
	All-purpose flour	

1. *Confit:* Blanch onions and fava beans in boiling water, then drain and cool down by plunging into cold water before peeling. Peel onions and fava beans. Place onions in a saucepan with half of the butter and sugar. Cover and cook over low heat until tender, about 20 minutes. Drain and set aside.

2. Braise fava beans in poultry or vegetable stock over low heat until tender, about 30 minutes. Set stock aside.

3. Heat remaining butter in a skillet over medium-high heat. Do not burn the butter. Sear chanterelles for 2 to 3 minutes, then add pearl onions and sauté until lightly caramelized, 2 to 3 minutes more.

Recipe continues, page 200...

Filet of Virginia Deer on Gingerbread Loaf with Confit of Onions, Fava Beans and Chanterelles *(continued)*

4. Stir in fava beans with some of their juice and cook for 1 to 2 minutes to blend the flavors. Adjust seasoning. Set aside.

5. *Venison:* Season venison medallions with salt and pepper. Heat half of the butter and oil in a skillet and sear venison over medium-high heat. Cook to taste, about 4 minutes per side so meat is medium-rare or rare.

6. Meanwhile, to make sauce, sauté onion in remaining butter until lightly browned. Add sugar and continue cooking until an amber caramel forms. Deglaze with vinegar then pour in Madeira wine. Reduce slightly and add game stock. Reduce again by half.

7. Thicken sauce with 2 slices of gingerbread loaf until desired texture is reached, then pass through a fine-mesh strainer or a sieve. Whisk butter, if using, into sauce and set aside.

8. Toast remaining gingerbread slices and keep warm. Cut 4 slices of foie gras, season, dredge in flour and cook quickly at high heat in a nonstick skillet.

9. *To Serve:* Place venison medallions on toasted gingerbread loaf. Top with slices of foie gras. Pour sauce on top of meat and garnish with the vegetable confit.

Venison vs. Deer

The word *venison* comes from the Latin verb *venari,* meaning "to hunt." At one time it meant all hunted animals but today *venison* refers primarily to deer and sometimes antelope. In this chapter we use the terms venison and deer interchangeably.

Roasted Rack of Boileau Deer with Fall Vegetables

Serves 4

Tips

Le Cerf de Boileau (Boileau deer) is a private brand of venison raised by Les Fermes Harpur in the Outaouais region of Quebec.

Thicken stock with 2½ tsp (12 mL) cornstarch and 5 tsp (25 mL) water.

If you prefer, cook the meat to the USDA recommendations (160°F/71°C).

Variations

Instead of deer, use rack of moose, caribou or elk.

- Preheat oven to 500°F (260°C)

2½ lbs	bone-in rack Boileau deer (see Tips, left)	1.25 kg
	Salt and freshly ground black pepper	
⅓ cup	peanut oil	75 mL
⅓ cup	unsalted butter	75 mL
2	Spanish onions	2
2	Cortland apples	2
8	baby carrots	8
1	bay leaf	1
2	sprigs thyme	2
4	cloves garlic	4
⅔ cup	white wine	150 mL
¾ cup	thickened brown venison stock or store-bought equivalent (see Tips, left)	175 mL

1. Remove rack of venison from refrigerator, wrap in plastic food wrap and wait for it to come to room temperature. Season with salt and black pepper.

2. Place peanut oil and butter on oven's broiler pan tray and heat in preheated oven. Place meat on sizzling hot pan and return to the hot oven to sear meat until golden brown. Reduce temperature to 350°F (180°C) and cook for 15 minutes.

3. Meanwhile, cut each onion into 6 lengthwise wedges. Blanch, rinse in cold water and pat dry with a paper towel. Cut each apple into 6 wedges. Surround rack of venison with onions, apples, carrots, bay leaf, thyme sprigs and garlic and continue cooking, 5 to 10 minutes. Remove cooking fat. Add white wine and brown venison stock and continue cooking until desired temperature at the center is reached (see below and Tips, left).

4. *To Serve:* Cut generous portions of the ribs and serve immediately with the vegetables surrounding the rack.

My Preferred Internal Temperatures for Cooked Meats

Rare: 125°F (52°C), after resting 130°F (54°C)
Medium: 130°F (54°C), after resting 136°F (58°C)
Well-done: 136°F (58°C), after resting 140°F (60°C)

Venison Tartare Bites

12 oz	venison filet mignon	375 g
¼ cup	extra virgin olive oil	60 mL
⅓ cup	finely minced shallots	75 mL
½	bunch parsley, finely minced	½
3 tbsp	small marjoram leaves	45 mL
	Salt and freshly ground black pepper	
1	loaf baguette bread	1
2 tbsp	Dijon mustard	30 mL

Variations

Instead of venison, use bison, moose, caribou, elk or muskox.

Parsley

Parsley is an essential ingredient of the famed *bouquet garni* used to flavor stocks, fumets and essences. With its subtle and delicate aroma, this condiment can be used to accentuate the blandest sauces and meats or add zest to herb omelets, drab salads, starchy dishes and ordinary soups.

1. Finely dice venison filet on chilled cutting board (see Precautions, below). Marinate meat in olive oil with shallots, chopped parsley, marjoram, salt and freshly ground black pepper. Place in refrigerator for 1 or 2 hours.

2. Cut baguette into ¼-inch (0.5 cm) slices and toast lightly. Set aside and let cool.

3. *To Serve:* Just before serving, spread mustard on each slice of bread and top with tartare.

Precautions

Certain precautions must be taken when handling raw meat. The cutting board used for chopping the meat should be placed in the freezer at least 2 hours ahead of time and the knife should be carefully washed and chilled.

Venison and Root Vegetable Patties

Serves 4

Recipe by Chef Myriam Pelletier, winner of the Gold Medal at the 1996 Berlin Culinary Olympics

Tips

If you do not have a lid that is tight-fitting enough, make a seal with foil or sealing pastry (see Tips, page 92).

Purchase pre-cut cubes of venison or select a cut with a gelatinous texture (like the shank) or protected by bone (like the neck). Ask your butcher to section it lengthwise in half, then ³⁄₄ inch (2 cm) in thickness. Cut vegetables into slightly larger cubes than the meat so they don't dissolve while cooking.

Variations

Use bison, muskox, caribou, moose or beef instead of venison.

- Preheat oven to 325°F (160°C)
- Dutch oven with tight-fitting lid (see Tips, left)

6 tbsp	butter	90 mL
¼ cup	peanut oil	60 mL
1¼ lbs	venison cubes (shank or neck) (see Tips, left)	625 g
2 cups	unthickened brown game stock or store-bought equivalent	500 mL
2	carrots	2
2	parsnips	2
2	parsley roots	2
1	onion	1
3	cloves garlic	3
4 oz	celery root	125 g
2½ tbsp	lemon zest	37 mL
3½ tbsp	chopped flat-leaf parsley	52 mL
	Salt and freshly ground black pepper	
½ cup	flax seeds, divided	125 mL
7 oz	rolled oats (about 2 cups/500 mL), divided	210 g
7 oz	Kamut flakes (about 2 cups/500 mL), divided	210 g
1½ cups	bread crumbs	375 mL
	All-purpose flour	
4	eggs	4
	Butter	
¼ cup	vegetable oil	60 mL

1. Heat butter and oil in a sauté pan and sear pieces of venison over low heat. Allow meat juices to stick to bottom of pan. Deglaze with water once the juices have caramelized; otherwise they may develop a bitter flavor.

2. Place meat in a Dutch oven with a tight-fitting lid. Add cooking juices, brown game stock, carrots, parsnips, parsley roots, onion, garlic and celery root. Bring to a simmer on stovetop over medium heat. Cover with tight-fitting lid and place in preheated oven, about 2 hours, depending on thickness of pieces. (Venison is a lean meat so it should be braised until medium-rare and over low heat to avoid drying it out.)

3. Remove meat from pan and shred it. Coarsely mash the vegetables. Place meat and vegetables back into the braising liquid, allowing them to soak it up (all of the liquid doesn't necessarily have to be absorbed, just enough to form a juicy patty without excess liquid). Add lemon zest and chopped parsley. Season with salt and pepper. Once mixture has cooled, form patties and place in freezer for 30 minutes.

Recipe continues, page 208...

Venison and Root Vegetable Patties *(continued)*

Serving Tip

Serve patties topped with the salad of your choice. For example, a living salad with sprouts, such as alfalfa, clover, radishes and a julienne of raw vegetables drizzled with hemp oil.

Celery Root

The Greeks and Romans used celery root (aka celeriac) as a blood purifier. This ball-shaped variety of celery grows up to 4 inches (10 cm) in diameter and weighs in at 1¾ to 3¼ lbs (875 to 1.625 g). Its culinary claim to fame is celery root *rémoulade*.

4. To make bread crumb mix, place half of the flax seeds, rolled oats and Kamut flakes in a coffee grinder and grind to a powder, then add bread crumbs. Coarsely crush remaining half of the flax seeds, rolled oats and Kamut flakes and set aside.

5. To bread, dredge patties in flour, eggs and bread crumb mix. Set aside for 30 minutes in freezer, then coat with the mixture of coarsely crushed flax seeds, rolled oats and Kamut flakes.

6. Preheat oven to 400°F (200°C). Pan-fry patties in butter and oil in a nonstick pan over medium heat. Brown on one side, flip carefully and finish cooking in preheated oven. Serve immediately with salad topping (see Serving Tip, left).

Venison vs. Deer

The word *venison* comes from the Latin verb *venari*, meaning "to hunt." At one time it meant all hunted animals but today *venison* refers primarily to deer and sometimes antelope. In this chapter we use the terms venison and deer interchangeably.

Heart Braised in Red Wine with Parsnip and Pearl Onion Garnish

Serves 4

To Pierre Vaillon, a great chef

Tip

Thicken stock with 3½ tsp (22 mL) cornstarch and 7 tsp (35 mL) water.

Serving Tip

Serve with boiled potatoes.

Variations

Instead of caribou heart, use the heart of deer, moose, bison, muskox, elk, beef or veal.

- Cast-iron Dutch oven

⅓ cup	vegetable oil	75 mL
1	caribou heart	1
1¼ cups	red wine	300 mL
1⅔ cups	thickened brown game stock or store-bought equivalent (see Tip, left)	400 mL
1	carrot	1
4	cloves garlic	4
2	stalks celery, stalks attached	2
1	bouquet garni	1
	Salt and freshly ground black pepper	
10 oz	parsnip, cut into strips	300 g
20 to 25	pearl onions	20 to 25
½ cup	finely chopped parsley	125 mL

1. Heat vegetable oil in Dutch oven over medium-high heat and brown heart evenly until nicely colored, about 3 minutes per side.

2. Remove excess cooking fat, add red wine and reduce by two-thirds to decrease the acidity. Then add game stock. Heat over medium heat until boiling point. Add carrot, garlic, celery stalks and bouquet garni. Season with salt and black pepper. Reduce heat to low and cook for 50 minutes. Remove the aromatics and set aside.

3. Add parsnip strips and pearl onions and continue to cook on low until meat is completely cooked. (The tip of a knife inserted in the meat should come out easily.) Or cook according to USDA recommendations, see Tips, page 244. During the second stage of cooking, finely dice celery and carrot and add at the end of cooking.

4. Cut heart quarters lengthwise, pour braising liquid over top and sprinkle with chopped parsley.

Whole Filet of Caribou Roasted in the Style of the Himbeault Family with Blueberry Sauce Poivrade

Serves 4

Tips

Marinate the filet only if you wish to impart the specific flavor of the marinade into the meat.

The Himbeault family owns Himbeault Gibier, Le Boucher du Chasseur, in Saint-Stanislas-de-Kostka, a small municipality in Quebec. It is a butcher specializing in game animal and game bird cuts.

Variations

Instead of caribou, use deer, moose, bison, muskox, wild boar piglet, elk, beef, pork or veal. Since caribou filet is much smaller than moose or deer filet, it can be cooked and served whole, depending on the animal's size. Deer and moose filets will need to be sliced before cooking and serving: approximately 5 oz (150 g) of meat per person.

- Preheat oven to 400°F (200°C)
- Meat thermometer

1¼ lbs	caribou filet	625 g
¼ cup	peanut oil	60 mL
¼ cup	Cognac	60 mL
1	onion, finely diced	1
1	stalk celery, finely diced	1
1	carrot, finely diced	1
	Several sprigs dried thyme	
1	bay leaf	1
⅔ cup	red wine	150 mL
1 cup	Sauce Poivrade (page 355)	250 mL
⅔ cup	blueberries	150 mL
¼ cup	butter	60 mL
	Salt and freshly ground black pepper	

1. Remove all the nerves from the filet and reserve the trimmings for another use.

2. Heat oil in a roasting pan over medium-high heat. Sauté filet until golden brown, about 2 minutes per side. Cook in preheated oven until thermometer inserted into the center of the filet registers 130°F (54°C) for medium (see Tips, page 211). Remove excess fat and flambé filet with Cognac. Remove filet and set aside on a warm grill and keep warm.

3. Transfer onion, celery, carrot, thyme, bay leaf and red wine to roasting pan. Cook until alcohol evaporates, 4 to 5 minutes. Then add Sauce Poivrade. Simmer for 3 to 4 minutes. Pass through a fine-mesh strainer, pressing vegetables against the sides to release all the flavors of the aromatics. Heat again and add blueberries and butter. Simmer for 2 to 3 minutes more. Season with salt and pepper to taste.

4. *To Serve:* Cut large slices of the filet and place on top of the sauce.

Roasted Round with Wild Mushroom Sauce

Per person
(see Tip, below)

Tips

Since the size of each animal varies, the recipe lists the ingredients per person. The amounts will need to be adjusted based on the cut of meat if a whole round is used or based on the number of guests.

If you prefer, cook the meat to the USDA recommendations (160°F/71°C).

Variations

Instead of caribou, use deer or moose.

- Meat thermometer
- Strainer, lined with cheesecloth

7 oz	untrimmed caribou meat	210 g
	Marinade of your choice (page 346)	
2 tbsp	vegetable oil	30 mL
1/3 cup	butter, divided	75 mL
1/2	shallot, minced	1/2
1 1/2 oz	hedgehog mushrooms	45 g
1 1/2 oz	chanterelle mushrooms	45 g
1 1/2 oz	black trumpets	45 g
	Salt and freshly ground black pepper	
1/3 cup	unthickened brown game stock or store-bought equivalent	75 mL

1. Remove large nerves from the round. Let marinate in the refrigerator for 2 days for a young animal and 5 to 7 days for an adult animal.

2. Preheat oven to 400°F (200°C). Pat dry round with a paper towel. Drain the aromatics from the marinade and set aside. Reserve marinade liquid. Heat oil in a roasting pan over medium-high heat. Sear the round until golden brown, about 2 minutes per side. Place in preheated oven and roast, basting frequently, until a thermometer inserted into the center reaches 113°F (45°C). Add the aromatics from the marinade. Continue cooking while basting frequently, until center of round reaches 130°F (54°C). At this stage, remove the round and let rest (see page 202 and Tips, left).

3. Heat half of the butter over medium heat. Slowly sweat shallot and mushrooms until all liquid has evaporated. Season with salt and black pepper to taste. Set aside.

4. To make sauce, remove excess cooking fat from roasting pan, then add marinade liquid until cooking residue comes loose. Pour liquid into a saucepan. Add game stock and cook over medium heat for 30 minutes. Filter through a fine-mesh strainer, then through a cheesecloth-lined strainer. Pour sauce over mushrooms. Season with salt and pepper and finish with remaining butter.

5. *To Serve:* Pour mushroom sauce onto a serving plate. Cut large slices of the round, place over sauce and garnish with vegetables.

Haunch of Venison with Grand Veneur Sauce

Serves 4

To Madame Micheline Delbuguet, a culinary pioneer in Montreal and owner of Chez la Mère Michel, a highly esteemed restaurant featuring Quebec cuisine

Tips

Estimate about 10 oz (300 g) with bone per person depending on the animal's size and age.

In general, one should cut up a haunch. If the haunch is small, however, leave it whole or cut it as in the illustration below.

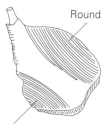

Round

Outside round

Serving Tip

Serve with a chestnut or celery purée.

Variations

Instead of venison, use wild boar piglet.

Gooseberry jelly can also be added to the sauce.

- Meat thermometer

1	haunch venison (see Tips, left)	1
2	carrots, minced	2
1 cup	minced Spanish onions	250 mL
1	stalk celery, minced	1
4	cloves garlic, crushed	4
1	bay leaf	1
	Sprigs dried thyme	
2	whole cloves	2
4	juniper berries	4
	Sprigs parsley	
	Salt and freshly ground black pepper	
3 cups	tannic red wine	750 mL
3 cups	high-quality red wine vinegar	750 mL
⅓ cup	peanut oil	75 mL
1½ cups	Grand Veneur Sauce (page 356)	375 mL

1. Thoroughly remove nerves from venison haunch. Place in a dish so the liquid covers less than 1 inch (2.5 cm) of the meat. Garnish with carrots, onions, celery, garlic, bay leaf, thyme, cloves, juniper berries and parsley sprigs. Lightly season with salt and black pepper. Add red wine and vinegar, cover with plastic wrap and refrigerate, turning haunch over twice a day, for 2 to 3 days.

2. Remove haunch from marinade and let drain for 30 minutes to release excess liquid. Carefully drain aromatics from marinade and set aside. Reserve marinade liquid.

3. Preheat oven to 450°F (230°C). Heat peanut oil in a roasting pan over medium-high heat and sear haunch on each side. Place in preheated oven. Halfway through cooking, when a thermometer inserted into the center registers 118°F (48°C), arrange the aromatics around the haunch and cook until meat reaches 130°F (54°C) at the center, about 45 minutes in total (see Tips, page 211). Take haunch out of oven and let rest for at least 30 minutes before serving.

4. Remove excess cooking fat from pan and add marinade liquid. Reduce by half, then add Grand Veneur Sauce. Cook for 2 to 3 minutes and pour through a fine-mesh strainer, pressing against the sides to extract all of the flavors. Adjust seasoning.

5. *To Serve:* Put a spoonful or two of sauce on each plate, slice deer haunch and place on top of sauce.

Tuktoyaktuk Caribou Sirloin and Sauce Poivrade with Sea Buckthorns

Tip

A *mirepoix* is a mixture of equal amounts of chopped celery, onions and carrots. Raw, roasted or sautéed with butter or olive oil, it is the flavor base for a wide variety of dishes, such as stocks, soups, stews and sauces.

Serving Tip

Serve with a celery and parsnip purée.

Variations

Instead of caribou sirloins, use bison, muskox, deer, moose, elk, beef or veal.

Sea Buckthorn

Sea buckthorn berries come from a prickly, deciduous shrub with the scientific name *Hippophae*. The shrub has a very pleasant fragrance.

- Strainer, lined with cheesecloth

4	caribou sirloins (each 5 oz/150 g)	4
2 tbsp	butter	30 mL
1½ tbsp	vegetable oil	22 mL
	Salt and freshly ground black pepper	

Sauce Poivrade with Sea Buckthorns

¼ cup	vegetable oil	60 mL
2¼ cups	diced mixed vegetables (see Tip, left)	550 mL
½ cup	diced parsley roots	125 mL
1	sprig thyme	1
1	bay leaf	1
	Game trimmings	
⅓ cup	wine vinegar	75 mL
1⅔ cups	unthickened game stock or store-bought equivalent	400 mL
3 tbsp	sea buckthorn jelly	45 mL
2 tbsp	sea buckthorn berries (fresh or frozen)	30 mL
1	pat butter	1
	Salt and freshly ground black pepper	

1. Remove all the nerves from the sirloin and reserve the trimmings. Heat butter and oil in a skillet over medium heat. Sear caribou sirloin, about 3 minutes per side. Cook to desired doneness (see page 217 and Tips, page 211). Season with salt and black pepper. Set aside and keep warm.

2. *Sauce Poivrade with Sea Buckthorns:* In the skillet used to sear caribou steaks, add oil, diced mixed vegetables, diced parsley roots, thyme, bay leaf and reserved game trimmings and brown over medium heat. Then deglaze with wine vinegar. Reduce to nearly dry. Add game stock and reduce until creamy consistency is reached. Pass through strainer, lined with cheesecloth.

3. Add sea buckthorn jelly and berries. Heat over low heat while adding butter. Season with salt and pepper.

4. *To Serve:* Spoon sauce over sirloins.

Braised Shank Scented with Cedar Shoots and Chicoutai

Serves 4

To Chef Régis Hervé of Les Saveurs Oubliées in Charlevoix, winner of the 2008 Renaud Cyr Award, which recognizes artisanal contributions to Quebec culinary culture

Tip

The thickness of the shanks will vary according to the type of animal and its size: if the shank is too large, it should be cut into pieces.

Variations

Instead of deer shanks, use caribou, bison, muskox, wild boar piglet, elk, beef or veal.

- Dutch oven with tight-fitting lid

40	cedar shoots	40
1 cup	cloudberry liqueur, such as Chicoutai	250 mL
1/3 cup	peanut oil	75 mL
10 to 14 oz	bone-in deer shank per person (see Tip, left)	300 to 420 g
1 1/4 cups	white wine	300 mL
6 cups	unthickened brown game stock or store-bought equivalent	1.5 L
1	whole clove	1
4	juniper berries	4
1	garlic head, unpeeled	1
1	bouquet garni	1
	Salt and freshly ground black pepper	
6	potatoes	6
2	carrots, diced	2
2	stalks celery, diced	2
2	onions, diced	2

1. A few days before making the recipe, slice cedar shoots with a knife and soak in an airtight container with cloudberry liqueur.

2. Heat peanut oil in a Dutch oven with a tight-fitting lid over medium-high heat. Sauté shank until golden brown, about 2 minutes per side. Remove excess fat. Add white wine and brown stock. Place clove, juniper berries, garlic and bouquet garni around the meat. Season with salt and black pepper.

3. Preheat oven to 400°F (200°C). Begin cooking on the stovetop, then cover tightly and place Dutch oven in preheated oven for 15 minutes. Reduce heat to 200°F (100°C) and simmer until meat around the bone is completely tender, 2 to 3 hours.

4. Once shanks are cooked, remove them. Add mixture of cedar shoots and liqueur to Dutch oven. Adjust seasoning and simmer for 5 minutes. Pass through a fine-mesh strainer and return to Dutch oven. Cook potatoes in the cooking juices over low heat until potatoes are tender, about 20 minutes. After about 10 minutes, add diced carrots, celery and onions. Once vegetables are tender, add shanks and simmer, 2 to 3 minutes. Serve hot.

Grilled Loin with White Bean Purée

Serves 4

From the cookbook of master chef Auguste Escoffier

Tips

This cooking method of simply searing and cooking the meat over a stovetop with salt and pepper is the simplest way to showcase the meat's flavor. The bean purée further enhances the flavors.

Fresh bay leaves, which are quite fragrant, have been used throughout these recipes. If you have dry bay leaves double the amount called for in the recipes.

Variations

Use deer, moose, bison, muskox, wild boar piglet, elk, beef, pork or veal instead of caribou loin.

Thyme

Thyme can easily be dried and kept for later use. At the end of the summer, tie the sprigs in bundles and hang them upside down in a well-ventilated area until the leaves are completely dry. Store in an airtight container away from the light.

White Bean Purée

14 oz	dried white kidney beans	420 g
8 cups	unthickened poultry stock or store-bought equivalent	2 L
1	whole carrot	1
1	whole onion	1
1	bouquet garni	1
¼	bay leaf (see Tips, left)	¼
	Salt and freshly ground black pepper	
½	sprig thyme	½
	Heavy or whipping (35%) cream, warmed	
4	pieces caribou loin (each 5 to 6 oz/150 to 175 g)	4
	Sautéed chanterelles, optional	

1. *White Bean Purée:* Soak beans in cold water for 4 to 5 hours. Rinse thoroughly, then transfer to a saucepan with poultry stock. Add carrot, onion, bouquet garni, bay leaf and thyme. Cook over low heat (do not add salt) until beans are tender, 1 to 1½ hours. Once cooked, drain beans and discard bay leaf, thyme, carrot and onion. Mash beans in a vegetable mill or by hand with a potato masher, then add warmed cream. Season with salt and black pepper to taste. Set aside.

2. Season loin pieces with salt and black pepper. Heat a large pan and cook meat over high heat to desired doneness (see below; as noted elsewhere, if you prefer, cook the meat to 160°F/71°C to meet USDA recommendations). Place meat on serving plates. Make several large dumplings with the White Bean Purée and place by the meat. Surround with sautéed chanterelles, if using.

My Preferred Internal Temperatures for Cooked Meats

Rare: 125°F (52°C), after resting 130°F (54°C)
Medium: 130°F (54°C), after resting 136°F (58°C)
Well-done: 136°F (58°C), after resting 140°F (60°C)

Sautéed Tournedos with Wild Herb Béarnaise Sauce

Serves 4 to 6

Serving Tip

Cattail hearts or fingerling potatoes go well with *tournedos*.

Variations

Instead of caribou filets, use deer, moose, bison, muskox, wild boar piglet, elk, beef, pork or veal.

¼ cup	vegetable oil	60 mL
6 tbsp	unsalted butter	90 mL
4	caribou filets (each 5 oz/150 g)	4
	Salt and freshly ground black pepper	
1 cup	Béarnaise Sauce (page 353)	250 mL
	Dried wild herbs, such as chicory, burdock, coltsfoot or aromatic garden herbs	

1. Heat vegetable oil and butter in a skillet over medium-high heat. Season caribou filets with salt and black pepper and sauté until desired doneness. Let rest on a warm rack.

2. Add a pinch each of the finely chopped aromatic herbs to the Béarnaise Sauce.

3. *To Serve:* Serve the tournedos very simply on a plate. The Béarnaise Sauce should be served on the side. (It is a very delicate sauce and heat can cause it to separate.)

Tournedos

According to the *French Dictionary of the Academy of Gastronomes*, this term first appeared in 1864: "In the last century, the stalls backing onto *(tournant les dos)* the central alleys of the fresh fish pavilion, in the Paris Halles, were assigned fish of doubtful freshness. By analogy, the name tournedos was given to pieces of filet of beef that were kept for a few days in storage. An indiscretion is said to have led to the word's appearing on a restaurant menu one day; the public, not knowing its origin, adopted it."

Another version of the word's origin is tied to a filet mignon dish with foie gras and truffles ordered by composer Rossini, which surprised the headwaiter so much, he had the dish served behind the backs *(dans les dos)* of the other customers. This cut of meat is among the most versatile in terms of the garnishes and sauces that can accompany it.

Roasted Venison Saddle with Wood Garlic, Crosnes and Wild Mushroom Jus

Serves 4

- Preheat oven to 400°F (200°C)
- Ovenproof skillet
- Meat thermometer

Tips

Estimate 9 to 10 oz (270 to 300 g) of meat with bone per person.

Good choices for wild mushrooms include chanterelles, meadow mushrooms or hedgehog mushrooms.

If you prefer, cook the meat to the USDA recommendations (160°F/71°C).

Variations

Use wild boar piglet, bear, elk, lamb or veal instead of venison.

Wood Garlic
Also known as wild garlic, ramsons and bear's garlic, possibly because bears are so fond of them. Wild boars like them, too. The cooked leaves can be used as a vegetable. Chives or garlic scapes are a good substitute.

1¼ lbs	crosnes	625 g
	Salt	
2	leaves wood garlic (see left)	2
1	entire venison saddle (about 3 to 4 lbs/1.5 to 2 kg or more depending on the animal's size) (see Tips, left)	1
	Salt and freshly ground black pepper	
⅓ cup	vegetable oil	75 mL
1	carrot, finely diced	1
4	shallots, finely diced	4
1	stalk celery, finely diced	1
¼	sprig thyme	¼
⅛	bay leaf	⅛
1¼ cups	tannic red wine	300 mL
1 cup	unthickened brown game stock or store-bought equivalent	250 mL
⅔ cup	unsalted butter, divided	150 mL
14 oz	porcini (cep) mushrooms or other wild mushrooms (see Tips, left)	420 g
½ cup	finely chopped chives	125 mL

1. Thoroughly clean crosnes by rubbing them with salt to remove all the dirt. Wash and cook in salted water over medium heat, about 10 minutes. They should remain crunchy.

2. Blanch wood garlic in salted water. Set aside.

3. Season interior of saddle with salt and black pepper, then truss (page 365). Heat vegetable oil in an ovenproof skillet over medium-high heat and brown saddle. Place skillet in preheated oven and roast, basting saddle frequently, until a thermometer inserted into the center registers 118°F (48°C). At this stage, remove excess fat and arrange carrot, shallots and celery around saddle. Add thyme and bay leaf. Baste frequently until thermometer inserted into the center registers 130°F (54°C) (see Tips, left). Cover saddle with foil and keep warm on top of the stove.

4. To make sauce, remove cooking fat from the skillet and deglaze with red wine. Reduce cooking stock by 70 percent over medium-high heat. Stir in brown game stock. Reduce by one-quarter, then add thoroughly drained crosnes and wood garlic. Let simmer over medium heat, 2 to 3 minutes. Finish with half of the butter. Adjust seasoning.

5. Slice porcini mushrooms into strips, wash well and pat dry with a paper towel. Heat remaining butter over medium-high heat and sear mushrooms. Reduce heat to low and finish cooking until mushrooms are golden brown. Season with salt and black pepper and sprinkle with chives. Set aside.

6. *To Serve:* Slice the meat and serve immediately with the sauce and vegetables.

Roasted Loin
with Blueberry Sauce
and Potato and Pear Gratin

Serves 4

Tip

If you prefer, cook the meat to the USDA recommendations (160°F/71°C).

Variations

Use deer, moose, bison, muskox, wild boar piglet, elk, beef, pork or veal instead of caribou.

Bosc Pear

This juicy and grainy variety of white pear stands up well to baking and can be cooked like a vegetable.

- Preheat oven to 400°F (200°C)
- Meat thermometer

1	piece caribou loin (about 2 lbs/1 kg)	1
⅓ cup	peanut oil	75 mL
	Salt and freshly ground black pepper	
1	carrot, diced	1
1	onion, diced	1
1	stalk celery, diced	1
1	sprig thyme	1
¼	bay leaf	¼
1⅔ cups	white wine, divided	400 mL
1¼ cups	unthickened brown game stock or store-bought equivalent	300 mL
2	shallots, chopped	2
⅓ cup	fresh or frozen blueberries	75 mL
½ cup	butter	125 mL

Potato and Pear Gratin

4	potatoes	4
4	cooking pears, such as Bosc	4
1	clove garlic, finely chopped	1
1¼ cups	heavy or whipping (35%) cream	300 mL
Pinch	ground nutmeg	Pinch
⅔ cup	butter	150 mL
	Salt and freshly ground black pepper	

1. Remove meat from refrigerator 1 hour prior to cooking so that it reaches room temperature. Heat oil in a sufficiently large roasting pan over medium-high heat. Season meat with salt and black pepper, then sear in hot oil until golden brown, about 2 minutes per side. Place in preheated oven for 15 minutes.

2. Remove excess cooking fat and add carrot, onion, celery, thyme and bay leaf. Reduce oven temperature to 300°F (150°C). Return roasting pan to oven, about 10 minutes, depending on meat's thickness. Check doneness by inserting thermometer into the thickest part until it registers 136°F (58°C) for medium or 130°F (54°C) for rare (see Tip, left). Remove meat from oven, cover and let rest on a rack so the air can circulate around it.

3. Add half of the white wine to the roasting pan. Let reduce on the stovetop. Add brown game stock and cook until reduced by one-quarter, about 10 minutes. Pass through a fine-mesh strainer. Set aside.

Recipe continues, page 224...

Roasted Loin with Blueberry Sauce and Potato and Pear Gratin *(continued)*

4. Place remaining white wine, finely minced shallots and blueberries in a saucepan over medium heat. Let evaporate slowly for 7 to 8 minutes, then add the reduced stock. Cook for 5 minutes. Pass through a fine-mesh strainer. Season with salt and pepper and whisk in butter.

5. *Potato and Pear Gratin:* Peel potatoes and pears and remove seeds. Cut into $\frac{1}{8}$-inch (3 mm) thick slices. Don't wash slices but pat dry with a paper towel and keep dry, about 10 minutes.

6. Reduce oven temperature to 275°F (140°C). Place potatoes, pears, chopped garlic, cream, ground nutmeg, butter, salt and pepper in a large saucepan over medium heat. Slowly bring to a boil and cook, stirring continuously, until thickened, about 10 minutes. At this stage, place in a baking dish and cook slowly in preheated oven over a bain-marie. Check doneness by gently poking the gratin with a knife; if the knife comes out easily, the gratin is done.

7. *To Serve:* Place a slice of meat on top of the sauce and serve with potato and pear gratin.

Resting

How and why do you let meat "rest"? If the animal has been dead for several days, or even one or two weeks, it will have a tendency to become hard once cooked, hence the importance of letting the meat rest after cooking. To do this, place the meat on a rack so that the air can circulate all around it. Cover with a sheet of foil to keep warm.

Venison Tartlets with Wild Herb Emulsion

Tips

If you don't have a meat grinder, use a food processor. The meat will be finer.

To thicken: For every 1 cup (250 mL) light stock, you need 2 tsp (10 mL) cornstarch mixed with 4 tsp (20 mL) water.

Use wild herbs such as wild thyme, nettle, mustard or burdock flower. Or garden herbs, such tarragon, chervil, parsley, sorrel or sage.

Variations

Instead of caribou, use moose, deer or beef.

- Preheat oven to 350°F (180°C)
- Meat grinder (see Tips, left)
- Six to eight 4-inch (10 cm) individual tartlet pans

1¼ lbs	caribou shoulder or neck with fat	625 g
4	slices bread without crust, diced	4
⅔ cup	heavy or whipping (35%) cream	150 mL
⅓ cup	unsalted butter	75 mL
½ cup	finely minced shallots	125 mL
1 cup	red wine	250 mL
⅔ cup	thickened brown game stock or store-bought equivalent (see Tips, left)	150 mL
3	whole eggs	3
¼ cup	potato starch	60 mL
1 tsp	minced gingerroot	5 mL
1 tsp	granulated sugar	5 mL
2 tsp	chopped dates	10 mL
2 tsp	chopped dried currants	10 mL
2½ tsp	salt	12 mL
	Freshly ground black pepper	
1½ lbs	shortcrust pastry	750 g

Wild Herb Emulsion

3 oz	wild and garden herbs (see Tips, left)	90 g
⅔ cup	unthickened light game stock or store-bought equivalent	150 mL
2	egg yolks	2

1. Remove nerves from meat and cut meat into small cubes. Soak bread slices in cream. Grind meat and bread twice in a grinder.

2. Heat butter in a heavy-bottomed skillet over medium heat. Sweat shallots until soft, about 5 minutes. Add meat mixture, wine and brown game stock. Bring to a boil over medium heat and cook, for 10 minutes. Drain and reserve cooking juices. Set aside and let cool.

3. Remove hardened fat. Stir eggs, potato starch, ginger, sugar, dates, dried currants, salt and black pepper into meat mixture.

4. Line tartlet pans with dough. Fill with mixture, then cook in preheated oven, 20 to 30 minutes.

5. *Wild Herb Emulsion:* Finely chop herbs. Set aside. Heat light game stock and cooking juices over medium heat. Add egg yolks and stir into mixture, then add herbs.

6. *To Serve:* Drizzle wild herb emulsion over tartlets.

Moose Medallion Filets with Cider Sauce

Recipe by Chef
Isabelle Talbot

Serves 4

Variations

You can use bison, muskox, caribou, venison, wild boar piglet, elk, beef, pork or veal instead of moose filets.

Eggplant

This vegetable fruit from the nightshade family originated in India. The eggplant is deep purple in color and looks like a large pear. It is eaten hot or cold and is used in the preparation of many dishes, such as ratatouille, moussaka and fritters.

- Pastry bag
- Meat thermometer

8	moose medallion filets (each 2 oz/60 g)	8
2 cups	boiling water	500 mL
1/3 cup	finely diced carrot	75 mL
1/3 cup	finely diced celery	75 mL
1/3 cup	finely diced red bell pepper	75 mL
1/3 cup	finely diced zucchini	75 mL
1/4 cup	finely diced eggplant	60 mL
1/4 cup	chopped onion	60 mL
1 tbsp	vegetable oil	15 mL
1/4 cup	crushed peeled tomato	60 mL
1/4 cup	chopped mushrooms	60 mL
1/4 tsp	minced garlic	1 mL
1/2 tsp	powdered chicken bouillon base	2 mL
1/4 tsp	freshly ground black pepper	1 mL
1	bay leaf	1
1/4 tsp	chopped thyme	1 mL
Sauce		
1	shallot, chopped	1
1/2 cup	butter, divided	125 mL
1 1/4 cups	apple cider	300 mL
1 cup	brown game stock or veal stock (demi-glace)	250 mL
1 tsp	honey	5 mL
3 tsp	salt	15 mL
1/4 tsp	freshly ground black pepper	1 mL
1/4 tsp	heavy or whipping (35%) cream	1 mL

1. Insert the blade of a paring knife into the center of each medallion. Cut a pocket in the meat, cutting out the inside but only making a small hole on the outside; be sure to leave the sides of the medallion intact.

2. In a pot of boiling water, blanch carrot, celery, bell pepper, zucchini, eggplant and onion, 2 to 3 minutes. Drain.

3. Heat vegetable oil in a nonstick skillet over low heat. Add blanched vegetables, cover and cook, stirring often, until sweated, about 5 minutes. Add tomato, mushrooms, garlic, powdered chicken bouillon base, black pepper, bay leaf and thyme. Place mixture in a pastry bag. Fill medallions and set aside.

4. *Sauce:* Sweat shallot in 1/4 cup (60 mL) of butter in a saucepan over medium heat. Deglaze skillet with cider to dissolve cooking juices. Pour in game stock, honey, salt and pepper. Allow sauce to reduce by half, then add cream. Strain sauce through a sieve, whisk in the remaining butter, then set aside to keep warm.

Tip

If you prefer, cook
the meat to the USDA
recommendations
(160°F/71°C).

5. On a greased grill or in a skillet over medium-high heat, pan-fry
medallions until a thermometer inserted into the center registers
130°F (54°C) for medium, about 3 minutes per side (see Tips, left).

6. *To Serve:* Serve medallions topped with sauce.

Sautéed Filet of Loin with Wild Vegetable Jus and Chestnut Purée

Serves 4

Variations

Instead of caribou, use venison, moose, bison, muskox, wild boar piglet, elk, beef, pork or veal.

Wild Vegetable Jus

These spring roots should be picked in May or June. Wash thoroughly and use a juice extractor to extract juice from wild carrots, wild parsnips and cattail roots. Stir well and store in freezer so that the juices can be used during hunting season. Garden-grown vegetables can be used as substitutes for the wild carrot and parsnip, and Jerusalem artichokes can replace the cattail roots.

- Preheat oven 350°F (180°C)
- Meat thermometer
- Ovenproof skillet

1 or 2	caribou loin filets (each about 6 oz/175 g per person)	1 or 2
	Salt and freshly ground black pepper	
¼ cup	vegetable oil	60 mL
2	wild carrots	2
1	wild parsnip	1
2	cattail roots	2
¼ cup	Armagnac	60 mL
⅔ cup	white wine	150 mL
⅔ cup	unsalted butter	150 mL

Chestnut Purée

1¾ lbs	chestnuts	875 g
8 cups	water	2 L
4 cups	milk	1 L
	Salt and freshly ground black pepper	
⅓ cup	heavy or whipping (35%) cream, warmed	75 mL

1. Season filet with salt and black pepper. Heat vegetable oil in an ovenproof skillet over medium-high heat. Sear meat about 3 minutes per side. Continue cooking in preheated oven until thermometer inserted into the center registers 130°F (54°C), depending on the thickness (see Tips, page 230). Let meat rest on top of the warm stove for 15 minutes.

2. Cook carrots, parsnip and cattail roots in water over medium heat until vegetables are tender, about 30 minutes. Drain, discard vegetables and set aside the cooking juices.

3. Remove cooking fat, deglaze with Armagnac and white wine and reduce to dry. Pour in vegetable jus and whisk in butter.

4. *Chestnut purée:* Using a sharp knife, make an incision in the chestnut shell and remove the first layer. Heat water in a saucepan over medium-high heat. Using a slotted spoon, drop 3 or 4 chestnuts at a time in boiling water for approximately 30 seconds, then remove and place in cold water. Repeat process with remaining chestnuts.

5. Heat milk with salt and black pepper in a saucepan over low heat. Cook chestnuts in milk over low heat, stirring frequently to prevent them sticking to bottom of saucepan. Once cooked, drain, saving milk. Mash chestnuts while warm in a vegetable mill or by hand with a potato masher. Gradually stir in warm milk to obtain a smooth purée. Season, cover and keep warm. When ready to serve, stir in warm cream. The purée can be prepared several days ahead of time.

6. *To Serve:* Arrange loin slices on top of sauce and serve with purée.

Caribou Chops Sautéed and Flambéed in Apple Cider with Porcini Mushroom Essence

Tips

If you prefer, cook the meat to the USDA recommendations (160°F/71°C).

To thicken stock, use 1¾ tsp (8 mL) cornstarch and 2½ tsp (12 mL) water.

Variations

Instead of caribou chops, use bison, muskox, wild boar piglet, elk, beef, pork or veal.

Boletus Edulis
Also known as porcini and cep. This family of fleshy mushrooms is distinguished by their stout stalks. Found in woodland clearings in late summer and autumn. They are also called Penny Buns because their light brown color and large heads make them look like freshly baked bread.

● Meat thermometer

Porcini Mushroom Essence

1¼ lbs	porcini (cep) mushrooms	625 g
4 cups	unthickened light game stock or store-bought equivalent	1 L
⅓ cup	vegetable oil	75 mL
⅓ cup	butter, divided	75 mL
4	bone-in caribou chops (each about 5 oz/150 g)	4
	Salt and freshly ground black pepper	
2	shallots, very finely chopped	2
⅓ cup	non-sparkling cranberry-flavored apple cider	75 mL
¾ cup	thickened brown caribou stock or store-bought equivalent (see Tip, left)	175 mL
½ cup	finely chopped chives	125 mL

1. *Porcini Mushroom Essence:* Separate mushroom caps and stems. Wash stems and thinly slice. Thinly slice mushroom caps and set aside. Heat light game stock in a saucepan over medium heat. Add thinly sliced mushroom stems and cook for 15 to 20 minutes. Pass through a fine-mesh strainer and reduce by 90 percent.

2. Heat vegetable oil and half of butter in a large saucepan over medium-high heat. Season caribou chops with salt and pepper. Cook until a thermometer inserted into the center registers 136°F (58°C) or USDA suggested 160°F (71°C) for medium. Remove cooking fat. Sprinkle with shallots, then flambé with cider. Remove caribou chops. Add mushroom essence and brown stock and simmer for 4 minutes.

3. Meanwhile, heat remaining butter in a skillet over medium-high heat. Sauté thinly sliced mushroom caps. Season with salt and pepper. At the last minute, stir in finely chopped chives.

4. *To Serve:* Arrange mushrooms in a circle, place caribou chops on top and spoon mushroom essence over meat.

Rack of Moose Stuffed with Duck Foie Gras, Dried Currants and Swiss Chard

Tips

If you prefer, cook the meat to the USDA recommendations (160°F/71°C).

When cooked in salted water, Swiss chard becomes translucent. To give it more body, cook it in cold water, flour and salt brought to a boil.

For this amount of water, use flour mixed with about 1¾ tsp (8 mL) salt and 6½ tbsp (97 mL) lemon juice.

Variations

Instead of moose, use bison, muskox, caribou, venison, wild boar piglet, elk, beef, pork or veal.

- Ovenproof skillet
- Meat thermometer

½ cup	dried currants or golden raisins	125 mL
⅔ cup	white wine	150 mL
2 lbs	Swiss chard	1 kg
4 cups	water	1 L
1 cup	all-purpose flour and salt (see Tips, left)	250 mL
	Lemon juice	
1	moose rack (3¼ to 4 lbs/1.625 to 2 kg), trimmed with bone	1
	Salt and freshly ground black pepper	
⅓ cup	vegetable oil	75 mL
2½ cups	mixture finely diced celery, carrots and onions	625 mL
¾ cup	unthickened brown game stock or store-bought equivalent	175 mL
4	slices duck foie gras (each about 3 oz/90 g)	4
⅓ cup	butter	75 mL

1. Soak dried currants in white wine for 1 or 2 hours.

2. Remove veins from Swiss chard and cut into 2-inch (5 cm) strips. Combine chard in a saucepan with water, flour mixture and lemon juice over low heat. Stir well until boiling.

3. Preheat oven to 350°F (180°C). Season rack of moose with salt and black pepper. Heat vegetable oil in an ovenproof skillet over medium-high heat. Sear moose rack, then cook in preheated oven until thermometer inserted into the center registers 118°F (48°C). At this point, add dried currants and white wine mixture. Let alcohol evaporate, then add finely diced vegetables and game stock. Continue cooking until thermometer registers 130°F (54°C) at the center (see Tips, left).

4. Remove rack of moose from skillet, then transfer Swiss chard to skillet and simmer over low heat, about 5 minutes. During this process, cut moose ribs three quarters of the way through and insert seasoned slices of foie gras in the openings. Tie top of ribs with kitchen string. Place rack back in skillet, add several small knobs of butter and cover. Keep warm for 10 minutes. The meat's temperature will cook the foie gras.

5. *To Serve:* Serve this dish hot with Swiss chard, finely diced vegetables and dried currants.

Oven-Cooked Rack of Caribou, Jus Scented with Labrador Tea and Cloudberries

Serves 4

Variations

Instead of caribou rack, use bison, muskox, venison, moose, wild boar piglet, elk, beef, pork or veal.

Labrador Tea

This small shrub from the Ericaceae family grows in the wetlands. The young shoots are picked then infused. Chilled and served over ice with sugar and lemon juice, these infusions are delicious.

Cloudberry

This small, tart fruit grows wild in parts of Scotland and Ireland, Scandinavia and the western U.S. and Canada, where it is known as baked apple berry. It is a distant relative of the raspberry. It produces a small red fruit that turns yellow, then amber-colored and translucent when ripe. Since the fruit isn't naturally sweet, it is eaten chilled, candied or as a jam.

- Dutch oven
- Meat thermometer

4 cups	Marinade (page 346)	1 L
1 cup	cloudberry liqueur, such as Chicoutai	250 mL
¾ cup	dry white wine	175 mL
1 tsp	Labrador tea	5 mL
4	shallots, finely minced	4
1	stalk celery, very finely diced	1
	Salt and freshly ground black pepper	
2 tbsp	olive oil	30 mL
2¾ to 3¼ lbs	bone-in caribou rack	1.375 to 1.625 kg
⅓ cup	vegetable oil	75 mL
⅔ cup	unsalted butter	150 mL
1⅓ cups	cloudberries	325 mL

1. Combine Marinade, liqueur, white wine, Labrador tea, shallots, celery, salt, black pepper and olive oil in a very large container. Add caribou. Cover and marinate for 48 hours in the refrigerator, turning twice a day.

2. After 48 hours, drain caribou rack (reserving marinade) and wrap in a towel so excess moisture can be soaked up for at least 1 hour.

3. Preheat oven to 350°F (180°C). Heat vegetable oil in a Dutch oven over medium-high heat. Sear caribou rack. Cook in preheated oven until thermometer inserted into the center registers 130°F (54°C) (see Tips, page 231). Set aside on a warm grill.

4. Meanwhile, reduce marinade juice by 75 percent. Pour through fine-mesh strainer, then whisk in butter. Adjust seasoning.

5. *To Serve:* Cut caribou ribs, pour jus over meat and top with cloudberries.

Rack of Venison with Sorrel Berries, Ground Cherries and Sautéed Cattail Hearts

Serves 4

To Marcel Kretz, a great Sainte-Adèle chef

Variations

Use bison, muskox, caribou, moose, elk, beef or veal instead of venison.

Ground Cherries

Physalis pruinosa grows in limestone soils. The papery husk protects the fruit until it reaches maturity. This delicate fruit pairs well with all game recipes.

- Preheat oven to 350°F (180°C)
- Large ovenproof skillet
- Meat thermometer

⅓ cup	maple syrup	75 mL
¼ cup	maple vinegar	60 mL
1 cup	ground cherries	250 mL
⅔ cup	elderberries	150 mL
1	rack of venison (about 3 to 4 lbs/1.5 to 2 kg) with rib bones	1
	Salt and freshly ground black pepper	
⅓ cup	vegetable oil	75 mL
¼ cup	mixture diced celery, carrot and onion	60 mL
¾ cup	unthickened brown game stock or store-bought equivalent	175 mL
⅓ cup	unsalted butter	75 mL
8 oz	cattail hearts	250 g

1. Place maple syrup, maple vinegar and ⅓ cup (75 mL) of water in a saucepan over medium heat and cook until caramelized, about 15 minutes. Stop cooking process immediately by carefully pouring 3 tbsp (45 mL) cold water into the pan, then add ground cherries and elderberries and let soak, about 15 minutes. This will help to reduce the acidity of the elderberries.

2. Unless the animal is old, do not marinate the venison rack. Season meat with salt and black pepper. Heat oil in a large ovenproof skillet big enough to accommodate the rack of venison and sear meat. Place in preheated oven and continue to cook until thermometer inserted into the center registers 118°F (48°C). At this stage, remove excess fat, add celery, carrot and onion mixture and continue to cook, basting regularly, until meat reaches 136°F (58°C) (see Tips, page 231). Remove rack from oven and set aside and keep warm. Add brown game stock to pan and cook for 6 to 8 minutes. Pass through a fine-mesh strainer.

3. After soaking in Step 1, heat maple syrup mixture in saucepan over medium-high heat and reduce by half. Drain ground cherries and elderberries and set aside. Gradually add maple syrup mixture to brown game stock, tasting regularly to achieve a balanced flavor that is both tart and sweet.

4. Heat butter in a skillet over medium-high heat. Sauté cattail hearts, about 5 minutes. Season with salt and pepper. A few minutes before serving, add ground cherries and elderberries to sauce.

5. *To Serve:* Arrange sauce and berries on a serving plate. Cut large slices of venison rack with bone and place on top of the berries. Garnish with cattail hearts.

Venison Chops Sautéed with Blackcurrants and Shredded Green Papaya

Tips

Shredded green papaya can sometimes be found in specialty Asian stores. Their delicate and subtle flavor pairs well with various game recipes.

To obtain 3½ oz (105 g) chops with bone, you will need to use a young deer. If the animal is larger, use a 7- to 8-oz (210 to 250 g) chop with bone.

To thicken stock, use 2¼ tsp (11 mL) cornstarch mixed with 4½ tsp (22 mL) water.

Variations

Instead of venison chops, use muskox, caribou, wild boar piglet, moose, beef or veal.

- Meat thermometer

10 oz	shredded green papaya (see Tips, left)	300 g
¼ cup	vegetable oil	60 mL
8	bone-in venison chops (each about 3 to 3½ oz/ 90 to 105 g) (see Tips, left)	8
	Salt and freshly ground black pepper	
1 cup	blackcurrants (fresh or frozen)	250 mL
¼ cup	pomace brandy (marc) or preferred spirits, such as Cognac or Armagnac	60 mL
¼ cup	crème de cassis	60 mL
1¼ cups	thickened brown game stock or store-bought equivalent (see Tips, left)	300 mL
3½ tbsp	duck fat	52 mL
3½ tbsp	butter	52 mL

1. Add shredded green papaya to a large pot of boiling salted water. Cook until al dente. Rinse in cold water, drain and set aside.

2. Heat vegetable oil in a skillet over medium-high heat. Season venison chops with salt and black pepper and sear on each side, then remove from skillet and set aside (they are not finished cooking).

3. To make sauce, remove excess cooking fat from skillet, add blackcurrants and flambé with brandy. Add crème de cassis and brown game stock. Gently cook over low heat so blackcurrants don't burst.

4. Adjust seasoning, then place venison chops back in skillet with the sauce. Use a spoon to pour sauce over chops. Cover and keep warm at low temperature (150°F/70°C). The heat from the sauce will finish cooking the chops until a thermometer inserted into the center registers 136°F (58°C) (see Tips, page 231).

5. Heat duck fat and butter in a skillet over medium-high heat. Sauté shredded green papaya. Season with salt and black pepper.

6. *To Serve:* Arrange venison chops by crossing the ribs to form a circle around the shredded green papaya. Pour blackcurrant sauce over the chops.

Venison Chops with Asian Spices

Serves 4

Recipe by Stéphane Tremblay, chef in China

Tip

To make Asian spice mix, combine 2½ tbsp (37 mL) five-spice powder, 1 tsp (5 mL) crushed coriander seeds, 4 tsp (20 mL) curry powder and 1½ tsp (7 mL) crushed black pepper.

Variations

Use chops from bison, muskox, caribou, wild boar piglet, moose, beef or veal instead of venison chops.

Vegetable Essence

Vegetable essences are concentrations of flavors that have been extracted from one or several ingredients. One can make celery essence, for an example. One can also make essences from a mixture of vegetables. It simply requires cooking the basic ingredient in water, and then, after cooking, allowing the liquid to reduce in order to concentrate the flavors.

- Meat thermometer

5 oz	sliced cabbage	150 g
3½ oz	snow peas	105 g
3½ oz	sliced red bell pepper	105 g
7 oz	sliced bok choy	210 g
4	bone-in venison chops (each 7 oz/210 g)	4
¼ cup	Asian spice mix (see Tip, left)	60 mL
4 tsp	olive oil	20 mL
¾ cup	balsamic vinegar	175 mL
⅓ cup	Vegetable Essence (see left)	75 mL
1 tsp	chopped parsley	5 mL
2 tsp	chopped garlic	10 mL
1 tsp	soy sauce	5 mL
½ tsp	cornstarch	2 mL
	Salt and freshly ground black pepper	
1 cup	steamed rice	250 g

1. Blanch cabbage, snow peas, bell peppers and bok choy in boiling salted water. Cool and drain. Set aside.

2. Season chops with Asian spice mix. Heat oil in a heavy-bottomed skillet over medium-high heat and cook chops until a thermometer inserted into the center registers 130°F (54°C) for medium (see Tips, page 231). Set aside and keep warm.

3. Deglaze cooking juices in skillet with balsamic vinegar and reduce by half. Add vegetable essence (reserving 1½ tsp/7 mL to thicken cornstarch), parsley and garlic. Bring to a boil and reduce by half. Add soy sauce and reserved vegetables. Thicken sauce with cornstarch diluted in 1½ tsp (7 mL) vegetable essence. Season with salt and pepper.

4. *To Serve:* Arrange chops on plates with rice and vegetables, then drizzle sauce on top.

Venison vs. Deer

The word *venison* comes from the Latin verb *venari*, meaning "to hunt." At one time it meant all hunted animals but today *venison* refers primarily to deer and sometimes antelope. In this chapter we use the terms venison and deer interchangeably.

Heart Strips
Sautéed in Rosé Apple Cider

Tip

This recipe is an appetizer rather than a main course. This is a quick method for cooking heart. Take care not to overcook the heart. If the heart is cooked beyond medium, it will become hard and chewy.

Serving Tip

Cooked mushrooms can be added to this recipe.

Variations

Use the heart from venison, caribou, bison, muskox, beef or veal instead of moose heart.

- Large tray or roasting rack for resting meat

1¼ lbs	moose heart	625 g
¼ cup	vegetable oil	60 mL
¼ cup	butter	60 mL
	Salt and freshly ground black pepper	
8	shallots, finely minced	8
⅓ cup	apple brandy, such as Michel Jodoin Calijo	75 mL
1 cup	rosé apple cider, such as Michel Jodoin Cidrerie	250 mL
1¼ cups	thickened brown game stock or store-bought equivalent	300 mL
	Apple cider vinegar, optional	
4	baked tartlet crusts (shortcrust pastry)	4

1. Cut heart into 2 by ½-inch (5 by 1 cm) strips. Heat vegetable oil and butter in a heavy-bottomed skillet over medium-high heat. Season heart strips with salt and pepper. Sear immediately at high heat while shaking skillet vigorously. Remove strips while still very rare (or according to USDA recommendations, see Tips, page 244) and place on large tray or roasting rack.

2. To make sauce, pour cooking fat and butter from skillet. Add shallots and flambé with apple brandy. Add rosé apple cider. Reduce by 75 percent over medium-high heat. Add game stock and cook, 3 to 4 minutes. Adjust seasoning and, if necessary, add 1 or 2 drops of apple cider vinegar to balance the sauce's flavor.

3. Two minutes before serving, place heart strips in the boiling sauce. Remove from heat. Serve in tartlet crusts.

Cubes of Braised Neck with Fall Vegetables

Serves 4

Tip
Some people like onions cooked whole.

Serving Tip
This braised meat can also be served with potatoes cooked in the cooking juice of the neck.

Variations
Instead of moose, use bison, muskox, caribou, deer or veal.

- Slow cooker

1/3 cup	vegetable oil	75 mL
1 1/2 lbs	moose neck, cut into 1 1/2-inch (4 cm) cubes	750 g
1 1/4 cups	red table wine	300 mL
6 cups	unthickened brown game stock or store-bought equivalent	1.5 L
3	onions, spiked with cloves (1 clove per onion) or 16 small onions (see Tip, left)	3
4	cloves garlic	4
1/2 cup	tomato paste	125 mL
1	bouquet garni	1
2	pinches cumin powder	2
2	pinches nutmeg powder	2
4	juniper berries	4
	Salt	
4	carrots	4
4	stalks celery or 10 oz (300 g) Jerusalem artichokes	4
1	turnip or rutabaga	1
	Freshly ground black pepper	

1. Heat oil in a heavy-bottomed skillet over medium-high heat. Add meat and carefully brown. For best results, leave bones attached to the neck meat.

2. Place meat in slow cooker stoneware. Add red wine and let alcohol evaporate. Add game stock, onions, garlic cloves, tomato paste, bouquet garni, cumin, nutmeg, juniper berries and salt to taste, stir well. Cook for 2 to 3 hours on High, depending on the tenderness of the meat. After 2 hours of cooking, verify doneness every 20 minutes by inserting a knife into the meat. It should be tender and offer no resistance.

3. While meat is cooking, wash and peel carrots, celery and turnip. Cut into sticks measuring 1 1/2 by 1 inch (4 by 2.5 cm). After 2 hours of cooking, add carrots, celery, turnip and pepper to slow cooker with pieces of neck. All should be ready at the same time.

4. Adjust seasoning and serve.

Licorice-Scented Short Ribs Cooked with Baby Yellow Beets

Serves 4

Tips

Short ribs are used here. Meat cooked on the bone always has more flavor because the flesh shrinks less during cooking.

Thicken stock with 1/4 cup (60 mL) cornstarch mixed with 1/2 cup (125 mL) water.

Variations

Instead of moose short ribs, use venison, caribou, bison, muskox, elk, beef or veal.

Licorice

This abundantly available rhizome plant (licorice root) is used to prepare a very popular beverage. Its unique flavor pairs very well with caribou meat.

- Preheat oven to 200°F (100°C)
- Dutch oven

2 lbs	bone-in moose short ribs (see Tips, left)	1 kg
1	star anise	1
3	licorice sticks	3
8	whole shallots	8
6	cloves garlic	6
1	bouquet garni	1
1	fennel bulb, sliced in half	1
6 cups	thickened brown game stock or store-bought equivalent (see Tips, left)	1.5 L
2 lbs	yellow beets, cut into pieces	1 kg

1. Place short ribs in a saucepan with cold water and blanch over high heat. As soon as water reaches a boil, rinse ribs quickly in cold water.

2. In a Dutch oven, place short ribs, star anise, licorice sticks, whole shallots, garlic, bouquet garni, fennel bulb and game stock. Cook in preheated oven until meat comes off the bone easily. At this stage, using a skimmer, retrieve pieces of meat and whole shallots. Strain sauce, then cook yellow beets in the sauce.

3. *To Serve:* Add short ribs to the sauce at the end of the cooking process. Adjust seasoning and serve hot. Serve with whole shallots.

Osso Bucco-Style Venison Shank

Braised according to my friend Serge Yelle, an outstanding hunter

Tip

Sauce-based dishes are best if allowed to rest 24 hours before serving.

Variations

Use bison, muskox, caribou, moose, beef or veal instead of venison.

Shanks

Like osso bucco, these are ¾ to 1¼-inch (2 to 3 cm) round pieces of shank cut with a saw by a butcher.

● Preheat oven to 250°F (120°C)

2½ to 3½ lbs	venison shank, sliced ¾-inch (2 cm) thick	1.25 to 1.75 kg
	Salt and freshly ground black pepper	
	All-purpose flour	
⅔ cup	butter	150 mL
2	onions	2
5	carrots, peeled and thinly sliced	5
12	cloves garlic	12
2	sprigs rosemary	2
1⅓ cups	white wine	325 mL
4 cups	unthickened brown game stock or store-bought equivalent	1 L
1 cup	Game Stock Reduction (demi-glace) (Variations, page 347)	250 mL
12	baby carrots with tops on	12

Polenta

½	bunch broccoli rabe	½
2 cups	water	500 mL
½ cup	fine polenta	125 mL
⅔ cup	grated Parmesan	150 mL
	Salt and freshly ground black pepper	
	Butter	

1. Season shanks with salt and pepper and dredge in flour. Heat butter in a Dutch oven over medium-high heat and brown meat. Remove shanks and set aside.

2. Add onions, sliced carrots, garlic and rosemary. Cook until browned, then add shanks. Deglaze with white wine and reduce by half. Add brown stock and game stock reduction (demi-glace) until the liquid covers shanks. Bring to a boil.

3. Cover and cook in preheated oven until meat releases its juices, about 45 minutes. The stock should be barely simmering.

4. To make sauce, remove shanks from Dutch oven and reduce cooking juices by half. Pour cooking juices through fine-mesh strainer, then back into the Dutch oven.

5. Peel baby carrots and save tops. Salt cooking juices to taste and cook carrots, then the tops. Transfer shanks back to Dutch oven and keep warm.

6. *Polenta:* Cook broccoli rabe in salted water. Run under cold water, drain and chop into pieces. Salt water and bring to a boil in a large saucepan over high heat. Gradually sprinkle in polenta and cook, about 15 minutes. Stir in Parmesan cheese. Season with salt and pepper. At the very end, add broccoli rabe. The polenta should be creamy and pliable, not stiff.

7. Spoon polenta onto a serving platter and top with shanks and carrots. Whisk butter into cooking juices and pour sauce over meat. Garnish with carrot tops.

Kidneys with Mustard Seeds

Serves 4

Tips

As a chef, taste and texture considerations are paramount in my mind when I prepare food. However, organizations such as the USDA put food safety considerations at the forefront. With that in mind, they recommend all organ meats, such as kidney, liver, stomach, tongue and tripe from red meats should be cooked to a minimum internal temperature of 160°F (71°C).

Kidneys (caribou, moose or venison) are very delicate. Before using them, it is important to ensure that they have been properly harvested and stored.

Only use the kidneys of farm-raised animals or refer to Tips on Using the Meat and Offal of Game Animals (page 178).

Variations

Instead of moose kidneys, use caribou, venison, bison, muskox, beef, pork or veal kidneys.

Mustard Seeds
Though it may seem paradoxical, most of the mustard seeds used to make Dijon mustard actually come from Canada.

- Meat thermometer

2 lbs	whole moose kidneys (see Tips, left)	1 kg
1/3 cup	white wine	75 mL
3/4 cup	thickened brown game stock or store-bought equivalent (see Tips, left)	175 mL
2 1/2 tbsp	mustard seeds	37 mL
1/3 cup	vegetable oil	75 mL
6 tbsp	butter	90 mL
4	shallots, finely minced	4
	Cognac	
1/3 cup	Dijon mustard	75 mL

1. Trim fat off kidneys, cut in half lengthwise and completely remove urinary tract. Do not soak the kidneys in any liquid; instead, pat dry with a paper towel.

2. Place white wine, game stock and mustard seeds in a small saucepan over medium heat until mustard seeds are completely cooked, about 12 minutes.

3. Cut kidneys into about 1-oz (30 g) lobes. Heat oil and butter in a heavy-bottomed skillet. Sear kidneys at high heat. Drain immediately on a rack to stop the cooking process.

4. In same skillet, add shallots and sweat, 1 to 2 minutes. Then flambé with Cognac. Add Dijon mustard and whisk for a few moments to remove mustard's acidity. Next, gradually add mustard seed stock, tasting regularly until desired mustard flavor is achieved. Adjust seasoning. Set aside.

5. Five minutes before serving, heat sauce. Add kidneys and simmer until a thermometer inserted in the center registers 195°F (91°C), 3 to 4 minutes. Be careful not to reach boiling point; the kidneys could become tough if overcooked. Serve with sauce.

6. Serve in a deep dish with rice or mashed potatoes.

Venison Liver in Persillade

Serves 4

Tips

Cut the liver into slices of the same thickness. For liver to retain its unique taste and texture, it should be neither undercooked nor overcooked, but cooked medium. Each slice should thus have the same thickness. If overcooked, the liver will become rubbery.

If you prefer, cook the meat to the USDA recommendations (160°F/71°C).

Serving Tip

Serve with mashed potatoes.

Variations

Instead of venison liver, use bison, caribou, muskox, moose, elk, lamb or veal.

¾ cup	unsalted butter, divided	175 mL
8	venison liver slices of equal thickness (see Tip, left)	8
	All-purpose flour	
2	shallots, chopped very finely	2
¼ cup	red wine or raspberry vinegar	60 mL
⅔ cup	unthickened brown game stock or store-bought equivalent	150 mL
2 tbsp	chopped parsley	30 mL
	Salt and freshly ground black pepper	

1. In a heavy and sufficiently large skillet, heat ⅓ cup (75 mL) of the butter over medium-high heat. Flour liver slices and shake to remove excess flour. Sear quickly in warm butter, about 1 minute per side (or according to USDA recommendations, see Tips, left). Remove liver slices and arrange on serving plates.

2. For the sauce, remove excess fat from skillet. Add shallots and red wine vinegar. Reduce until all liquid has evaporated. Add game stock and whisk in remaining butter. Add parsley. Season with salt and pepper. Pour sauce over liver slices.

Venison vs. Deer

The word *venison* comes from the Latin verb *venari*, meaning "to hunt." At one time it meant all hunted animals but today *venison* refers primarily to deer and sometimes antelope. In this chapter we use the terms venison and deer interchangeably.

Poached Tongue with Gribiche Sauce

Serving Tip
Serve with boiled potatoes.

Variations

Use the tongue of venison, moose, bison, muskox, elk, beef or veal instead of caribou.

Juniper Berries
Juniper plants produce dark berries that are used for cooking, among other things. These berries are highly prized in game animal and game bird dishes.

1¾ lbs	caribou tongue	875 g
16 to 20 cups	water	4 to 5 L
2	onions, studded with 1 clove each	2
2	leeks	2
3	carrots	3
1	head garlic	1
4	stalks celery	4
1	bouquet garni	1
4	juniper berries	4
	Salt and freshly ground black pepper	
	Gribiche Sauce (page 360)	

1. Soak tongue by placing in a bowl under cold running water for at least 1 hour to remove all impurities (blood, etc.).

2. Place water in a saucepan over medium heat. Add onions, leeks, carrots, garlic, celery, bouquet garni and juniper berries and cook for 45 minutes. Add tongue to vegetable stock and simmer over low heat until cooked through. (The tip of a knife inserted in the meat should come out easily) (see Tips, page 244). While still hot, remove white skin covering the tongue and reserve in the warm cooking broth. Discard vegetables.

3. *To Serve:* Cut large slices of tongue and pour Gribiche Sauce over the tongue.

Fried Moose Ribs with Red Cabbage, Poached Pears and Candied Chestnuts

Serves 4

To Martin Picard at Au Pied de Cochon restaurant, who created a new approach to Québécois cuisine

Variations

Instead of moose ribs, use bison, muskox, caribou, deer, elk, beef or veal.

2 lbs	red cabbage, finely sliced	1 kg
3 tbsp	vinegar	45 mL
2	lemons, divided	2
2	Russet apples, peeled and finely diced	2
2 tbsp	chopped horseradish	30 mL
½ cup	granulated sugar, divided	125 mL
2½ tbsp	duck fat	37 mL
1	onion, minced	1
1½ oz	cranberries	45 g
4 tsp	all-purpose flour	20 mL
¾ cup	red wine	175 mL
4	Bosc pears	4
2 cups	unthickened light game stock or store-bought equivalent	500 mL
¾ cup	butter, divided	175 mL
¼ cup	vegetable oil	60 mL
4	bone-in moose ribs (each 5½ to 7 oz/160 to 210 g)	4
5	juniper berries, finely crushed	5
½ cup	Madeira wine	125 mL
2 cups	unthickened dark game stock or store-bought equivalent	500 mL
10	porcini or other mushrooms	10
	Salt and freshly ground black pepper	
4	candied chestnuts	4

1. Place sliced cabbage in a large bowl. Add vinegar, juice of 1 lemon, diced apples and horseradish. Marinate for 1 hour.

2. Make a light caramel with half the sugar. In a saucepan, combine ¼ cup (60 mL) sugar and 2 tbsp (30 mL) water and bring to a boil over medium-high heat. Once it comes to a boil, continue to cook, about 5 minutes. Add warm duck fat, then onion. Lightly brown. Add red cabbage mixture, remaining sugar and cranberries. Add 1¼ cups (300 mL) water and cook over low heat, stirring frequently with a spoon, for 1 hour. Sprinkle with flour. Add red wine and cook until red cabbage is fork-tender.

3. Peel pears, cut in half and remove stems and seeds. Add pears and light game stock to a saucepan and cook over medium heat until pears are fork-tender.

Recipe continues, page 252…

Fried Moose Ribs with Red Cabbage, Poached Pears and Candied Chestnuts *(continued)*

4. Heat $1/3$ cup (75 mL) of the butter and oil in a heavy-bottomed skillet over medium-high heat. Add moose ribs and sear until golden brown on the outside but still very rare on the inside. Remove excess cooking fat and add juniper berries. Deglaze saucepan with Madeira wine. Pour in dark game stock and reduce by half. Adjust seasoning, pour through a fine-mesh strainer, then whisk in $1/4$ cup (60 mL) of butter. Set aside.

5. Clean and thoroughly wash mushrooms. Season with salt and black pepper. In a skillet over medium heat, add $1/4$ cup (60 mL) of butter, juice of remaining lemon and mushrooms and fry quickly until softened. Set aside.

6. Place half a candied chestnut inside each pear and heat in microwave oven.

7. *To Serve:* Place a half pear stuffed with a candied chestnut in a dish. Arrange moose rib on top, pour sauce over and add mushrooms on the side. Serve red cabbage separately on a small plate.

Game Animal Terrine

**Serves
12 to 15**

*To my friend Gilbert
Roffi, a famous
Montreal charcutier*

Tips

When butchering
game meat, remove
as many nerves as
possible from the
meat selected. If
a butcher cuts the
meat, ask him to set
aside the fat. Wrap
it well and freeze it.
That way, the next
time you need game
fat, as in this terrine
recipe, you will have
some handy.

This recipe is
homemade. As such,
the terrine will not
have the pinkish
color of industrial
charcuterie because
it does not contain
any sodium nitrite,
dextrose or sodium
polyphosphate.

Variations

**Instead of moose,
use caribou, venison,
elk or bear.**

- Preheat oven to 425°F (220°C)
- Meat grinder
- Meat thermometer
- Ovenproof terrine dish

4	slices bread, crust removed	4
¾ cup	heavy or whipping (35%) cream	175 mL
1¾ lbs	moose meat from shoulder or above neck, nerves removed (see Tips, left)	875 g
1 lb	veal meat from the shoulder or above the neck, nerves removed	500 g
¾ cup	game fat or pork throat fat	175 mL
	Salt and white pepper	
2	whole eggs	2
	Potato starch	
½ cup	dried unsweetened cranberries or blueberries	125 mL
⅔ cup	shelled pistachios or pine nuts	150 mL
¼ cup	unsalted butter	60 mL
7 oz	game or veal liver strips	210 g
½ cup	brandy	125 mL
1	bay leaf	1
1	sprig thyme	1
1 cup	light Game Stock Reduction (Variations, page 347) or commercial gelatin	250 mL

1. Soak bread slices in cream.

2. Using a grinder with a medium screen, grind together moose and veal meat, bread dipped in cream and game fat twice consecutively. Weigh mixture and season, adding 2½ tsp (12 mL) salt and ¼ tsp (1 mL) pepper per 2 lbs (1 kg). Mix everything together, adding eggs and 2 tsp (10 mL) potato starch per 2 lbs (1 kg). If desired, add dried unsweetened cranberries or pistachios. Let sit for 2 hours in the refrigerator.

3. Heat butter in a heavy skillet, then sear game or veal liver strips at high heat. Season with salt and white pepper. Remove cooking fat and flambé with brandy. Set aside. Spread half of the meat in an ovenproof terrine dish, then arrange the liver strips lengthwise. Add remaining meat. Press bay leaf and thyme sprig on top and cover. Cook in preheated oven in a bain-marie until a knife can be inserted in the terrine. The mixture should be hot in the center or between 165 and 170°F ((74 and 77°C) according to thermometer. Set aside and let cool to room temperature, then place in refrigerator.

4. After removing terrine from oven, place a small board over it that fits the inside of the terrine and place a weight on top of the board (2 large tin cans can be used). This way, the fat will rise to the surface. If you have any light game stock reduction (demi-glace) or commercial gelatin available, pour it over the top and let it percolate into the terrine. When the mixture cools down, the fat will harden, preventing oxidation.

Wild Boar recipes

Wild Boar Piglet Haunch with Highbush Cranberries

Serves 4

- Preheat oven to 350°F (180°C)
- Roasting pan
- Meat thermometer

Tips

If you prefer, cook the meat to the USDA recommendations (160°F/71°C).

Since the recipe calls for a wild boar piglet, the animal will be young and won't need to be marinated, unless a specific flavor is to be imparted to the meat. If a wild boar is used (thus, an older animal), it would be best to marinate the haunch for 48 hours and to reserve the marinated vegetables.

Thicken stock with 2 tsp (10 mL) cornstarch and 4 tsp (20 mL) water.

Serving Tip

Serve with a chestnut purée.

Variations

Use chamois, mouflon, young deer, elk or lamb instead of wild boar.

5 oz	pork belly (uncured)	150 g
1	wild boar piglet haunch (see Tips, left)	1
	Salt and freshly ground black pepper	
⅓ cup	vegetable oil	75 mL
1	onion, diced	1
1	carrot, diced	1
1	stalk celery, diced	1
1	sprig thyme	1
½	bay leaf	½
3	juniper berries	3
¾ cup	red wine	175 mL
⅓ cup	pomace brandy (marc), such as Marc de Bourgogne, or preferred spirits, such as Cognac or Armagnac	75 mL
1 cup	thickened brown game stock or store-bought equivalent (see Tips, left)	250 mL
⅓ cup	highbush or regular cranberries	75 mL
	Highbush or regular cranberry jelly, optional	

1. Select a roasting pan that is neither too small nor too large, so the aromatic vegetables can be arranged around the haunch.

2. Cut long strips of pork belly. Bard the haunch (page 366) with the strips. Season with salt and black pepper. Heat vegetable oil in a skillet over medium-high heat and sear haunch.

3. Place haunch in preheated oven, basting regularly with cooking fat, for 20 minutes. Reduce temperature to 300°F (150°C). Halfway through cooking process, when thermometer inserted into the center registers approximately 125°F (52°C), place diced onion, carrot, celery, thyme, bay leaf and juniper berries around haunch. Continue cooking, basting regularly, until thermometer inserted into the center registers 140°F (60°C) (see Tips, left). Remove haunch and keep warm on a rack on the warm stovetop. (Allowing the meat to rest will enhance its flavor.)

4. To make sauce, pour red wine and brandy in the roasting pan and reduce by half. Add game stock and cook for 7 to 8 minutes. Pour sauce through a fine-mesh strainer, pressing hard against sides to extract the flavors. A few minutes before serving, add cranberries to sauce. The berries will burst. Taste, if sauce is too acidic, add some cranberry jelly. Cut haunch when ready to serve.

Wild Boar Chops with Currants and Sauerkraut Marinated in Cumin and Maple Syrup

Serves 4

To David McMillan, from the Montreal restaurant Joe Beef, which focuses on splendid ingredients

Variations

Instead of wild boar, use caribou, chamois, deer, mouflon, moose, elk or veal.

Wild Currants

Cultivated currant bushes come from wild currant bushes. Red currant bushes grow to a height of 4 to 5 feet (1.2 to 1.5 m). In July and August, the fruit form pretty bunches of bright berries that are pink, red or a dazzling whitish yellow. The currants are very delicate and need to be picked at the right moment. If picked too early, the fruit will be too acidic; if picked too late, it will go to seed. Be careful not to confuse wild currant with spurge laurel, which is toxic.

- Preheat oven to 350°F (180°C)
- Dutch oven with tight-fitting lid

12 cups	water	3 L
1¼ lbs	store-bought sauerkraut, uncooked	625 g
⅓ cup	duck fat	75 mL
2	Russet or Cortland apples, peeled and diced	2
2	onions, finely minced	2
¾ cup	dry white wine	175 mL
⅓ cup	maple syrup	75 mL
2 tbsp	ground cumin	30 mL
4	juniper berries	4
3	cloves garlic, unpeeled	3
	Salt and freshly ground black pepper	
⅓ cup	peanut oil	75 mL
8	bone-in wild boar piglet chops (each 3 oz/90 g)	8
5½ oz	red currants or gooseberries	165 g
¼ cup	pear or Saskatoon berry eau de vie	60 mL
⅔ cup	brown game stock reduction (demi-glace)	150 mL
⅔ cup	heavy or whipping (35%) cream	150 mL
⅓ cup	butter	75 mL

1. Heat water in a saucepan over high heat. Add sauerkraut and bring to a boil. Immediately remove sauerkraut and plunge into cold water and drain.

2. Heat duck fat in a heavy-bottomed Dutch oven over medium heat. Sweat apples and onions. Add sauerkraut. Add white wine and maple syrup. Add cumin, juniper berries and garlic cloves. Season with salt and black pepper. Cover with a tight-fitting lid and cook in preheated oven until sauerkraut is tender, about 40 minutes. When ready to serve, remove garlic cloves and juniper berries.

3. Heat peanut oil a large heavy skillet over medium-high heat. Season chops with salt and black pepper. Cook until rare, about 2 minutes per side. Set aside.

4. Remove all cooking fat from skillet and prepare sauce. Add red currants and flambé with eau de vie. Add game stock reduction and heat for 1 minute. Season with salt and pepper. Finish by adding cream and butter and heat until sauce coats the back of a spoon, about 1 minute more.

5. *To Serve:* Form a small mound of sauerkraut, place chops on each side and pour sauce on top.

Wild Boar Piglet Sweetbreads with Port Wine and Mushrooms

Serves 4

Tips

Only use sweetbreads from farm-raised animals or refer to Tips on Using the Meat and Offal of Game Animals (page 178).

As soon as a young animal has been killed, it is important to harvest the sweetbreads immediately and to degorge them. To do this, place them under running water to remove blood and other impurities. If the sweetbreads are small, they can be cooked immediately after this procedure.

Thicken stock with 1¾ tsp (8 mL) cornstarch and 3¼ tsp (16 mL) water.

Serving Tip

Serve in a puff pastry shell, on a bed of greens or with rice pilaf.

Variations

Instead of sweetbreads from wild boar, use caribou, moose, elk, veal, lamb or deer (all very young).

Court-Bouillon

8 cups	water	2 L
1	onion, studded with a clove	1
1	carrot	1
3	cloves garlic	3
3	juniper berries	3
1	bouquet garni	1
1	stalk celery	1
	Salt and freshly ground black pepper	

1½ to 1¾ lbs	wild boar piglet sweetbreads (see Tips, left)	750 to 875 g
¾ cup	unsalted butter, divided	175 mL
5	shallots, chopped	5
1¼ cups	red port wine	300 mL
¾ cup	thickened brown game stock or store-bought equivalent (see Tips, left)	175 mL
14 oz	mushrooms, diced	420 g
⅔ cup	heavy or whipping (35%) cream	150 mL
⅓ cup	Cognac	75 mL

1. *Court-Bouillon:* Combine water, studded onion, carrot, garlic, juniper berries, bouquet garni, celery stalk, salt and black pepper in a saucepan over medium heat. Cook for 30 minutes to allow court-bouillon to absorb flavor of the aromatics.

2. Add sweetbreads and poach for 10 minutes. Turn off heat and leave in court-bouillon for 1 hour.

3. Press sweetbreads under a weight (so they become less porous and less absorbent). Refrigerate for 12 hours. Remove surrounding membranes and small nerves.

4. Heat half of the butter in a skillet over medium heat. Braise chopped shallots, about 3 minutes. Add sweetbreads and braise, 3 to 4 minutes. Add port wine and reduce by three-quarters. Mix in game stock and simmer for 15 minutes on low heat (internal temperature of braising liquid should register 185°F/85°C).

5. Heat remaining butter in a heavy skillet and sauté mushrooms until liquid evaporates completely, about 6 minutes. Season with salt and black pepper, then add to sweetbreads.

6. *To Serve:* Just before serving, add cream and Cognac to the preparation. Adjust seasoning.

Wild Boar Piglet Saddle with Cloudberry Liqueur, Labrador Tea and Sautéed Salsify

To Chef Marie-Sophie Picard

Tip

The number of portions will depend on the size of the saddle.

Variations

Instead of wild boar piglet saddle, use young caribou, young chamois, young deer, young mouflon, young elk or lamb.

Saddle

The saddle of a wild boar piglet, lamb, young deer, hare and other young animals runs from the end of the rib cage to the hind legs. It is usually cooked on the bone. (See photograph of bear saddle on page 307).

- Strainer, lined with cheesecloth
- Ovenproof skillet
- Meat thermometer

2½ lbs	bone-in wild boar piglet saddle (see Tip, left)	1.25 kg
1	carrot, finely minced	1
1	stalk celery, finely minced	1
4	shallots, finely minced	4
2	cloves garlic	2
1¼ cups	cloudberry juice	300 mL
⅔ cup	cloudberry liqueur, such as Chicoutai	150 mL
1¼ cups	white wine	300 mL
⅓ cup	grapeseed oil	75 mL
1 tsp	dried Labrador tea	5 mL
1½ tsp	dried summer savory	7 mL
8	peppercorns	8
	Celery salt	
2 lbs	salsify	1 kg
3	lemons, divided	3
12 cups	cold water	3 L
¾ cup	all-purpose flour	175 mL
	Salt and freshly ground black pepper	
1 cup	butter, divided	250 mL
⅓ cup	papaya juice	75 mL
⅓ cup	peanut oil	75 mL
	Celery salt and freshly ground white pepper	
1⅓ cup	cloudberries	325 mL

1. Carefully remove nerves from wild boar piglet saddle. Select a container in which the saddle won't be completely covered by the marinade liquid.

2. Arrange carrot, celery, shallots and garlic cloves around saddle. Add cloudberry juice, liqueur, white wine, grapeseed oil, Labrador tea, summer savory and peppercorns. Season with celery salt to taste. Cover with plastic wrap and marinate in the refrigerator for 48 hours, turning saddle over 2 or 3 times during this period.

3. When you are ready to make the recipe, peel salsify (wearing gloves, otherwise your hands will be stained black) and wash. Combine with juice of 1 lemon and set aside, about 10 minutes. Cut into 2-inch (5 cm) sticks and then cut in half lengthwise.

Salsify
Salsify
This vegetable has been known for over 2,000 years in Europe. Its long, fleshy root is appreciated for its sweet and mucilaginous flavor. It is said to taste slightly like asparagus or artichoke, with a coconut aftertaste.

4. Combine cold water, flour, juice of 2 lemons, salt and black pepper in a large saucepan over high heat. Bring to a boil, stirring constantly. Add salsify sticks and cook until crunchy, about 15 minutes.

5. Remove saddle from marinade, reserving marinade. Drain, pat dry with a paper towel and set aside.

6. To make stock, heat $1/4$ cup (60 mL) of the butter in a large pot over medium heat and sweat marinade ingredients. Add papaya juice and marinade liquid. Cook until simmering and reduced by half, about 25 minutes. Pour through prepared strainer and reserve stock. Set aside.

7. Preheat oven to 350°F (180°C). Tightly truss wild boar piglet saddle (page 365). Heat peanut oil in an ovenproof skillet over medium-high heat. Gently brown wild boar piglet saddle. Season with celery salt and black pepper. Place in preheated oven and cook, basting frequently, until thermometer inserted into the center registers 154°F (68°C). Remove and keep warm on a rack on the warm stovetop.

8. Remove cooking grease from skillet, deglaze with reserved stock and simmer over medium heat. Whisk in $1/3$ cup (75 mL) of butter and add cloudberries.

9. Heat remaining butter in a skillet over medium-high heat and sauté well-drained salsify. Season with celery salt and white pepper.

10. *To Serve:* Debone saddle and serve a piece of loin and a small piece of filet per person, topped with cloudberry sauce and surrounded by salsify.

Baby Wild Boar and Fried Chanterelle Mushrooms with Parsley

Serves 4

*For Nicolas Gauthier
of the Rieur Sanglier
farm in Yamachiche,
a Quebec municipality*

Tip

If you prefer,
cook the meat
to the USDA
recommendations
(160°F/71°C).

Variations

**Use filet from
caribou, deer,
moose, elk, veal
or beef instead of
wild boar filet.**

Chanterelle mushrooms

Chanterelle
(Cantharellus) is a
yellow mushroom
with white flesh
and slightly fruity
flavor. Prized
by gourmets, it
is a wonderful
accompaniment
to game.

- Preheat oven to 350°F (180°C)
- Ovenproof skillet
- Large roasting pan
- Meat thermometer

1/3 cup	peanut oil	75 mL
1	wild boar filet (about 1 1/4 lbs/625 g), trimmed	1
1/3 cup	finely diced carrots	75 mL
1/3 cup	finely diced celery	75 mL
1/4 cup	finely diced shallots	60 mL
1/3 cup	finely diced leek, white part only	75 mL
3/4 cup	dry white wine	175 mL
1/3 cup	unthickened light game stock or store-bought equivalent	75 mL
1 3/4 lbs	fresh chanterelle mushrooms	875 g
1/3 cup	butter	75 mL
	Salt and freshly ground black pepper	
1 2/3 cups	fresh chopped parsley	400 mL

1. Heat peanut oil in an ovenproof skillet over medium-high heat. Sauté filet on all sides until golden brown. Place in preheated oven until thermometer inserted in the center registers 130°F (54°C).

2. Remove excess fat from skillet. Surround filet with carrots, celery, shallots and leek and continue to cook, basting with juices, until thermometer inserted in the center registers 135°F (57°C) (see Tip, left). Remove meat and set aside and keep warm on a rack on warm stovetop.

3. Pour white wine into roasting pan and cook over high heat to reduce by 90 percent to remove acidity, 2 to 3 minutes. Then add game stock and cook for 1 to 2 minutes. Set aside.

4. Thoroughly wash chanterelle mushrooms, changing water several times to remove any sand or grass. Thoroughly strain and dry. Heat butter in a skillet over medium-high heat. Sauté chanterelles until mushrooms are golden brown, about 5 minutes. Season with salt and black pepper. Top with fresh chopped parsley.

5. *To Serve:* Form a mound of chanterelle mushrooms in middle of plate. Cut large slices of baby wild boar fillet and arrange on top of mushrooms. Pour cooking juice around it.

Sautéed Medallions of Wild Boar Piglet with Sauce Diane

Variations

Use medallions from caribou, deer, moose or elk instead of wild boar.

Chives

Chives come from small bulbs that grow in bunches, with pink or purplish flowers peeking out from beneath the leaves. Their flavor is similar to that of an onion, but is subtler and delicately nuanced.

- Dutch oven

14 oz	Le Puy green lentils	420 g
1	onion, studded with a clove	1
1	carrot	1
2	cloves garlic, unpeeled	2
	Salt and freshly ground black pepper	
8	medallions from loin wild boar piglet (each 2½ oz/75 g)	8
¾ cup	butter, divided	175 mL
⅓ cup	Armagnac	75 mL
1 cup	Sauce Diane (page 355)	250 mL
3 tbsp	butter	45 mL
16	stems chive	16

1. Carefully wash lentils and place in a Dutch oven and cover with cold water. Add clove-studded onion, carrot and garlic cloves and cook over medium heat until simmering, about 30 minutes. When lentils are cooked, leave them in their cooking juice. Remove onions, carrots and garlic, setting carrots aside. Season with salt and black pepper.

2. Season wild boar piglet medallions with salt and black pepper. Heat ⅓ cup (75 mL) of the butter in a heavy skillet over medium-high heat. Sauté wild boar piglet medallions to desired doneness (see below), then flambé with Armagnac. Remove medallions and keep warm. Pour Sauce Diane into skillet, heat and whisk in remaining butter.

3. Drain lentils and finely dice carrots. Heat 3 tbsp (45 mL) butter and sauté lentils with carrots. Adjust seasoning.

4. *To Serve:* Place lentils in center of plate, arrange wild boar piglet medallions around them and coat with Sauce Diane. Garnish with chive stems.

My Preferred Internal Temperatures for Cooked Meats

Rare: 125°F (52°C), after resting 130°F (54°C)

Medium: 130°F (54°C), after resting 136°F (58°C)

Well-done: 136°F (58°C), after resting 140°F (60°C)

Sautéed Wild Boar Piglet Shoulder with Wild Cherries

Serves 4

To Martin Champagne, a chef living in Kuwait

Tip

Fresh bay leaves, which are quite fragrant, have been used throughout these recipes. If you have dry bay leaves double the amount called for in the recipes.

Variations

Instead of wild piglet shoulder, use caribou, chamois, deer, mouflon, moose or elk shoulder.

- Preheat oven to 350°F (180°C)
- Heavy-bottomed Dutch oven

⅓ cup	peanut oil	75 mL
1¾ lbs	wild boar piglet shoulder, cut into 2-oz (60 g) cubes	875 g
1	carrot, finely diced	1
1	stalk celery, finely diced	1
7 oz	wild cherries or Montmorency tart cherries, fresh or canned	210 g
4 cups	unthickened brown game stock or store-bought equivalent, divided	1 L
½ cup	granulated sugar	125 mL
⅓ cup	apple cider vinegar	75 mL
1	bouquet garni	1
4	juniper berries	4
¼	bay leaf	¼
½ cup	tomato paste	125 mL
1¼ cups	white wine	300 mL
12	fingerling or baby potatoes	12
⅓ cup	Kirsch	75 mL
	Salt and freshly ground black pepper	
⅔ cup	finely chopped chives	150 mL

1. Heat peanut oil in a heavy skillet over medium-high heat and gently brown cubes of meat, about 5 minutes per side. Transfer to a heavy-bottomed Dutch oven.

2. Sauté carrot and celery in same skillet over medium-high heat. Add to meat. Set aside.

3. Cook cherries (or drain canned cherries and set aside juice) and 1 cup (250 mL) of the game stock in a saucepan over medium heat. Add sugar and apple cider vinegar.

4. Heat cooking juice from cherries (or juice of canned cherries) over high heat until caramelized, about 8 minutes. Stop cooking process immediately by pouring cold water over the caramel.

5. Pour remaining 3 cups (750 mL) of stock and cherry cooking juice over meat. Add bouquet garni, juniper berries, bay leaf, tomato paste and white wine. Season lightly with salt. Bring to a boil and stir well. Cover tightly and cook in preheated oven, about 90 minutes. Add potatoes halfway through cooking time. Everything should finish cooking at the same time.

6. *To Serve:* A few minutes before serving, add Kirsch and cherries. Season with salt and pepper. Sprinkle with chopped chives. Serve in a soup plate.

Wild Boar Head Cheese

**Serves
8 to 10**

Tip

This recipe was very common in the rural areas of Quebec when pigs were slaughtered before winter. This way, the animal's head could be used. Since wild boar has the same morphology as pork, this recipe is a perfect match.

Serving Tips

Serve on baguette slices.

Serve with mayonnaise and dill pickles.

Variations

Use caribou snout or moose instead of wild boar.

- Preheat oven to 200°F (100°C)
- Terrine mold

1	wild boar or pork head	1
8 cups	Court-Bouillon (page 348)	2 L
2	carrots	2
1	head garlic	1
2	pork trotters	2
	Salt and freshly ground black pepper	
1 tsp	garlic powder	5 mL
1 tsp	onion powder	5 mL
½ tsp	bay leaf powder	2 mL
1⅓ cups	finely chopped parsley	325 mL

1. Singe all remaining hairs on wild boar or pork head. Cut head in half, remove tongue and brain. Reserve brain for another recipe. Rinse tongue under running water, then place head and tongue in cold water. Bring to a boil over high heat, then plunge in cold water. (The purpose of this process is to remove all impurities.)

2. Prepare court-bouillon. Add whole carrots, garlic, head and tongue of boar and pork trotters and cook in preheated oven until a sharp knife inserted in meat comes out easily, 4 to 5 hours. Remove meat from oven. Debone head and remove skin from tongue. Dice meat into ½-inch (1 cm) cubes. Set aside. Remove carrots and dice into ¼-inch (0.5 cm) cubes. Set aside.

3. Pour contents of pan through a mesh colander into a saucepan. Cook over high heat and reduce by 70 percent. Test stock's jellification by placing ¾ cup (175 mL) of stock in refrigerator. When chilled, it should "harden naturally." If it hasn't hardened, continue reducing the stock. (The natural collagen present in bones and meat tissues is called gelatin, so the stock will be like a jelly once cooled.) At this stage, season remaining stock with salt, black pepper, garlic powder, onion powder and bay leaf powder.

4. Mix together meat cubes and carrots, then add cooking stock. Let cool, stirring regularly, about 40 minutes. Add chopped parsley. Adjust seasoning and pour into a terrine mold, checking that all the ingredients are immersed in the stock. Refrigerate for at least 24 hours.

5. *To Serve:* Cut meat into ¾-inch (2 cm) thick slices, then into points. The thickness of the slices will make it easy to pick up each bite with a fork.

Whole Rack of Wild Boar with Verjuice and Apples Stuffed with Parsnip Purée

Serves 8

To Chef Ian Perreault

Tips

Estimate 8 oz (250 g) per portion.

Verjuice (an ingredient in mustard) is the acidic juice of unripe grapes. It contains a large amount of tartaric acid (or cream of tartar). This makes it both tonic and astringent, but without the corrosive effects of acetic acid, the main ingredient in vinegar.

Variations

Instead of wild boar rack, use rack of young deer, young caribou, young moose or milk-fed veal.

Nutmeg

Nutmeg is the seed of the nutmeg tree. Brown and wrinkled with an ovoid shape, it has a unique fragrance and a flavor that is subtle yet distinct. Nutmeg can enhance many foods but should be used in moderation.

- Large heavy-bottomed roasting pan
- Meat thermometer

1	wild boar rack (see Tips, left)	1
1	onion	1
1	carrot	1
1	stalk celery	1
12	cloves garlic, finely minced	12
12	whole shallots	12
1	sprig thyme	1
¼	bay leaf	¼
8	juniper berries	8
1	sprig rosemary	1
¾ cup	verjuice (see Tips, left)	175 mL
¾ cup	white wine	175 mL
2½ tbsp	apple cider vinegar	37 mL
⅓ cup	olive oil	75 mL
	Salt and freshly ground black pepper	
½ cup	butter, divided	125 mL
1⅔ cups	Sauce Poivrade (page 355)	400 mL
70	fresh skinless seedless red grapes	70
⅓ cup	vegetable oil	75 mL
8 cups	water	2 L
8	Russet apples	8
1	potato	1
2 lbs	parsnips	1 kg
½ cup	heavy or whipping (35%) cream, warmed	125 mL
Pinch	ground nutmeg	Pinch
½ cup	chopped chives	125 mL

1. Remove nerves, trim wild boar rack and clean ribs. Place wild boar rack in a container large enough to lay flat. Add onion, carrot, celery stalk, garlic, whole shallots, thyme, bay leaf, juniper berries and rosemary sprig. Add verjuice, white wine, apple cider vinegar and olive oil. Lightly season with salt and black pepper. Cover with plastic wrap and marinate in the refrigerator for 2 to 3 days, turning rack twice a day.

2. Drain all ingredients thoroughly in a colander, reserving marinade. Set aside meat and vegetables separately.

Recipe continues, page 270…

Whole Rack of Wild Boar with Verjuice and Apples Stuffed with Parsnip Purée *(continued)*

Parsnip
The parsnip belongs to the umbellifer family. It was widely used by the Greeks and Romans. This root vegetable is very nutritious. Among other attributes, it is a diuretic. Because its flavor is delicate, it is preferable to cook parsnips without liquid.

3. To make sauce, heat $4\frac{1}{2}$ tbsp (67 mL) butter in a saucepan over medium-high heat and sweat vegetables from marinade. Add marinade stock and reduce by half. Add Sauce Poivrade and cook gently over medium heat, about 8 minutes. Remove shallots when cooked and keep warm. Taste sauce. Once it has taken on the flavor of the aromatic ingredients, pour through a fine-mesh strainer, pressing hard to extract the maximum amount of flavor. Place cooked shallots back in sauce and add grapes. Whisk in remaining butter.

4. Preheat oven to 400°F (200°C). Select a heavy-bottomed roasting pan large enough for the piece of meat. Heat vegetable oil over medium-high heat and gently brown wild boar rack. Place in preheated oven and cook, basting frequently.

5. Meanwhile, heat water in a saucepan high heat. Peel and core apples (keeping whole) and blanch in boiling water, then plunge in cold water. Wrap in a damp cloth to keep from oxidizing and help to maintain its natural form. In the same water used to cook the apples, cook potato and parsnips, then pass through a vegetable mill or by hand with a potato masher. Season with salt and black pepper. Mix in cream, then add nutmeg and chopped chives. Stuff apples with parsnip purée.

6. When a thermometer inserted into center of meat registers 118°F (48°C), arrange stuffed apples around meat. Continue cooking until thermometer inserted into center of meat registers 160°F (71°C). The apples should be cooked by then.

7. *To Serve:* Cut a large wild boar chop with its rib, place apple in middle of plate, lean chop against apple and pour sauce on top. Garnish with shallots and grape mixture.

Wild Boar Shank Stew with Fava Beans

Tip

If you are fortunate enough to kill a wild boar, have the shanks immediately placed in a vacuum-sealed bag in order to use them later. Similarly, you can cook the shanks wrapped in plastic wrap, but the stock will need to be prepared separately.

Variations

Instead of wild boar shanks, use shanks of caribou, deer, moose, elk, veal or lamb.

- Sous vide machine
- Dutch oven
- Candy/deep-fry thermometer

4	wild boar shanks (2 front shanks and 2 hind shanks) (see Tip, left)	4
10 lbs	coarse salt	5 kg
2	carrots	2
2	Spanish onions	2
4	cloves garlic	4
2	stalks celery	2
2	whole cloves	2
$\frac{1}{2}$	bay leaf	$\frac{1}{2}$
1	sprig thyme	1
14	peppercorns	14
4 cups	unthickened brown game stock or store-bought equivalent	1 L
24 to 28 cups	water	6 to 7 L
$1\frac{3}{4}$ lbs	potatoes	875 g
$1\frac{3}{4}$ lbs	fava beans	875 g

1. Place 4 wild boar shanks in a container, cover with coarse salt and let stand in the refrigerator for 12 hours.

2. Run cold water over shanks for 1 to 2 hours. If you or your butcher has a machine to vacuum-seal meat (sous-vide), prepare 2 bags: one bag with the 2 front shanks and one bag with the 2 hind shanks. In each bag, place 1 whole carrot, 1 onion, cut in half, 2 garlic cloves, 1 celery stalk, 1 clove, $\frac{1}{4}$ bay leaf, $\frac{1}{2}$ sprig thyme, 7 peppercorns and 2 cups (500 mL) game stock. Seal bags with vacuum-sealing machine.

3. Place water in a stockpot and bring its temperature to 160°F (71°C). Maintain this temperature during the entire cooking process. The temperature must not fluctuate. Plunge bags into water and cook slowly for 10 to 12 hours. Then, open bags, save cooking juices and keep shanks warm.

4. One hour before serving, peel and dice potatoes. Place diced potatoes and fava beans in a Dutch oven over medium heat. Add cooking stock from shanks and simmer like a stew, about 40 minutes. The carrots and celery can also be cut into large cubes and added to the stew.

5. Serve shanks with potatoes and fava beans.

Wild Boar Cheeks Braised with Sparkling Cider

Serves 4

Tip

Thicken stock with 2½ tsp (12 mL) cornstarch and 5 tsp (25 mL) water

Variations

Instead of wild boar cheeks, use veal, pork, beef, moose, caribou or muskox.

- Preheat oven to 350°F (180°C)
- Ovenproof skillet

4	wild boar cheeks	4
	Salt and crushed black peppercorns	
⅓ cup	peanut oil	75 mL
⅓ cup	butter	75 mL
1½ cups	sparkling rosé cider	375 mL
1¼ cups	diced vegetables, such as carrots, celery, onion	300 mL
1	bouquet garni	1
12	small grape tomatoes	12
1½ cups	thickened brown stock of wild boar or veal or store-bought equivalent (see Tip, left)	375 mL
12	fingerling potatoes	12

1. Score the meat by making several ⅛-inch (3 mm) slits in a crisscross pattern on each side of the cheeks. Season with salt and black pepper. Heat peanut oil and butter in a heavy ovenproof skillet over medium-high heat. Sear cheeks on each side until nicely browned, about 2 minutes per side.

2. Remove cooking fat and add cider. Boil liquid over high heat to remove alcohol, then reduce by three-quarters.

3. Add diced vegetables, bouquet garni and tomatoes and simmer for 10 minutes. Add brown stock. Cover and cook in preheated oven until tip of knife can be inserted into meat and easily removed. Adjust seasoning. Cook fingerling potatoes in cooking juices of cheeks or in salted water.

4. *To Serve:* Serve immediately with fingerling potatoes.

Bison recipes

Bison Roast
with Milkweed Sauce

Tips

Ask your butcher to cut a roast from the bison's inner thigh, as this majestic animal always falls on the outer part of its thigh when it lies down, causing this area to become tougher.

If you prefer, cook the meat to the USDA recommendations (160°F/71°C).

Serving Tip

A sweet potato purée pairs very well with this dish.

Variations

Instead of bison, use muskox, caribou, deer, moose, elk or beef.

- Preheat oven to 350°F (180°C)
- Heavy-bottomed roasting pan
- Meat thermometer

1	onion, diced	1
1	carrot, diced	1
2	stalks celery, diced	2
	Salt and freshly ground black pepper	
3½ to 4 lbs	roast from bison inner thigh (see Tip, left)	1.75 to 2 kg
8 oz	pork fatback	250 g
3 tbsp	vegetable oil	45 mL
1	sprig thyme	1
½	bay leaf	½
1 cup	dry white wine	250 mL
⅔ cup	water	150 mL
1¼ cups	Sauce Poivrade (page 355)	300 mL
6 tbsp	unsalted butter	90 mL
8 oz	milkweed, fresh or canned	250 g

1. Season diced onion, carrot and celery with salt and pepper.

2. Bard bison with pork fatback and truss (page 366).

3. Heat oil in a heavy-bottomed roasting pan over medium-high heat. Gently brown bison roast, 2 minutes per side. Place in preheated oven. When thermometer inserted into the center of meat registers 118°F (48°C), surround meat with diced vegetables. Add thyme and bay leaf. Continue cooking until thermometer inserted into the center registers 130°F (54°C) (see Tips, left). Remove roast and set aside on a rack.

4. Deglaze pan with white wine and water and cook for 2 to 3 minutes. Pour through a fine-mesh strainer, pressing vegetables against the side to extract the maximum amount of flavor. Add Sauce Poivrade and thicken sauce with butter. A few minutes before serving, add milkweed to sauce.

5. *To Serve:* Cut large slices of bison roast and pour sauce around them.

Grilled Double-Cut Bison Chops with Mushroom-Stuffed Tartlets

Serves 4

Tips

Since bison is a large animal, ask your butcher to cut about 1½ lbs (750 g) of trimmed meat with bone for the chops. The chops should be at least ¾ to 1 inch (2 to 2.5 cm) thick.

Burdock is seasonal. The pistils can be preserved, either dehydrated or frozen. Edible hyssop flowers can be used instead.

Variations

Use muskox, chamois, deer, mouflon, moose or beef chops instead of bison chops.

- Preheat oven to 350°F (180°C)
- Food processor

14 oz	white mushrooms	420 g
⅓ cup	butter	75 mL
	Salt and freshly ground black pepper	
7 oz	crosnes	210 g
2	bone-in bison chops (1¾ lbs/875 g total) (see Tips, left)	2
3 tbsp	olive oil	45 mL
4	tartlet shells, homemade or store-bought	4
1⅓ cups	Grand Veneur Sauce (page 356)	325 mL
3 tbsp	Cognac	45 mL
⅓ cup	burdock pistils, optional (see Tips, left)	75 mL

1. Carefully wash mushrooms and chop in food processor. Heat butter in a large saucepan over medium-high heat. Add chopped mushrooms and cook until liquid evaporates completely, about 8 minutes. Season with salt and pepper and keep warm.

2. Thoroughly wash crosnes, cook in salted water and keep warm.

3. In summer, fire up the barbecue; in winter, a stovetop grill pan or an electric grill will do the job. Heat the grill pan or electric grill.

4. Season bison chops with salt and black pepper. Brush with olive oil, then mark chops on hot side of grill. Once meat has been marked, move to cooler side of grill.

5. Stuff tartlet shells with chopped mushrooms and bake in preheated oven.

6. Heat Grand Veneur Sauce and stir in Cognac. Before serving, add burdock pistils, if using.

7. *To Serve:* Cut the meat against the grain. Spoon sauce into each plate, then arrange bison chops on top. Place tartlets on the side and garnish with hot crosnes.

Bison Stew with Kumquats

Serves 4

To Josée Toupin and Alain Demontigny, La Terre des Bisons, a bison farm in Rawdon, Quebec

Tip
If oven heat is too strong, the stew will become cloudy.

Variations
Instead of bison, use muskox, caribou, deer, moose, beef or veal.

If kumquats are not in season, substitute with black olives, making this recipe a Provençal daube.

A pig's trotter can be added, if desired.

Kumquat
The fruit is eaten whole: its skin is edible because it does not have the bitter taste characteristic of other citrus fruits. The flesh is pleasantly tart. There are 2 kumquat species, *Fortunella margarita* and *F. japonica*: one oval and the other round. A hybrid also exists, *F. crassifolia*, which has a milder flavor. For this stew, select equal amounts of 2 types of kumquats to achieve a balanced flavor.

- Preheat oven to 300°F (150°C)

2¾ lbs	bison cubes, cut from the shoulder (each 2 oz/60 g)	1.375 kg
7 oz	pork belly (uncured)	210 g
5 oz	bison or veal fat (around the kidneys)	150 g
8	cloves garlic	8
1	bay leaf	1
2	whole cloves	2
3	dried orange peels	3
7 oz	kumquats	210 g
4 cups	red wine	1 L
	Salt and freshly ground black pepper	
	Cooked large macaroni noodles	

1. Place bison, pork, bison fat, garlic, bay leaf, cloves, orange peels and kumquats in a stoneware casserole, an ovenproof stockpot or a Dutch oven with a recessed lid that has a small hole. Cover with red wine. Season with salt and pepper.

2. Place lid on pot, upside down, and fill with ½ cup (125 mL) water. Cook in preheated oven, 2 to 3 hours. Make sure there is always water in the upside-down lid during the entire cooking process. Note that none of the ingredients are browned and no vegetables are added to the stew.

3. Serve stew in a soup plate with large macaroni noodles.

Sautéed Double Bison Rib-Eye Steak with Wild Cherry Sauce

Tips

As with bison chops, it is very important to use a thick rib-eye steak (¾ inch/2 cm) for the best results.

Once the meat is cooked, you should be able to slice it against the grain. The meat of a young animal does not need to be marinated. However, if the meat is from an adult bison, marinating for 48 hours will improve the quality.

Wild cherries are readily available from the end of July to early August. They can be picked on the bush and preserved in various ways: frozen whole, boiled in water, pitted and canned, or dehydrated.

Serving Tip

Artichoke hearts make an excellent accompaniment.

Variations

Instead of bison, use muskox, caribou, deer, moose, beef or elk.

- High-sided skillet
- Meat thermometer

2	double bison rib-eye steak, trimmed (about 1¼ lbs/625 g total) (see Tips, left)	2
	Salt and freshly ground black pepper	
⅓ cup	licorice powder	75 mL
⅓ cup	peanut oil	75 mL
⅓ cup	Kirsch	75 mL
1 cup	Sweet-and-Sour Highbush Cranberry Sauce (page 359)	250 mL
6 tbsp	butter	90 mL
2⅔ cups	pitted wild cherries or canned sour cherries	650 mL
⅓ cup	cherry jelly, optional	75 mL

1. Season steaks with salt and black pepper and sprinkle with licorice powder. Heat oil over medium-high heat in a high-sided skillet (its higher sides will retain the moisture required for the cooking process). Gently brown steaks until golden brown, about 2 minutes per side. Reduce temperature to medium heat and cook until thermometer inserted into the center registers 136°F (58°C) for medium.

2. Remove cooking fat from skillet. Flambé with Kirsch. Remove steaks and set aside. Add cranberry sauce to pan and heat. Whisk in butter, then mix in pitted cherries. If sauce is too acidic, add some cherry jelly.

3. *To Serve:* Cut meat against the grain. Spoon sauce and cherries on plate and place meat on top.

Beer-Braised Bison Neck

Serves 4

Variations

Instead of bison neck, use muskox, caribou, deer, moose, beef or elk.

2¾ lbs	bison neck, cut into 2- to 3-oz (60 to 90 g) cubes	1.375 kg
4	medium-size leeks	4
2	Spanish onions, coarsely diced	2
2	carrots, coarsely diced	2
6	cloves garlic, unpeeled	6
4 cups	blonde (pale) ale	1 L
⅓ cup	maple syrup	75 mL
	Salt and freshly ground black pepper	
3 tbsp	olive oil	45 mL
⅓ cup	vegetable oil	75 mL
14 oz	turnips or rutabaga, cut into 2- to 3-oz (60 to 90 g) cubes	420 g
¾ cup	unthickened game stock or brown veal stock or store-bought equivalent	175 mL

1. Place meat in a large container. Wash leeks thoroughly, then tie together. Add onions, carrots, garlic and leeks to container with meat. Baste meat with beer and maple syrup. Season with salt and pepper. Add olive oil. Marinate in the refrigerator for at least 24 hours.

2. The next day, heat vegetable oil in a heavy skillet. Drain meat cubes, garlic and leeks from marinade, reserving marinade, and pat dry. Gently brown meat over medium-high heat until golden brown.

3. Select one of these two cooking methods:

   In a slow cooker: Place all marinated items including browned meat and reserved marinade in a slow cooker stoneware. Add turnips and game stock. Close lid and cook over Medium for at least 7 hours.

   In the oven: Preheat oven to 300°F (150°C). Place all ingredients including browned meat and reserved marinade in a casserole or Dutch oven and cook in preheated oven. Obviously, the meat will cook faster. This is what differentiates the two methods. Slow cooking is much more suitable for this type of preparation since the meat won't be "rushed."

4. *To Serve:* Season with salt and pepper and serve in a soup plate with country bread.

Sautéed Bison Tournedos with Blueberry Sauce

Serves 4

Tips

If you prefer, cook the meat to the USDA recommendations (160°F/71°C).

To thicken stock, use 2 tsp (10 mL) cornstarch and 4 tsp (20 mL) water.

During blueberry season, dry the berries in the sun without any added sugar or in an oven on low heat. This way, the blueberries can be kept all winter and used to prepare a recipe like this one year-round.

Bison filet mignon is a large cut of meat. If you prefer rare meat, cut a thick piece, then slice it in half from top to bottom.

Variations

Instead of bison, use muskox, deer, beef, moose or caribou.

- Preheat oven to 350°F (180°C)
- Heavy-bottomed ovenproof skillet

Blueberry Sauce

½ cup	shallots, finely chopped	125 mL
¾ cup	dry white wine or blueberry wine	175 mL
½ cup	blueberry juice	125 mL
1 cup	thickened brown veal stock or store-bought equivalent (see Tips, left)	250 mL
	Salt and freshly ground black pepper	
½ cup	unsweetened dried blueberries (see Tips, left)	125 mL
¼ cup	diced unsalted butter	60 mL

Tournedos

1¾ lbs	bison filet mignon (see Tips, left)	875 g
	Salt and freshly ground black pepper	
¼ cup	peanut oil	60 mL
½ cup	unsalted butter	125 mL
⅓ cup	brandy	75 mL
10 oz	crosnes	300 g
10 oz	chanterelle mushrooms	300 g
⅓ cup	unsalted butter	75 mL

1. **Blueberry Sauce:** Place shallots in a saucepan over medium-high heat. Add white wine and blueberry juice and reduce by 90 percent. Mix in thickened brown veal stock and cook for 6 to 8 minutes. Season with salt and black pepper. Pour through a mesh colander. Add dried blueberries. Stir and top sauce with diced butter. Set aside.

2. **Tournedos:** Season bison with salt and black pepper. Heat peanut oil and ½ cup (125 mL) butter in a heavy-bottomed ovenproof skillet over medium-high heat. Sear tournedos on each side until nicely browned. Place in preheated oven and cook until desired doneness: for rare 130°F (54°C), medium 136°F (58°C), well-done 140°F (60°C) (see Tips, left).

3. Deglaze skillet with brandy. Remove tournedos and keep warm. Pour blueberry sauce into skillet. Stir and adjust seasoning. Set aside.

4. Cook crosnes in salted water until crunchy. Slice large chanterelle mushrooms. Heat ⅓ cup (75 mL) butter in a skillet over medium-high heat. Sauté chanterelle mushrooms until golden brown, about 6 minutes. Season with salt and black pepper. Just before serving, add crosnes.

5. **To Serve:** Arrange vegetables on a plate. Place tournedos on top of the vegetables and pour sauce on top, or serve sauce separately.

Bison Tail Parmentier

To Chef Laurier Therrien, game specialist

Variations

Instead of bison tail, use muskox, beef or veal.

Parmentier

Parmentier is a reference to dishes that feature potatoes. It is named after the pharmacist Antoine-Augustin Parmentier (1737-1813), who was an enthusiastic promoter of the potato.

1	bison tail (depending on animal's size), cut into pieces	1
1	bison trotter	1
2	onions, studded with one clove each	2
2½ tbsp	peppercorns	37 mL
2	stalks celery	2
2	carrots	2
1	bouquet garni	1
1	head garlic	1
2 lbs	potatoes, diced	1 kg
1 cup	butter, divided	250 mL
6	shallots, finely chopped	6
	Salt and freshly ground black pepper	
7 oz	tomato paste, divided	210 g
⅔ cup	heavy or whipping (35%) cream, warmed	150 mL
Pinch	ground nutmeg	Pinch
¾ cup	fresh white bread crumbs	175 mL
¾ cup	brown game stock reduction (demi-glace)	175 mL
	White Roux (page 351)	

1. Place tail pieces in a large stockpot and cover with cold water over high heat. When it comes to a boil, skim well. Add bison trotter, onions, peppercorns, celery stalks, carrots, bouquet garni and garlic head and cook until simmering and the tail is cooked through, 2 to 3 hours.

2. Remove tails, bison trotter, carrots and celery from broth. Pass remaining broth through a fine-mesh strainer and reduce by 90 percent to make a cooking stock.

3. While meat is still warm, remove all flesh and shred. Finely dice celery and carrots. Add to meat and set aside. Cook potatoes in salted water.

4. Meanwhile, heat ⅓ cup (75 mL) of the butter over medium heat. Slowly sweat shallots, then add shredded meat. Season with salt and black pepper. Add 1 tsp (5 mL) of the tomato paste. Set aside.

5. Purée potatoes. Add 4½ tbsp (67 mL) of butter and warm cream. Season with salt and black pepper. Add nutmeg. Set aside.

6. Preheat oven to 450°F (230°C). Arrange bison meat in an ovenproof platter, then cover with the potato purée. Sprinkle with bread crumbs and top with dollops of remaining butter. Place in preheated oven until bread crumbs are golden brown.

7. Add remaining tomato paste and brown game stock reduction to cooking stock. Thicken with White Roux. Cook over low heat for 10 minutes. Adjust seasoning.

8. *To Serve:* Place a generous portion of bison parmentier on a plate and drizzle sauce around it.

Bison Tongue Braised in Papaya Juice with Cloudberry Juice Emulsion

Serves 8

To Chef Jean-Claude Belmont, a master and instructor

Serving Tip

Serve very simply with a boiled potato and vegetables.

Variations

Instead of bison tongue, use muskox, caribou, deer, moose, beef, veal or pork.

Wood Garlic

Wood garlic are also known as wild garlic, ramsons and bear's garlic, possibly because bears are so fond of them. Wild boars like them, too. The cooked leaves can be used as a vegetable. Garlic chives or garlic scapes are a good substitute.

Amaranth

Amaranth is a weedy green available in the summer. It is said to taste like a mild mustard leaf.

- Preheat oven to 350°F (180°C)
- Braising pan with tight-fitting lid
- Food processor

1	bison tongue (6 oz/175 g per person)	1
8 cups	fresh papaya juice	2 L
8 cups	unthickened white game stock or store-bought equivalent	2 L
20	leaves wood garlic, chopped (see Tips, left)	20
4	amaranth leaves (see Tips, left)	4
4	wild parsnip roots	4
2 tbsp	mustard seeds	30 mL
1	sprig rosemary	1
½	bay leaf	½
10 oz	pork belly (uncured)	300 g
¾ cup	cloudberry juice	175 mL
¾ cup	grapeseed oil	175 mL

1. Place bison tongue, papaya juice and white game stock in braising pan. Bring to a boil over medium-high heat. Skim, then add wood garlic, amaranth leaves, parsnip roots, mustard seeds, rosemary sprig, bay leaf and pork. Bring to a boil.

2. Cover and place in preheated oven. Check doneness periodically by inserting a needle in the meat. If needle comes out easily, the tongue is cooked (see Tips, page 244). Set aside tongue in its broth.

3. Place cloudberry juice and grapeseed oil in a food processor and process at high speed.

4. *To Serve:* Remove tongue from broth and peel off white skin. Cut into large and fairly thick slices. Lay a slice of pork on top of each slice of tongue and spoon emulsion on top.

Muskox
recipes

Muskox Tournedos with Cherimoya Cream

Serves 4

To Colombe St-Pierre, chef at Chez Saint Pierre in Le Bic, Quebec, a highly esteemed restaurant which focuses on local products

Tip

To thicken stock, use 1½ tsp (7 mL) cornstarch and 3 tsp (15 mL) water.

Serving Tip

Serve with warm palm hearts or root vegetables.

Variations

Instead of muskox, use bison, caribou, deer, moose, bear, elk or beef.

Cherimoya

Also known as "custard apples." This exceptional fruit looks somewhat like an artichoke. It is green and heart-shaped and contains large, dark seeds. Its subtle flavor will enhance the delicate qualities of the muskox meat.

- Juicer

2	cherimoyas (see left)	2
4	muskox tournedos (each 6 oz/175 g)	4
	Salt and freshly ground black pepper	
⅓ cup	butter, divided	75 mL
3 tbsp	Cognac	45 mL
⅔ cup	thickened white game stock or store-bought equivalent (see Tip, left)	150 mL
½ cup	heavy or whipping (35%) cream	125 mL

1. Extract juice of cherimoyas and set aside in refrigerator.

2. Season tournedos with salt and black pepper. In a heavy-bottomed skillet (cast-iron, if possible), heat 4½ tbsp (67 mL) of the butter over medium-high heat. Sear tournedos and cook to taste. Flambé with Cognac. Remove muskox and keep warm.

3. Transfer cherimoya juice and thickened game stock to skillet. Whisk in cream and remaining butter and heat. Adjust seasoning.

4. *To Serve:* Place tournedos on plate and pour sauce on top.

Sautéed Muskox Short Ribs with Cranberry Juice

Serves 4

In memory of André Bardet, a great chef

Tip

Leave the meat on the muskox ribs. Slightly more effort will be required to eat the meat, but it won't lose its moisture during cooking and will remain juicy and tender.

Serving Tip

Serve in a soup plate with steamed potatoes.

Variations

Instead of muskox ribs, use bison, caribou, moose, bear, elk or beef.

Cranberries

Cranberries grow wild in bogs and are also cultivated commercially. These red fruits taste better if picked after several light frosts. They can be used to make jams or jellies served with poultry dishes, as well as pies, cookies and cakes. A full-bodied rosé wine is also produced using cranberries.

4 cups	unsweetened cranberry juice, preferably fresh	1 L
1/3 cup	non-sparkling cranberry-flavored apple cider	75 mL
2 1/2 cups	cranberries	625 mL
1 tsp	dried Labrador tea	5 mL
3 to 4 lbs	bone-in muskox short ribs (see Tip, left)	1.5 to 2 kg
	Salt and freshly ground black pepper	
1/3 cup	vegetable oil	75 mL
2	Spanish onions	2
20	leaves wood garlic, chopped (see Tips, page 286)	20
1/3 cup	tomato paste	75 mL
1	bouquet garni	1
2	sage leaves	2
1/2	recipe White Roux (page 351)	1/2
2 tbsp	chopped parsley	30 mL

1. Heat cranberry juice and cider. Poach cranberries, if fresh. Drain and set aside. Add Labrador tea to cranberry cooking juices, cover and let infuse, about 1 hour.

2. Season muskox ribs with salt and black pepper. Heat vegetable oil in a heavy-bottomed skillet over medium-high heat. Gently brown meat on all sides. Set aside. Dice onions and sweat in the cooking fat.

3. Transfer meat, onions, wood garlic, cranberry cooking juices, tomato paste, bouquet garni and sage leaves to a saucepan. Cover and cook on low heat until meat is cooked through, about 2 hours. Remove meat and wood garlic. Pour remaining ingredients through a fine-mesh strainer, then thicken with white roux and cook, about 10 minutes. Adjust seasoning and sprinkle with chopped parsley. Add cranberries.

Springtime Muskox Pot-au-Feu with Wild Vegetables

Serves 4

To Chef Jean-Philippe St-Denis

Variations

Use caribou, deer, wild boar, moose, bear, elk or beef short ribs instead of muskox.

3½ to 4½ lbs	bone-in muskox short ribs	1.75 to 2.25 kg
2 lbs	muskox bones and, if possible, several pieces bone marrow	1 kg
3	leeks, white parts only	3
8	leaves wood garlic or garlic (see Tips, page 286)	8
7 oz	primrose	210 g
14 oz	wild or cultivated carrots	420 g
14 oz	wild or cultivated parsnips	420 g
10 oz	rutabaga or turnip	300 g
2	stalks celery or wild celery	2
3	onions, studded with a clove	3
1	bouquet garni	1
20	crushed peppercorns	20
4	cooking potatoes	4
	Salt and freshly ground black pepper	
	Toasted croutons	
	Coarse salt	
	Strong mustard	
	Dill pickles	
	Country bread	

1. Place muskox ribs and bones in a saucepan filled with cold water. Bring to a boil, then skim. Reduce heat to low and cook meat, about 2 hours.

2. Meanwhile, thoroughly wash leeks, wood garlic leaves and primrose, then tie together. Peel carrots, parsnips, rutabaga and celery stalks. Chop vegetables into equal-size pieces and wrap each type of vegetable in cheesecloth or another cloth.

3. Place tied and wrapped vegetables in saucepan with meat along with onions, bouquet garni and peppercorns. Cook over low heat, regularly checking doneness of each ingredient. Once a vegetable ingredient is tender, remove and keep warm. After 60 to 90 minutes, add potatoes. They should finish cooking at the same time as the meat. Season with salt and black pepper.

4. *To Serve:* Serve cooking broth in a soup plate with toasted croutons. Then, on a large plate, arrange 2 muskox short ribs and 1 bone marrow. Elegantly surround them with warm vegetables. Serve with coarse salt, strong mustard, sour pickles and country bread.

Whole Roasted Rack of Muskox with Vegetable Juice Emulsion and Baby Potatoes

Serves 8

In memory of Rodolphe Doseger, a great chef

Tip

If you prefer, cook the meat to the USDA recommendations (160°F/71°C).

Variations

Instead of muskox rack, use caribou, deer, wild boar piglet, moose, bear, elk or veal.

Parsnip

The parsnip belongs to the umbellifer family. It was widely used by the Greeks and Romans. This root vegetable has a high nutritional value as well as diuretic properties. Delicately flavored, it is best cooked without added liquid.

- Preheat oven to 450°F (230°C)
- Medium-size roasting pan
- Meat thermometer
- Blender

5 to 5½ lbs	bone-in muskox rack	2.5 to 2.75 kg
	Salt and freshly ground black pepper	
⅓ cup	vegetable oil	75 mL
2 lbs	baby potatoes	1 kg
16	slices smoked bacon, cut into ¼-inch (0.5 cm) strips	16
4½ tbsp	duck fat	67 mL
6	shallots, coarsely chopped	6
¾ cup	white wine	175 mL
⅓ cup	parsnip juice	75 mL
⅓ cup	carrot juice	75 mL
⅓ cup	celery juice	75 mL
⅓ cup	Game Stock Reduction (demi-glace) (Variations, page 347)	75 mL

1. Trim rack, removing meat and fat from the ends of the bones. Season with salt and black pepper.

2. Heat vegetable oil in roasting pan. Place meat fatty side down and cook in preheated oven, basting frequently, until a thermometer inserted into the center of the rack registers 130°F (54°C) (see Tip, left).

3. Meanwhile, blanch potatoes. Blanch bacon, drain and gently fry. Heat duck fat and brown potatoes until golden brown. Place in oven with meat. Add bacon towards end of cooking process. Degrease, then season with salt and black pepper before serving.

4. Remove meat and keep warm on a rack on the stovetop. Remove cooking fat. Place shallots and white wine in roasting pan. Reduce to dry. Add juice from parsnips, carrot and celery. Reduce by three-quarters, then mix in game stock reduction. Heat, then purée in blender.

5. *To Serve:* Cut large ribs and arrange elegantly on a plate. Garnish with roasted potatoes and pour vegetable emulsion on top.

Muskox Tagine with Moroccan Truffles

Serves 4

To Estrella Schiff, an outstanding cook

Tip

Potato cocotte is a French cooking term referring to potatoes that have been peeled and cut into finger shapes and then trimmed into oblongs, about 2 inches (5 cm) long. Fingerling potatoes would also work here.

Variations

Instead of muskox, use bison, caribou, deer, wild boar piglet, moose, elk or lamb.

White Truffle

Larger than other types of truffles, the white truffle has a white or marbled yellow-white flesh. Its fragrance and flavor are reminiscent of garlic. It is the most prized and most expensive truffle of all.

- Preheat oven to 350°F (180°C)
- Cast-iron skillet
- Tagine

1¾ lbs	muskox (butt)	875 g
⅓ cup	vegetable oil	75 mL
	Salt and freshly ground black pepper	
⅓ cup	olive oil	75 mL
¾ cup	minced shallots	175 mL
1 tsp	Arabica coffee powder	5 mL
½ tsp	chile powder	2 mL
¾ cup	unthickened brown game stock or store-bought equivalent	175 mL
⅔ cup	Moroccan white truffle juice	150 mL
6	cloves garlic	6
12 oz	potato cocotte or fingerling potatoes (see Tip, left)	375 g
3 oz	Moroccan white truffles, quartered	90 g
	Truffle oil	

1. Cut muskox into 2-oz (60 g) cubes. Heat vegetable oil in cast-iron skillet over medium-high heat and gently brown muskox cubes. Season with salt and black pepper.

2. Meanwhile, in bottom of the tagine dish, gently heat olive oil and sweat minced shallots. Add coffee powder and chile powder.

3. Place browned muskox cubes over shallots. Add brown game stock and truffle juice. Surround with garlic cloves. Cover and cook in preheated oven, basting occasionally.

4. Halfway through the cooking time, when muskox pieces are semi-firm, add potatoes and white truffles. Simmer in oven until fully cooked, basting frequently.

5. *To Serve:* Place tagine in center of table, sprinkle with a few drops of truffle oil and serve.

Tagine

This term designates a stew made with braised meat, vegetables and even fruits, as well as the ceramic pot with a cone-shaped lid in which the stew is cooked. This dish originated in North Africa, particularly Morocco.

Muskox Liver with Blueberry Vinegar Sauce, Sautéed Chayotes and Blueberries

● Preheat oven to 350°F (180°C)
● Dutch oven
● Meat thermometer

Tip
Thicken stock with 3 tsp (15 mL) cornstarch and 6 tsp (30 mL) water.

WARNING
It is best to wear latex gloves when peeling chayotes, otherwise you will get sap on your hands that will irritate your skin.

Variations
Instead of muskox liver, use the liver of bison, veal, lamb, elk, deer or moose.

Chayote
Originally from Mexico and Central America, the chayote is a member of the gourd family. Its skin is thin and has a pale green, white or dark green color. Its flesh is white and contains a soft, flat seed. The plant's fruit is eaten, as well as its leaves, flowers and roots. When cooked, the flesh of the chayote fruit has a crisp and crunchy taste that pairs well with many dishes.

9 oz	fatty bacon	270 g
	Salt and freshly ground black pepper	
2 lb	muskox liver (lobe)	1 kg
9 oz	pork caul fat	270 g
9 oz	unsalted bacon	270 g
⅓ cup	butter	75 mL
1½ cups	thickened brown game stock or store-bought equivalent (see Tip, left)	375 mL
½ cup	white wine	125 mL
⅓ cup	Madeira wine	75 mL
3 tbsp	brown game stock reduction (demi-glace) (Variations, page 347)	45 mL
2	chayotes	2
⅓ cup	blueberry vinegar	75 mL
¾ cup	fresh or frozen blueberries	175 mL

1. Cut fatty bacon into thin, long strips. Season with salt and black pepper. Using a larding needle (page 367), lard muskox liver lengthwise with the strips, then wrap caul fat around liver.

2. Cut unsalted bacon into small cubes. In a Dutch oven, gently fry bacon cubes in butter. Add muskox liver wrapped in caul fat. Add thickened brown game stock, white wine and Madeira wine. Add game stock reduction. Cover and cook in preheated oven until a thermometer inserted into the center registers 154°F (68°C). (The USDA recommends an internal temperature of 160°F/71°C, see Tips, page 244.)

3. Meanwhile, peel chayotes (see Warning, left). Dice chayotes, then steam in a vegetable steamer. Season with salt and black pepper. Keep warm.

4. When liver is cooked, remove and keep warm. Add blueberry vinegar and blueberries to cooking stock. Simmer for 2 to 3 minutes and adjust seasoning.

5. *To Serve:* Place blueberry cooking stock on a large plate. Place diced chayotes on the side, then cut large slices of liver and arrange over the chayotes.

Bear recipes

Sautéed Young Bear Chops with Grand Veneur Sauce and Quince Purée

Serves 4

To Chef Michel Bush, restaurateur and great hunter

Variations

Instead of bear chops, use caribou, deer, wild boar piglet, moose or elk.

Chops or Cutlets

"Cutlets" designates the ribs of medium-size animals (sheep, pork), while "chops" is used for larger animals (bear, beef, moose).

Quinces

Also known as "golden apple," the quince first appeared in North America in the 17th century. A member of the rose family, it is related to the apple and the pear. Native to the Middle East, it is found from Turkey to Iran. Quinces can be round or pear-shaped with fuzzy or smooth skin. Its color changes from green to yellow when it ripens. Quinces have a pleasant and fruity flavor and are a wonderful accompaniment to game.

2	quinces	2
1/4	bay leaf	1/4
	Salt and freshly ground black pepper	
1/3 cup	heavy or whipping (35%) cream, warmed	75 mL
8	bone-in bear chops (each about 3 oz/90 g)	8
1/3 cup	vegetable oil	75 mL
2/3 cup	white wine	150 mL
1 cup	Grand Veneur Sauce (page 356)	250 mL
1/3 cup	butter	75 mL

1. Peel quinces well and finely dice. Cook in salted water with bay leaf. Drain, then run through vegetable mill or by hand with a potato masher. Mix well, season with salt and pepper and add warm cream until desired consistency is obtained. Set aside and keep warm.

2. Season bear chops on each side with salt and black pepper. Heat oil in a very heavy-bottomed skillet. Sear chops and cook through. Remove excess fat and deglaze with white wine. Mix in Grand Veneur Sauce. Simmer for a few minutes and finish with a few pats of butter.

3. *To Serve:* Mound quince purée on individual serving plates. Arrange chops on each side. Pour sauce on top.

Leg of Young Bear in Beer

Serves 4

To chefs Gilbert Godbout and Renée Dupuis

Tip

When a bear comes out of hibernation, it hardly has any body fat so its meat is exceptionally good.

Variations

Instead of bear leg, use venison or wild boar piglet.

How to carve a small leg or haunch with bone:

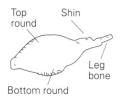

- Dutch oven with tight-fitting lid
- Meat thermometer

1	young bear leg	1
3	bottles (each 12 oz/341 mL) blonde (pale) ale	3
¾ cup	apple cider vinegar	175 mL
¾ cup	sunflower oil	175 mL
3	stalks celery	3
1	onion, cut into large cubes	1
1	carrot, diced	1
1	leek, cut into pieces	1
⅓ cup	peppercorns	75 mL
2	sprigs marjoram	2
2	sprigs rosemary	2
½	bay leaf	½
1	sprig thyme or wild thyme	1
¾ cup	butter, divided	175 mL
	Salt and freshly ground black pepper	
	Heavy or whipping (35%) cream	
1 cup	rowanberry or plum jelly	250 mL
⅔ cup	rowanberry eau-de-vie or equivalent	150 mL

1. Carefully remove fat from around bear leg, as it is quite unpalatable. Remove bone from the rump part and scrape clean the handle of bone part.

2. Prepare marinade with beer, vinegar, oil, celery, onion, carrot, leek, peppercorns, marjoram, rosemary, bay leaf and thyme. Add leg and marinate in the refrigerator for 36 hours, turning twice daily. After 36 hours, drain leg and wrap in a cloth to dry and place back in the refrigerator for at least 6 hours. Drain vegetables from marinade in a colander, reserving vegetables and marinade.

3. Preheat oven to 400°F (200°C). Using a braising pan or a Dutch oven with a tight-fitting lid, heat ⅓ cup (75 mL) of the butter and sweat vegetables from marinade (the butter will be absorbed by the vegetables). Place bear leg on top of vegetables. Season with salt and pepper. Cook in preheated oven for 15 minutes to sear meat. Add reserved marinade.

4. Reduce temperature to 350°F (180°C). Cover and cook, checking meat and basting occasionally, until a thermometer inserted into the center registers 190 to 194°F (88 to 90°C). Once cooked, remove bear leg and keep warm. Strain cooking stock, add cream and let boil. Season with salt and black pepper. Mix in jelly and eau-de-vie, stirring continuously. When sauce has reached desired consistency, whisk in remaining butter.

Young Bear Saddle with Corn Juice Essence and Pears Stuffed with Chestnuts

Serves 4

To my friend Bruno Sarles

Tip

Unfortunately, it is still very challenging to find vacuum-sealed bags equipped with meat probes. Should this be the case, cook the meat in the bag and estimate 4 hours of cooking at 185°F (85°C). Open bag and check cooking temperature.

Variations

Instead of bear, use young deer, young caribou, lamb or veal.

Saddle

The saddle of a bear, lamb or young deer (also wild boar piglet, hare and other small animals) runs from the end of the rib cage to the hind legs. It is usually cooked on the bone.

- Juicer
- Sous-vide machine
- Meat thermometer

1	young bear saddle	1
	Salt and freshly ground black pepper	
1/3 cup	vegetable oil	75 mL
4	carrots	4
2	onions	2
6	cloves garlic	6
2	stalks celery	2
1 cup	cranberries	250 mL
1 cup	corn	250 mL
24 cups	water	6 L
	Potato starch	

Stuffed Pears

4	Bosc pears	4
7 oz	unsweetened chestnut purée (canned)	210 g

1. Carefully remove fat from around bear saddle. Truss (page 365). Season with salt and black pepper. Heat oil in a large skillet over medium heat. Sear saddle on each side. Set aside.

2. Using a juice extractor, extract juice from carrots, onions, garlic, celery, cranberries and corn. Stir well. Season and set aside.

3. Ask your butcher to vacuum seal the saddle with juice in a bag equipped, if possible, with a meat probe (or do it yourself if you own a sous-vide machine, see Tip, left). Set aside in refrigerator for 48 hours.

4. Heat water in a large saucepan until temperature reaches 185°F (85°C). Since water needs to remain at this temperature, clip a thermometer to the side of the saucepan to constantly monitor temperature. Plunge bag with meat probe directly into water and cook until meat probe reaches 190 to 194°F (88 to 90°C) at center.

5. When bear saddle is cooked, open bag and transfer juices to a pan. Thicken with potato starch mixed with water. Reduce until sauce reaches desired consistency.

6. *Stuffed Pears:* Peel pears and remove core from the base using a melon baller. Cook in salted water, then drain. Heat chestnut purée and season with salt and black pepper. Stuff pears, then keep warm in oven.

7. *To Serve:* At the last minute, debone bear saddle and cut into portions. Arrange portions on plate, pour sauce on top and garnish with a pear stuffed with chestnuts.

Beaver recipes

Beaver Tail Consommé and Quenelles with Salted Herbs

Serves 8

In memory of Marcel Beaulieu, a great chef

Tips

Herbes salées, or herbs preserved in salt, is a mixture of finely chopped vegetables, such as carrots, leeks, celery and green onions, and fresh herbs, such as parsley, rosemary and thyme, layered in a jar and covered with salt. A good ratio is about 6 cups (1.5 L) chopped vegetables and herbs to 1 cup (250 mL) coarse salt. The fresh ingredients create their own brine when left for a few days in the refrigerator. The herbs will keep for several weeks in the refrigerator. Use in fish and meat dishes, soups and stews, or even added to mashed potatoes and salad dressings.

Quenelle is a kind of dumpling made of a minced meat and/or fish mixture and poached in a stock or water. It can also describe a small football-shaped scoop, such as ice cream.

- Food processor

2	beaver tails	2
6 cups	unthickened light poultry stock or store-bought equivalent	1.5 L
2 cups	light fumet (page 348)	500 mL
1 cup	herbes salées (see Tips, left)	250 mL
2	slices white bread, crusts removed	2
¾ cup	heavy or whipping (35%) cream	175 mL
1	chicken breast (about 7 oz/210 g)	1
1	egg yolk	1
	Salt and freshly ground black pepper	
½	carrot	½
½	onion	½
1	stalk celery	1
2	egg whites	2
8 cups	salted water	2 L
	Sprigs chervil	

1. Blanch beaver tails. Pour light poultry stock and fish fumet into a saucepan. Bring to a boil, then add beaver tails. Cook through.

2. Meanwhile, blanch salted herbs by plunging in cold water, then bring water to a boil. Immerse salted herbs in cold water, drain and pat dry with a paper towel. Soak bread in cream.

3. In a food processor, purée chicken breast with bread soaked in cream. Add egg yolk. Season with salt and black pepper. Strain filling, then add salted herbs. Cover and refrigerate for 1 to 2 hours.

4. Remove cooked beaver tails from broth. Remove meat from tails and cut into cubes; store covered in the refrigerator until serving. Place pot of broth in an ice bath to cool for a few hours before clarifying it.

5. To clarify broth, chop carrot, onion and celery in a food processor and add egg whites. Mix well with chilled broth. Place over medium heat and heat broth, stirring continuously, until the egg white particles coagulate (at 160°F/71°C) and rise to the surface. Skim off egg white mixture, then strain broth. Once clarified, the broth becomes a consommé.

6. Heat 8 cups (2 L) salted water in a saucepan. Using 2 tsp (10 mL), form small poultry and salted herb quenelles (see Tips, left). Immerse in hot water, 3 to 4 minutes. Once quenelles are cooked, set aside and keep warm.

7. *To Serve:* Reheat consommé over medium heat until steaming. Ladle into a soup plate. Add salted herb quenelles, beaver tail meat and chervil sprigs.

Pappardelle Pasta with Beaver and Shiitake Mushroom Stew

*Recipe by
Chef Pascale Vari*

Tip

Tradition holds that in northern Italy, pasta is served with butter and cream. In the south, it is served with olive oil, and in central Italy, tomatoes. In the Tuscany region, however, home of the Renaissance (and of avant-garde cuisine), pasta is accompanied by a game stew flavored with Chianti wine. Here is a lovely recipe from Italy, prepared with a game animal from North America that deserves recognition.

Pappardelle Pasta

2 cups	all-purpose flour	500 mL
1	whole egg	1
2	egg yolks	2
Pinch	salt	Pinch
1/3 cup	water	75 mL

Stew

10 oz	beaver meat, cut into cubes	300 g
3/4 cup	milk	175 mL
1/2 cup	olive oil, divided	125 mL
1/2 cup	chopped onion	125 mL
1	clove garlic, minced	1
2 cups	red wine	500 mL
1 cup	diced tomato	250 mL
1 2/3 cups	unthickened brown veal stock or store-bought equivalent	400 mL
3 oz	shiitake mushrooms, thinly sliced	90 g
1 tsp	chopped fresh thyme	5 mL
1 tbsp	fresh rosemary	15 mL
	Salt and freshly ground black pepper	
Pinch	nutmeg	Pinch

1. *Pappardelle Pasta:* Sift flour and form a mound. In center, add egg, egg yolks, salt and water. Thoroughly blend and knead for 10 minutes. The mound of dough should be firm. Cover dough with a cloth and let stand for 30 minutes in refrigerator before kneading it.

2. Roll out dough to 1/8-inch (3 mm) thickness. Using a knife, cut dough into pappardelle strips of 12 by 1 inches (30 by 2.5 cm). Store pappardelle pasta in freezer if not using the same day.

3. *Stew:* In a large bowl, place cubes of beaver in milk to soak in the refrigerator for 2 days.

4. When ready to cook, heat 1/3 cup (75 mL) of the olive oil in a skillet over medium heat and gently fry onion and garlic. Add meat and sauté until well browned. Add wine and reduce by half. Add diced tomato and pour veal stock on top. Season and cook, covered, for 50 minutes.

5. In a skillet over medium-high heat, add remaining olive oil and sauté shiitake mushrooms until tender.

6. Five minutes before meat has finished cooking, add shiitake mushrooms, thyme and rosemary to sauce. Season sauce with salt, black pepper and ground nutmeg.

7. In a large pot of boiling salted water, cook pappardelle pasta for 2 minutes. Drain, mix with stew and serve.

Roasted Beaver Loin Tartlets with Crayfish and Beaver Tail

Serves 4

Chives

Chives come from small bulbs that grow in bunches, with pink or purplish flowers peeking out from beneath the leaves. Their flavor is similar to that of an onion, but is subtler and delicately nuanced.

- High-sided skillet
- Meat thermometer

4 cups	Court-Bouillon (page 348)	1 L
1	beaver tail	1
32	whole crayfish	32
1¼ cups	unthickened brown game stock or store-bought equivalent	300 mL
12	whole shallots	12
14 oz	oyster mushrooms	420 g
⅓ cup	butter	75 mL
	Salt and freshly ground black pepper	
⅓ cup	vegetable oil	75 mL
1¼ to 1½ lbs	beaver loin (with or without bone)	625 to 750 g
4	tartlet shells	4
12	stems chive	12

1. Heat court-bouillon in a saucepan over high heat. Reduce to low and immerse beaver tail and let simmer until tail is cooked through and tender, about 2 hours. At the same time and in the same court-bouillon, cook crayfish. Drain, peel and de-vein. Set aside.

2. Heat game stock in a saucepan over medium-high heat. Add whole shallots and cook. Thoroughly wash oyster mushrooms and drain. Heat butter in a skillet over high heat. Sauté oyster mushrooms until golden. Season with salt and pepper and set aside.

3. When beaver tail is cooked, remove from court-bouillon and remove meat from tail. Set aside.

4. Heat vegetable oil in a high-sided skillet over medium-high heat. Season beaver loin with salt and black pepper and cook until thermometer inserted into center registers 160°F (71°C).

5. Place crayfish and beaver tail meat in a small saucepan. Add ¼ cup (60 mL) cooking stock from shallots and simmer for 5 minutes.

6. Preheat oven to 350°F (180°C). Heat mini tart shells in preheated oven. Fill with crayfish and beaver tail stew.

7. *To Serve:* Make a bed of oyster mushrooms on one side of a serving plate. Top with beaver loins. Place tartlets on other side of plate. Place 3 shallots on each plate, then pour shallot stock on top. Garnish with chive stems.

Types of Mushrooms for Cooking

Cep or porcini mushroom

This nutty-flavored mushroom is among the greatest in the bolete mushroom family.

Chanterelle

An explosion of flavors, the golden chanterelle is mild to the taste and has a very pleasant fruity fragrance.

Common or button mushroom

The most cultivated mushroom in the world. It is native to grasslands in Europe and North America.

Matsutake

A delicious, white-fleshed mushroom that is highly prized in Japan.

Morel

The mushroom of kings and the king of mushrooms. Relatively rare, it is highly valued for its delicious taste.

Oyster mushroom

Slightly more fragrant than the cultivated variety, the wild oyster mushroom has a flavor reminiscent of anise or tarragon.

Shiitake

Cultivated mushroom widely used in Asian cuisine.

Shimeji

An Asian mushroom with an elegant flavor. It grows in bunches or clusters.

Hare and Rabbit recipes

Hare with Blackcurrants

*In memory
of my friend,
Chef François Cara*

Tips

The pulp of the
blackcurrant contains
many seeds. Black-
currants are tart,
juicy and flavorful.
They are used in
cooking and to make
crème de cassis,
blackcurrant syrup
and fruit jelly.

We do not fry the
meat of a hare, we
"stiffen" it, which
means that we cook
it in hot fat just long
enough to stiffen
the fibers without
coloring the meat.

Serving Tips

Serve hot with
boiled potatoes,
crosnes, salsify or
chestnut purée.

Variations

**Instead of hare,
use rabbit or
Arctic hare.**

- Dutch oven

2	small hares (each 1½ to 1¾ lbs/750 to 875 g)	2
12	whole shallots	12
1	stalk celery	1
1	carrot, thinly sliced	1
1	bouquet garni	1
4	cloves garlic	4
1¼ cups	blackcurrant wine	300 mL
¼ cup	grapeseed oil	60 mL
2 tbsp	black peppercorns	30 mL
2 tbsp	salt	30 mL
¼ cup	vegetable oil	60 mL
1 cup	brown game stock	250 mL
	White Roux (page 351), optional	
160	blackcurrants (see Tips, left)	160

1. Cut hares into pieces. Set aside thighs, saddles and shoulders, and cut breasts into small pieces for the sauce.

2. Add pieces of hare breast, shallots, celery stalk, thinly sliced carrot, bouquet garni and garlic to a heavy-bottomed skillet. Pour in blackcurrant wine and grapeseed oil. Add peppercorns and salt. Cover with plastic wrap and let marinate in the refrigerator for at least 36 hours.

3. When you're ready to cook, remove hare breasts from marinade. Heat oil in a heavy-bottomed skillet over medium heat. Add 4 thighs, 4 shoulders and 2 saddles, each cut in two and cook, stirring, until firm, but not browned, about 5 minutes per side (see Tips, left). Place hare breast and its marinade in a large Dutch oven and heat. Add brown game stock and simmer gently until completely cooked. The blood of the animal will have slightly thickened the sauce.

4. Using a slotted spoon, drain pieces of hare and shallots. Set aside. Pour sauce through a fine-mesh strainer. If it is not thick enough, add a little white roux until desired consistency is achieved. Taste and adjust seasoning. Add pieces of hare, whole shallots and blackcurrants to the sauce. Simmer for about 10 minutes.

Hare with Dry Cider

To Michel Lambert, Quebec culinary historian

Tip

If the slow cooker is precise, it won't require any monitoring because it will never exceed the desired temperature and won't "stress" the meat.

- Slow cooker
- Cast-iron or heavy-bottomed skillet

4	hare saddles	4
3	cooking apples	3
4	cloves garlic	4
½	sprig rosemary	½
Generous pinch	nutmeg	Generous pinch
3 cups	dry cider, such as Champagnette or Du Minot	750 mL
	Salt and freshly ground black pepper	
¼ cup	vegetable oil	60 mL
6 tbsp	butter	90 mL
4	shallots, finely chopped	4
1	pork belly (uncured) (about 8 oz/250 g)	1
1⅔ cups	brown game or hare stock	400 mL
	Potato starch, optional	
	Boiled potatoes	
½ cup	chopped chives	125 mL

1. Remove legs and shoulders from hare saddles, and reserve for another recipe. The bones can be used to make a stock.

2. Peel and dice apples. Place saddles in a sufficiently large container, along with apples, garlic, rosemary and nutmeg. Add cider. Lightly season with salt and black pepper. Cover with plastic wrap and let marinate in the refrigerator overnight.

3. Heat oil in a cast-iron or heavy-bottomed skillet over medium heat. Season saddles with salt and black pepper, then cook, stirring, until firm, but not browned, about 5 minutes per side.

4. Heat butter in a small saucepan over medium heat. Sweat shallots. Cut piece of pork into small cubes, blanch and add to shallots. Set aside.

5. Transfer marinade ingredients and hare saddle and bacon to a slow cooker. Add brown hare stock. Cover and cook over Low heat until meat is tender, about 2 hours (see Tip, left). If cooking stock is too liquidy, thicken with potato starch right before serving.

6. *To Serve:* Place hare saddle on a plate. Spoon sauce and garnish over meat. Serve with boiled potatoes and top with chopped chives.

Hare Pie

Serves
4 to 6

*To my friend Marcel
Bouchard from the
Auberge des 21 in
La Baie, a chef and
skilled hunter*

Tip

Use a spice mixture
of equal amounts
cinnamon, nutmeg,
clove and ginger.

- Preheat oven to 250°F (120°C)
- Dutch oven
- 12-inch (30 cm) ramekin
- Meat thermometer

14 oz	cubes hare from thighs or saddle	420 g
3 oz	cubes chicken breast	90 g
1½ oz	salt pork, diced	45 g
1⅔ cups	chopped onions	400 mL
1¼ cups	white wine	300 mL
1⅔ cups	light game stock	400 mL
	Salt and freshly ground black pepper	
2 tbsp	mixed spices (see Tip, left)	30 mL
10 oz	potatoes, cut into cubes	300 g
8 oz	ground pork	250 g
1¼ lbs	shortcrust pastry	625 g

1. Blanch hare cubes and chicken breast in a saucepan of boiling water over medium-high heat.

2. Heat salt pork in a Dutch oven over medium heat until fat has rendered. Sweat chopped onions. Add hare and chicken cubes, then add white wine and reduce by 90 percent. Add game stock and cook very slowly in a preheated oven, about 2 hours.

3. Remove from oven. Season with salt, black pepper and mixed spices. Drain meats through sieve. Reserve the sauce.

4. Blanch potatoes in a saucepan of boiling water over high heat for about 2 minutes. Drain well. Mix together chicken and hare cubes, potatoes and ground pork. Season well.

5. Increase oven to 400°F (200°C). Roll out shortcrust pastry and divide in half. Press one-half into a porcelain ramekin. Spread filling evenly in ramekin, then cover with remaining half of dough. Cut a ½-inch (1 cm) vent hole in the dough. Cook in preheated oven until a thermometer inserted into the vent registers 185°F (85°C).

6. Meanwhile, pour sauce through a fine-mesh strainer, heat and adjust seasoning. Serve sauce with pie.

Hare as Prepared by My Friend Georges Boujard

Serves 4

Variations

Instead of hare, use rabbit or Arctic hare.

Clove

The Greeks and the Romans were very familiar with cloves and their distinct flavor. The leaves of the clove tree are similar to laurel. Clove's flavor profile is compatible with many dishes.

- Slow cooker
- 9-inch (23 cm) pie plate

1	hare (about 1¾ to 2 lbs/875 g to 1 kg)	1
4 cups	tannic red wine	1 L
5 oz	diced vegetables, such as onions, carrots, celery and leek whites	150 g
4	cloves garlic	4
8	juniper berries	8
½ tsp	black crushed black peppercorns	2 mL
1	whole clove	1
1	bouquet garni	1
1 tsp	sea salt	5 mL
¼ cup	olive oil	60 mL
1½ cups	brown hare or veal stock or store-bought equivalent	375 mL
12 oz	celery root	375 g
12 oz	rutabaga	375 g
	Salt and freshly ground black pepper	
1½ lbs	shortcrust pastry	750 g

1. Cut hare into 8 pieces. Place hare pieces in a large bowl and add red wine, diced vegetables, garlic, juniper berries, crushed peppercorns, clove, bouquet garni, salt and oil. Cover with plastic wrap and place in the refrigerator for 72 hours.

2. When ready to cook, place everything in a slow cooker. Add brown hare stock and cook on Low, 3 to 4 hours. Hare meat is very dry and so it must be cooked through. The tip of a knife inserted in the meat should come out easily. Remove pieces of hare and shred. Pour sauce through strainer and reserve.

3. Preheat oven to 325°F (160°C). Slice celery root and rutabaga into juliennes. Cook in salted water, then immerse in cold water. Drain and pat dry with a paper towel. Season with salt and black pepper.

4. Roll out dough and press into pie plate. Arrange 1 row celery root and 1 row rutabaga on the bottom and top with shredded hare. Place in preheated oven until bottom crust is baked, about 40 minutes. Ladle 2 to 3 spoonfuls of sauce over pie every 5 minutes (4 times at most). Serve immediately once bottom of pie is baked.

Braised Hare with Ham

To my friend Patrick, owner of the artisanal charcuterie shop Les Cochons Tout Ronds, on the Magdalen Islands

Tip

I did not add any salt to the recipe because the salt in the ham shank is sufficient to season the recipe. Taste and adjust seasoning as needed.

Juniper Berries

Juniper bushes produce dark blue berries used, among other things, for cooking. They are prized as an accompaniment for game birds and game animals.

● Slow cooker

1	hare (about 1 to 2 lbs/500 g to 1 kg)	1
4 cups	tannic red wine	1 L
¾ cup	diced vegetables	175 mL
4	cloves garlic	4
8	juniper berries	8
½ tsp	crushed black peppercorns	2 mL
1	whole clove	1
1	bouquet garni	1
¼ cup	olive oil	60 mL
1½ cups	brown hare or veal stock or store-bought equivalent	375 mL
2	slices ham shank, cut ¾-inch (2 cm) thick	2
10 oz	mushrooms	300 g
¼ cup	unsalted butter	60 mL
	Salt and freshly ground black pepper	
1	slice ham, ¼-inch (0.5 cm) thick	1
14 oz	chanterelle mushrooms	420 g
⅓ cup	shallots, finely chopped	75 mL

1. Cut hare into 8 pieces. Place pieces in a dish and add red wine, diced vegetables, garlic, juniper berries, crushed peppercorns, clove, bouquet garni and oil. Cover with plastic wrap and set aside in the refrigerator for 72 hours.

2. When you are ready to cook, transfer ingredients to a slow cooker. Add brown hare stock and ham shank. Cook on Low for 3 or 4 hours. Hare meat is very dry and must be cooked through. The tip of a knife inserted in the meat should come out easily.

3. Remove pieces of hare and ham shank slices. Strain sauce through a mesh strainer. Season with pepper and place meat back in sauce.

4. Meanwhile, place mushrooms in a heavy-bottomed skillet. Heat butter and cook until liquid is completely evaporated. Season with salt and pepper and keep warm.

5. Cut slice of ham into ¼-inch (0.5 cm) cubes. Blanch and add to mushrooms. Slice chanterelle mushrooms, if large, into quarters lengthwise, then sauté in a skillet over medium-high heat with finely chopped shallots. Season with salt and black pepper. Keep warm. Ten minutes before serving, add ham and mushroom mixture to the hare in its sauce.

6. *To Serve:* Portion out the pieces of hare. Pour sauce on top. Cut ham shank slices in half and place over the hare. Spoon chanterelle mushrooms on the side of each plate.

Arctic Hare with Water Chestnuts

Serves 6 to 8

To Raymond Ferry, a great chef

Variations

Instead of Arctic hare, use domestic rabbit or hare.

Water chestnut
A water chestnut—or water spinach—is the edible, underwater bulb of an aquatic plant that grows in the deep waters of streams. It has a thin black hull with tints of brown and a crisp white flesh.

- Dutch oven

1/3 cup	butter	75 mL
1	red onion, minced	1
1	Arctic hare (about 4 to 5 lbs/2 to 2.5 kg)	1
6	cloves garlic	6
2	carrots, finely diced	2
1 lb	celery root, finely diced	500 g
1	bouquet garni	1
1 2/3 cups	red wine	400 mL
10	crushed black peppercorns	10
	Salt	
1/4 cup	olive oil	60 mL
1/3 cup	vegetable oil	75 mL
16 cups	water	4 L
1 1/4 lbs	water chestnuts (fresh or canned)	625 g
	Cornstarch or rice flour, optional	
1/3 cup	chopped chives	75 mL

1. Heat butter in skillet over medium heat. Sweat onion. Let cool.

2. Cut Arctic hare into 8 pieces. Wrap minced onion and garlic cloves in cheesecloth. Place in a large bowl and add hare, carrots, celery root and bouquet garni. Add red wine, peppercorns, pinch of salt and olive oil. Cover with plastic wrap and let marinate in the refrigerator for at least 36 hours.

3. Remove hare from marinade. Reserving marinade. Heat vegetable oil in a large skillet over medium heat and cook rabbit, stirring, until firm, but not browned, about 5 minutes per side.

4. Heat water in a saucepan, then immerse water chestnuts, 6 at a time. Drain and remove skins. Repeat procedure as necessary.

5. Place marinated hare and marinade in a Dutch oven. Heat over medium-low heat. Cover and cook, about 40 minutes. Add water chestnuts and continue cooking. The Arctic hare should be cooked through. At this stage, remove pieces of hare and water chestnuts. Drain and set aside. Remove small bag of onion and garlic and press well to release the flavors.

6. Gently pour marinade through a fine-mesh strainer, reserving diced celery and carrots. If sauce isn't thick enough, add some cornstarch diluted in water, adding a little at a time until desired consistency.

7. Place hare, water chestnuts, diced celery and diced carrots back into the Dutch oven and simmer for 3 to 4 minutes. Serve in soup bowls and sprinkle with chopped chives.

Arctic Hare with Prunes

Serves 4

To Jacques Noeninger, pastry chef and friend

Variations

Instead of Arctic hare, use domestic rabbit or hare.

Prune

When cooking with prunes, it is best to stew them for a long time in white wine. Prunes can even be served with certain white meats or fatty fish.

- Preheat oven to 350°F (180°C)
- Porcelain or stoneware Dutch oven

8 oz	pitted prunes	250 g
⅓ cup	Armagnac	75 mL
⅔ cup	white wine	150 mL
2 to 4	Arctic hare thighs or saddles, cut into quarters	2 to 4
10 oz	rutabaga, diced	300 g
4	cloves garlic	4
1¼ cups	thickened brown game stock or store-bought equivalent	300 mL
1	bouquet garni	1
4½ oz	fingerling potatoes, optional	135 g
	Salt and freshly ground black pepper	

1. Soak pitted prunes overnight in Armagnac and white wine.

2. Blanch Arctic hare thighs to coagulate the blood inside the thighs and prevent the sauce from "breaking."

3. Place hare thighs in a porcelain or stoneware Dutch oven. Surround with soaked prunes and diced rutabaga. Add garlic cloves, brown game stock, bouquet garni and potatoes, if using. Cover Dutch oven and seal with sealing pastry, a tight-fitting lid or heavy-duty foil. Cook in preheated oven until thighs are tender and almost falling off the bone, about 90 minutes. Remove bouquet garni and garlic cloves. Season with salt and pepper.

Domestic Rabbit Saddles Stuffed with Dried Apricots and Pistachios

In memory of the great chef Carlo Dell'Olio

Tip

The apricot is one of the most widely cultivated fruit trees, for both the table and for preserves. The stone of the apricot, which is high in oil content, is edible when it is sweet, but is usually bitter.

Serving Tip

Serve with crosnes or pasta.

Variations

Use Arctic hare or hare instead of rabbits.

- Meat thermometer

6 oz	dried apricots, diced (see Tip, left)	175 g
2½ tbsp	crème d'abricot (French apricot liquor)	37 mL
2½ tbsp	Cognac	37 mL
⅓ cup	dry white wine	75 mL
3	slices bread	3
⅓ cup	heavy or whipping (35%) cream	75 mL
3½ tbsp	butter	52 mL
4	shallots, minced	4
2	domestic rabbits, deboned by the belly	2
8 oz	meat of two rabbit thighs	250 g
4 oz	fatty bacon	125 g
2 tbsp	chopped parsley	30 mL
1	egg white	1
3 tbsp	potato starch	45 mL
2 oz	blanched pistachio nuts	60 g
	Salt and freshly ground black pepper	
12 to 16 cups	water	3 to 4 L
1¼ cups	brown rabbit or game stock reduction, thickened	300 mL

1. Combine apricots, apricot liquor, Cognac and dry white wine in a large bowl and soak. Cover with plastic wrap and leave on counter for at least 24 hours.

2. Remove crusts from bread. Combine bread and whipping cream in a bowl and soak.

3. Melt butter in a skillet over medium heat. Add shallots and sweat. Let cool.

4. To make stuffing, chop rabbit thighs. Combine thighs, soaked bread and bacon in a large dish. Add apricots, parsley, shallots, egg white, potato starch and pistachios and mix by hand. Add salt and black pepper.

5. Lay out rabbit breasts, stuff and truss (page 365). Roll breasts in 3 or 4 layers of plastic wrap. Tie both ends and use a skewer to pierce 2 to 3 small holes in each breast.

6. In a large pot, heat water to 200°F (100°C). Place breasts in water, then maintain temperature at about 200°F (100°C). Cook until thermometer inserted the center registers 162°F (72°C). While rabbit breasts are cooking, heat rabbit stock reduction in another pot over medium heat.

7. *To Serve:* Pour 1 tbsp (15 mL) rabbit stock reduction on each plate. Lay three large slices of breast on top.

Squirrel
recipes

Roast Squirrel with Sauce Poivrade

Serves 4

Serving Tip

Serve with fried potatoes and green beans.

Variations

Instead of squirrel, use muskrat, young beaver, woodchuck or domestic rabbit.

2	whole squirrels	2
¾ cup	sunflower or other oil, divided	175 mL
18	black peppercorns, crushed	18
8	juniper berries, crushed	8
3	shallots, finely chopped	3
¾ cup	dry white wine	175 mL
2½ tbsp	Cognac	37 mL
	Fine sea salt	
1¼ cups	Sauce Poivrade (page 355)	300 mL

1. Prepare and age squirrels (see below). Leave the skin on during aging. After aging, remove the skin but leave the squirrels whole.

2. Place squirrels in a roasting pan. Add half of the oil, peppercorns, juniper berries, shallots, white wine, Cognac and salt. Cover with plastic wrap and refrigerate for 3 days, making sure to turn the meat over twice a day.

3. When you are ready to cook, strain squirrels thoroughly, reserving marinade, and pat squirrel meat dry.

4. Preheat oven to 450°F (230°C). Add remaining oil to roasting pan and heat in preheated oven. Sear squirrel meat on both sides until golden brown. Reduce temperature to 325°F (160°C) and cook, basting occasionally, until the tip of a knife can easily be inserted in the thigh, about 45 minutes.

5. Heat reserved marinade and Sauce Poivrade in a saucepan over low heat, about 8 minutes. Cut meat into equal portions and serve with hot Sauce Poivrade and marinade mixture.

Aging and Preparing Squirrel

Once the squirrels have been killed it is important that they are aged for some time to tenderize. First eviscerate and pat dry. Leave the skin and hair on the animal. Wrap in cheesecloth and hang them by their hind legs in a cool area (basement pantry or garage in the fall or spring and in the refrigerator in the summer) for 2 to 4 days, depending on the size of the animal. Hanging the animal is the natural process to tenderize the meat as just after killing the muscles stiffen. By hanging the body we let the meat and muscles relax. After this period, gently remove the skin and internal organs. If the recipe indicates, leave whole or cut squirrel into about 8 pieces as you would a rabbit or hare, then proceed with the recipe.

Squirrel Ragoût with Peanuts

Serves 4

Tips

Instead of a white roux, use a *beurre manie*—an equal amount of butter and flour mixed together and added to a hot stock to thicken.

We do not fry the meat of a squirrel, we "stiffen" it, which means that we cook it in hot fat just long enough to stiffen the fibers without coloring the meat.

Serving Tip

Serve with mashed potatoes and parsnips.

Variations

Instead of squirrel, use muskrat, beaver, woodchuck, domestic rabbit or hare.

- Dutch oven

2	squirrels, each cut into 8 pieces	2
	Marinade (page 346)	
⅓ cup	butter	75 mL
⅓ cup	peanut oil	75 mL
4 cups	unthickened brown game stock or store-bought equivalent	1 L
	White Roux (page 351) or similar (see Tips, left)	
	Salt and freshly ground black pepper	
4 oz	peanuts	125 g

1. Prepare and age squirrels (see 332).

2. Prepare marinade (uncooked) and marinate squirrel meat in the refrigerator for 48 hours.

3. After marinating, thoroughly strain squirrel meat, reserving marinade.

4. Heat butter and oil in a Dutch oven over medium heat. Add squirrel meat and cook, stirring, until firm, but not browned, about 5 minutes per side (see Tips, left). Remove squirrel meat from pot.

5. Strain marinade and pour into Dutch oven and reduce until liquid is completely evaporated. (This procedure is designed to remove the wine's acidity.) Preheat oven to 350°F (180°C).

6. Add squirrel meat and brown stock. Cover and cook in preheated oven for 30 to 40 minutes, depending on the size of the squirrels. To check doneness, insert the tip of a knife into the thigh. If it comes out easily it is done. Using a slotted spoon, remove squirrel meat and set aside to keep warm.

7. Pour stock through a mesh strainer into a saucepan. Thicken to desired consistency with White Roux. Season with salt and pepper. Return meat to sauce. Add peanuts and let simmer, about 10 minutes. Serve hot.

Squirrel Stew with Wood Garlic

Serving Tip

Serve with potatoes that have been boiled in salted water.

Wood Garlic

Also known as wild garlic, ramsons and bear's garlic, possibly because bears are so fond of them. Wild boars like them, too. The cooked leaves can be used as a vegetable. Garlic chives or garlic scapes are a good substitute.

- Large ovenproof Dutch oven
- Meat thermometer

2	squirrels	2
1½ cups	finely diced onions, celery and carrots	375 mL
1	head garlic, cut in half horizontally	1
6	juniper berries	6
1	whole clove	1
1	bay leaf	1
1	sprig fresh or dried thyme	1
2½ cups	dry white wine	625 mL
½ cup	olive oil, divided	125 mL
	Salt and freshly ground black pepper	
2 oz	butter	60 g
1⅔ cups	thickened brown game stock, or store-bought equivalent	400 mL
16	leaves wood garlic, finely chopped	16

1. Prepare and age squirrels (see page 332).

2. Cut squirrel into equal portions of about 8 cuts. Place meat in a large container with mixed vegetables, garlic, juniper berries, clove, bay leaf, thyme, white wine, ¼ cup (60 mL) of the olive oil, salt and black pepper. Cover and marinate in the refrigerator for 4 to 5 days.

3. When this procedure is completed, drain meat, reserving marinade and aromatics. In a heavy-bottomed Dutch oven, heat ¼ cup (60 mL) of olive oil and butter over medium heat until hot. Add squirrel meat and brown until golden, about 5 minutes per side. Add reserved marinade liquid and aromatics. Reduce liquid by 90 percent, then add thickened game stock.

4. Preheat oven to 350°F (180°C). Cook in preheated oven until thermometer inserted into the thickest part registers 185°F (85°C). (Note that we do not specify cooking time as squirrel size varies.)

5. When cooking is completed, remove meat. Pour sauce through a fine-mesh strainer. Adjust seasoning, if needed. Place squirrel meat in sauce and add wood garlic. Simmer for about 10 minutes. Serve hot.

Seal recipes

Seal Cubes with Lobster

To all my friends in the Magdalen Islands

CAUTION
Whatever part of the seal you prepare, you must first soak it in cold water for at least 2 to 3 hours for the blood to run out.

- Ovenproof saucepan

1¾ lbs	cubed seal loin	875 g
1	shallot or 1 small onion, finely minced	1
¾ cup	dry white wine	175 mL
¾ cup	brown veal stock	175 mL
14 oz	lobster bisque, homemade or store-bought	420 g
16	small potatoes	16
4	half lobster tails (each 4 oz/125 g), pre-cooked	4
1¼ cups	heavy or whipping (35%) cream, warmed	300 mL
¼ cup	Cognac	60 mL
12	stems chive	12

1. Soak seal cubes in cold water for 2 to 3 hours (see Caution, left). Drain well and pat dry.

2. When you are ready to make the recipe, preheat oven to 325°F (160°C). Place shallot in an ovenproof saucepan over medium-high heat. Pour in white wine and reduce by 90 percent. Add brown veal stock and lobster bisque and simmer gently for 10 minutes. Add soaked seal cubes. Cook in preheated oven until cubes are tender, about 2 hours. Keep warm.

3. Meanwhile, steam potatoes. Five minutes before serving, use same steamer to reheat lobster tails. Reheat seal cubes and add warmed cream and Cognac. Adjust seasoning.

4. Place seal cubes in a serving dish. Arrange half lobster tails and potatoes around them. Garnish with chive stems.

Seal Osso Bucco

Serves 4

In homage to the Inuit and North American Indians who live by the sea, to whom the seal is indispensable.

Tip

Fresh bay leaves, which are quite fragrant, have been used throughout these recipes. If you have dry bay leaves double the amount called for in the recipes.

Serving Tip

Serve on a soup plate with pasta.

Why Cook at 158°F (70°C)?

As a seal is normally shot, it retains most of its blood, even when "degorged." If you cook it at the temperature indicated, the blood coagulates without "granulating" the meat. If you have concerns about consuming game that has not reached 160°F (71°C) as recommended by the USDA, do not make this recipe.

- Dutch oven
- Meat thermometer

12	round slices seal (thigh or shoulder)	12
3	dried orange peels	3
14	fresh tomatoes	14
1/3 cup	vegetable oil	75 mL
2	shallots, finely diced or 1/3 cup (75 mL) small finely diced onions	2
2	carrots, finely diced	2
1	stalk celery	1
2	cloves garlic	2
3/4 cup	white wine	175 mL
4 cups	unthickened brown veal stock or store-bought equivalent	1 L
1/2	bay leaf	1/2
1/2 tsp	chopped thyme	2 mL
2 tbsp	chopped parsley	30 mL
	Salt and freshly ground black pepper	

1. Soak seal slices in cold water for 2 to 3 hours (see Caution, page 338). Drain well and pat dry.

2. Dehydrate orange peels on a tray at room temperature for 2 hours, then finely chop.

3. Immerse tomatoes in boiling water for a few seconds, then plunge in cold water. Peel skins off and remove seeds. Cut into small cubes. Set aside.

4. Preheat oven to 325°F (160°C). Heat oil in a skillet over medium heat. Add seal meat and cook, stirring, until firm, but not browned. Add shallot, carrots, celery, garlic and white wine to a Dutch oven over medium-high heat and reduce by 90 percent.

5. Add seal meat, then pour brown veal stock on top. Add chopped orange peel, bay leaf, thyme and parsley. Cook slowly in preheated oven until thermometer inserted into meat registers 122°F (50°C), about 1 1/2 hours. Add diced tomatoes and continue cooking until seal meat is tender, about 30 minutes more. (Do not allow the internal temperature to exceed 158°F/70°C.) Season with salt and pepper to taste.

Black Gold of the Magdalen Islands with Mustard Sauce

Serves 4

Serving Tip

Serve with baked potatoes in their skins.

Mustard

The mustard plant is an annual. The seeds inside can be red, brown, yellow or white, depending on the variety.

- Meat grinder

1¾ lbs	minced seal (thigh or saddle)	875 g
⅔ cup	white bread	150 mL
⅓ cup	heavy or whipping (35%) cream	75 mL
1	onion	1
1	clove garlic	1
1	sprig parsley	1
	Salt and white pepper	
¼ cup	butter	60 mL
¼ cup	vegetable oil	60 mL
1 cup	Mustard Sauce (page 351)	250 mL

1. Soak seal meat under cold running water for 2 to 3 hours (see Caution, page 338). Thoroughly drain meat and pat dry.

2. Soak bread with cream, onion, garlic and parsley. Run meat through grinder with a medium-size screen along with soaked bread. Season with salt and white ground pepper. Carefully wrap mixture in plastic wrap and refrigerate for 24 hours.

3. Shape meat into small square slab shapes (pavés). Heat butter and oil in a skillet over medium heat. Add seal mixture and cook until desired doneness. Drain and pour Mustard Sauce over the meat.

4. *To Serve:* Place seal pieces on a serving dish with Mustard sauce.

Seal Pavés with Green Peppercorns

Serves 6

To Marguerite and Charles-Claude Dion of Grande-Entrée in the Magdalen Islands

Serving Tip
Serve with steamed potatoes and vegetables in season.

Green peppercorn
The fruit of the peppercorn grows on a vine in tight clusters of 20 to 30 berries. The fruit is initially green, then yellow at the time of harvest.

6	pieces seal loin (each 6 oz/175 g)	6
	Milk, optional	
⅔ cup	unsalted butter, divided	150 mL
2½ tbsp	sunflower or other oil	37 mL
	Salt and freshly ground black pepper	
2 tbsp	Cognac	30 mL
½ cup	dry white wine	125 mL
4	shallots, minced	4
¾ cup	heavy or whipping (35%) cream	175 mL
2 cups	thickened brown veal stock or store-bought demi-glace	500 mL
	Green peppercorns	

1. Cut small square slab shapes (pavés) from seal loin. Soak seal squares in one of the following two ways: Soak for 24 hours in milk or cold water for 2 to 3 hours (see Caution, page 338). Thoroughly pat seal squares dry with cloths and set aside.

2. Heat 3½ tbsp (52 mL) of the butter and oil in a skillet over medium heat. Season seal squares with salt and pepper and sauté until cooked to desired doneness. Set aside.

3. Deglaze skillet with Cognac and white wine. Add shallots and reduce by half. Add cream and reduce by two-thirds. Add brown stock and green peppercorns and let cook for 2 to 3 minutes. Whisk remaining butter into sauce. Reheat seal squares and pour sauce over them.

Marinade, Stock, Roux and Sauce
recipes

Marinade

Variation

Cooked Marinade:
**The ingredients
and instructions
are the same as
for the uncooked
marinade. Boil
the mixture in a
saucepan over
medium heat for
10 minutes. Let
cool, then pour
over meat.**

4 cups	tannic red wine	1 L
⅔ cup	wine vinegar	150 mL
⅔ cup	grapeseed oil	150 mL
3	shallots, finely chopped	3
1	onion, finely chopped	1
6	juniper berries	6
12	black peppercorns	12
8	carrots, sliced into very thin rounds	8
1	stalk celery, finely chopped	1
½	clove garlic	½
2	bay leaves	2
10	sprigs parsley	10
1 tsp	dried thyme or 1 sprig fresh thyme	5 mL
	Salt and freshly ground black pepper	

1. Combine all ingredients together. Let stand for 5 to 6 hours on the counter. Pour over top the meat to be marinated.

Note: The liquid should never exceed one-third of the meat. Turn the piece of meat twice a day. If marinating more than 30 minutes, keep in the refrigerator. Cover with plastic wrap or a lid.

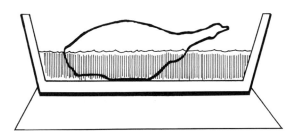

Brown Game Animal Stock

Makes about 24 cups (6 L)

- Preheat oven to 450°F (230°C)

6¾ lbs	chopped game bones	3.375 kg
⅓ cup	sunflower oil or butter	75 mL
2 lbs	trimmings (see Tips, left)	1 kg
1 cup	diced onions	250 mL
2 to 3	carrots, cut in pieces	2 to 3
1	stalk celery, cut in pieces	1
7 oz	mushrooms	210 g
	Bouquet garni	
2	stems parsley	2
1	sprig thyme	1
1	bay leaf	1
10	juniper berries	10

Tips

For the trimmings, combine meat and vegetable trimmings such as peelings from carrots and other vegetables from this recipe or whatever vegetable or meat trimmings you have available.

Game stock is the essential base of a good sauce to accompany game.

If you wish to make a more economical stock base, do not reduce stock and thicken it with cooked white roux (page 351).

Freezing Stock

Cooled stock can be frozen in airtight containers for up to 6 months. Leave 1-inch (2.5 cm) headspace when filling containers to allow for expansion. Let stock thaw overnight in the refrigerator, or defrost in the microwave before using.

1. Place a large roasting pan in preheated oven to heat. Chop bones with cleaver. Add oil to hot roasting pan and swirl to coat. Add bones and roast until golden, about 20 minutes.

2. Remove bones and place in a large stockpot. Repeat procedure with trimmings including onions, carrots, celery and mushrooms. When browned, add to large stockpot with bouquet garni, parsley, thyme, bay leaf and juniper berries and cover with water. Simmer, skimming frequently, 3 to 4 hours.

3. Pour through a fine-mesh strainer and return to heat and reduce by half.

Variations

Game Stock Reduction (demi-glace): Reduce stock by three-quarters. You will obtain a game stock reduction that has no thickening element.

Light Game Stock: Use the same ingredients as for the brown stock. However, do not brown the bones, but place them directly in the stockpot. Boil, skim and then add aromatic ingredients. The cooking time is the same.

White Poultry or Game Bird Stock

Makes
about
20 cups
(5 L)

4 lbs	poultry or game stock bones	2 kg
3 to 4	carrots, cut in medium-size cubes	3 to 4
1 cup	onions, cut in medium-size cubes	250 mL
2	leeks, white part only, cut in medium-size cubes	2
1	celery, cut in medium-size cubes	1
3	cloves garlic, minced	3
1	whole clove	1
	Freshly ground black pepper	
20	stems parsley	20
1	sprig thyme	1
½	bay leaf	½
	Bouquet garni	

Tips

This recipe is suitable for all types of poultry. The basic principle is always the same. Whether you use a hen or a rooster, boil the poultry whole. The long cooking time will bring out the maximum amount of flavor. If you use chicken bones, be sure to soak to remove the impurities such as blood.

Freezing Stock

Cooled stock can be frozen in airtight containers for up to 6 months. Leave 1-inch (2.5 cm) headspace when filling containers to allow for expansion. Let stock thaw overnight in the refrigerator, or defrost in the microwave before using.

1. Rinse poultry or game bird bones under cold water and then soak, about 1 hour. Drain.

2. Place carrots, onions, leeks, celery, garlic, clove, pepper, parsley, thyme and bay leaf in a stockpot with soaked bones. Cover with water and bring to a boil over medium heat. Skim, if necessary. Add bouquet garni. Simmer for 45 minutes. Pour through fine-mesh strainer and reduce if flavor isn't strong enough after straining.

Fumet or Game Essence

Fumet is a concentration of flavors that are extracted from trimmings or the bones of selected game animals or game birds. Fumet is always prepared with ingredients that have not been browned. An essence or fumet can constitute the liquid base for a brown game stock or serve as a base for a consommé of game.

Court-Bouillon

Court-bouillon is used more for cooking fish, mollusks and crustaceans than for game. It is prepared by extracting the flavors of a variety of vegetables (carrots, onions, celery and bouquet garni) cooked in white wine. It is then used to poach a food.

Vegetable Essence

Vegetable essences are concentrations of flavors that have been extracted from one or several ingredients. One can make celery essence, for example. One can also make essences from a mixture of vegetables. It simply requires cooking the basic ingredient in water, and then, after cooking, allowing the liquid to reduce in order to concentrate the flavors.

Brown Poultry or Game Bird Stock

Makes
about
20 cups
(5 L)

Tip

Before adding tomato paste to a stock, cook it in a microwave oven in 60-second intervals (4 to 6 times). Do not worry if the mixture turns brown. This procedure is to remove the acidity.

Freezing Stock

Cooled stock can be frozen in airtight containers for up to 6 months. Leave 1-inch (2.5 cm) headspace when filling containers to allow for expansion. Let stock thaw overnight in the refrigerator, or defrost in the microwave before using.

● Preheat oven to 450°F (230°C)

4 lbs	poultry or game bird bones	2 kg
⅔ cup	vegetable oil, divided	150 mL
3 to 4	carrots, cut in medium-size cubes	3 to 4
1 cup	onions, cut in medium-size cubes	250 mL
2	leeks, white parts only, cut in medium-size cubes	2
1	celery, cut in medium-size cubes	1
3	cloves garlic, minced	3
1	whole clove	1
20	parsley stems	20
1	sprig thyme	1
½	bay leaf	½
	Freshly ground black pepper	
	Bouquet garni	
	Warmed tomato paste (see Tip, left)	

1. Place a roasting pan in preheated oven to heat. Chop bones with cleaver. Place ⅓ cup (75 mL) of the oil in hot roasting pan and swirl to coat. Add bones and roast in preheated oven until golden, about 20 minutes.

2. At the same time, sweat carrots, onions, leeks, celery and garlic in the remaining oil in a large skillet over medium heat. Combine bones, sweated vegetables, clove, parsley, thyme, bay leaf, pepper and bouquet garni to a stockpot.

3. Cover with water and simmer, for 45 to 60 minutes. If the stock is not brown enough, add a little warmed tomato paste (see Tip, left), then pour through fine-mesh strainer.

Brown Veal Stock

Makes about 48 cups (12 L)

Tips

This weight is ideal, but if you do not have a sufficiently large stockpot, divide the quantities.

By reducing or concentrating the cooking juices, we obtain demi-glace sauce. If we reduce them even more, we obtain veal stock reduction or glace.

This veal stock is not thickened. We use white roux to obtain a thickened brown stock.

Freezing Stock

Cooled stock can be frozen in airtight containers for up to 6 months. Leave 1-inch (2.5 cm) headspace when filling containers to allow for expansion. Let stock thaw overnight in the refrigerator, or defrost in the microwave before using.

• Preheat oven to 400°F (200°C)

20 lbs	bones (preferably knees, finely diced by the butcher) (see Tips, left)	10 kg
2/3 cup	vegetable fat	150 mL
2/3 cup	vegetable oil	150 mL
5 1/2 cups	onions, cut into large cubes	1.375 L
5 1/2 cups	carrots, cut into large cubes	1.375 L
2 3/4 cups	celery stalks, cut into 2-inch (5 cm) lengths	675 mL
2	heads garlic, unpeeled	2
1	bay leaf	1
2 pinches	ground thyme	2 pinches
7 cups	parsley	1.75 L
25	black peppercorns	25
7 oz	warmed tomato paste (see Tip, page 349)	210 g

1. Place a roasting pan in preheated oven to heat. Chop bones with cleaver. Place vegetable fat in hot roasting pan and swirl to coat. Add bones and roast in preheated oven until golden, about 20 minutes. This step is very important, as it is these roasted cooking juices that will give the game or veal stock its nice color.

2. At the same time, heat oil in a sufficiently large saucepan over medium heat. Add onions, carrots and celery and sweat. Add garlic, bay leaf, thyme, parsley, peppercorns and tomato paste and cook until well coated with oil, about 8 minutes.

3. When these two procedures are complete, place vegetables and bones in a sufficiently large stockpot. Cover with water completely and let simmer for at least 6 hours.

Note: Never add salt to a stock, because if you eventually wish to reduce it, it will be too salty. While it is cooking, skim it regularly. If it is evaporating too much, add water. After cooking, pour through a fine-mesh strainer or fine sieve, let sit in a cool area, then fill up small containers that can be frozen. Stock can be made in winter and frozen for use later. When it cooks, it gives off a very nice scent and adds humidity to the house. To accelerate the cooling process, pour stock into a bowl, place it in the sink, and run a stream of cold water around the bowl. If the stock produces fat, degrease regularly during the cooking process.

White Roux

| ½ cup | butter | 125 mL |
| ½ cup | all-purpose flour | 125 mL |

1. Melt butter in microwave oven for 20 seconds. Add flour. Cook in 20-second intervals and blend thoroughly between each interval. Roux is cooked when it starts to foam, about 5 minutes.

Roux Substitutes

You can find commercial substitutes for thickening stocks and sauces. The one we use most is cornstarch. If you thicken with cornstarch, you must serve the sauce immediately. Otherwise, after about 20 minutes, it will separate. The same thing occurs with all starches (potato, rice, arrowroot, chestnut, etc.). The advantage of thickening with rice or potato starch is that they will not impart a secondary flavor.

Tip

It is much better to use roux than starch, as the gluten in the flour makes sauces bind more effectively.

Variation

Brown Roux:
Proceed as for white roux and cook until mixture turns brown.

Mustard Sauce

Makes
about
1³⁄₄ cups
(425 mL)

½ cup	minced onions or shallots	125 mL
1 tbsp	butter	15 mL
⅓ cup	Dijon mustard	75 mL
1 cup	brown veal stock, thickened	250 mL
⅔ cup	heavy or whipping (35%) cream	150 mL
	Salt and freshly ground black pepper	

1. Gently brown onions or shallots in butter over medium heat. Add mustard. Reduce heat to low and cook slowly to remove acidity. Add veal stock and let cook for 5 minutes. Add cream. Season with salt and pepper to taste.

Hollandaise Sauce (Quick Method)

Tip

We used unsalted butter because of its greater fat density.

¾ cup	unsalted clarified butter	175 mL
4	egg yolks	4
3 tbsp	white wine	45 mL
	Salt and freshly ground black pepper	
	Juice of ½ lemon	

1. Melt butter in a small saucepan over low heat.

2. In a deep stainless-steel mixing bowl, whisk together egg yolks, white wine, salt and black pepper. Set bowl over a saucepan of simmering water and whisk mixture at a constant steady speed until the consistency of whipped cream. This procedure is very important, as it is the emulsion of the egg yolks combined with the acidity of the white wine in the double boiler that will ensure the success of this sauce.

3. When this procedure is complete, gradually incorporate melted butter. The mixture should be smooth. Add lemon juice as needed.

Hollandaise Sauce (Classic Method)

Tip

The minced shallot reduction can be left in the sauce.

¾ cup	unsalted clarified butter	175 mL
⅓ cup	white wine	75 mL
¼ cup	minced shallots	60 mL
2 tsp	white wine vinegar or apple cider vinegar	10 mL
4	egg yolks	4
	Salt and ground white pepper	
	Juice of ½ lemon	

1. Melt butter in a small saucepan over low heat.

2. Reduce white wine, minced shallots and vinegar by 90 percent. Let reduction cool. Pour reduction through cloth strainer, pressing down to extract the maximum amount of juice.

3. In a deep stainless-steel bowl, thoroughly blend egg yolks and white wine mixture, then add salt and pepper. Set bowl over a saucepan of simmering water and whisk mixture at a constant steady speed until the consistency of whipped cream. This procedure is very important, as it is the emulsion of the egg yolks combined with the acidity of the white wine in the double boiler that will ensure the success of this sauce.

4. When this procedure is complete, slowly incorporate melted butter. Mixture should be smooth. Add lemon juice as needed.

Béarnaise Sauce

Makes about 1³/₄ cups (425 mL)

Tip

You can leave the shallots in, according to your taste, in which case do not strain the sauce in Step 3.

1¼ cups	unsalted clarified butter	300 mL
2½ tbsp	red wine vinegar	37 mL
1 cup	white wine	250 mL
1 tsp	black cracked peppercorns	5 mL
1 tbsp	chopped fresh tarragon	15 mL
3½ tbsp	minced shallot	52 mL
3	egg yolks	3
	Salt and freshly ground black pepper	
1 tbsp	finely chopped tarragon	15 mL
1 tbsp	finely chopped parsley	15 mL
2 tbsp	finely chopped chives	30 mL

1. Clarify unsalted butter in double boiler. Set aside.

2. Pour vinegar and wine into saucepan over medium heat. Add peppercorns, tarragon and shallot. Reduce by half and let cool. In a stainless-steel bowl set over a saucepan of simmering water, whisk egg yolks to blend. Add vinegar and wine reduction to egg yolks, then cook, whisking mixture at a constant steady speed until creamy and smooth. Gently incorporate clarified butter, ensuring that the butter is not too warm.

3. Pour sauce through cloth strainer. Season with salt and pepper to taste. If sauce is too thick, add a little warm water to slightly liquefy it. Top with tarragon, parsley and chives, then serve.

Béarnaise Sauce (other method)

Béarnaise sauce is a Hollandaise sauce made according to the classic method, to which chopped chives and tarragon are added. The sauce is not poured through a cloth strainer or through a fine sieve.

Béarnaise Sauce Derivatives

Choron Sauce: Béarnaise to which a cooked reduction of tomatoes that have been chopped or run through the blender (no tarragon or chervil at the end) are added.

Paloise Sauce: Béarnaise in which mint leaves replace the tarragon.

Valois or Foyot Sauce: Béarnaise and meat or game stock reduction (glace).

Cranberry Sauce

¾ cup	unsalted butter, divided	175 mL
4	shallots, minced	4
¾ cup	tannic red wine	175 mL
½ cup	cranberry juice	125 mL
1 cup	brown game stock	250 mL
1 cup	cranberries	250 mL
	Salt and freshly ground black pepper	

Tip

If the sauce needs a thickener or binder, add white roux or a starch-based thickener. You can also, at the last minute, add a few drops of alcohol of the same fruit.

Variation

You can make the same recipe, replacing cranberries with blueberries or cloudberries.

1. Heat half the butter in a small saucepan over medium heat and add shallots. Add red wine and cranberry juice and reduce by 90 percent. Add game stock and simmer, about 10 minutes Pour through fine-mesh strainer and set aside.

2. Meanwhile, sauté cranberries in remaining butter in a small skillet over medium heat until they burst, about 5 minutes. Place on paper towel. A few minutes before serving, add cranberries to the sauce. Season with salt and pepper to taste.

Labrador Tea or Eastern Teaberry Sauce

½ cup	dried Labrador tea leaves or Eastern teaberry leaves	125 mL
¾ cup	white wine	175 mL
¾ cup	water	175 mL
¾ cup	butter, divided	175 mL
6	shallots, finely minced	6
1 cup	thickened brown game stock (demi-glace) or store-bought equivalent	250 mL
	Salt and freshly ground black pepper	

1. The day before you plan to use, rehydrate Eastern teaberry or Labrador tea leaves in wine and water overnight. The next day, pour through a fine-mesh strainer, reserving liquid.

2. Heat ⅓ cup (75 mL) of butter in a saucepan over medium heat. Sweat shallots. Add soaking liquid and reduce by 90 percent. Add game stock and cook, about 10 minutes. Pour through a fine-mesh strainer. Season with salt and pepper to taste and add remaining butter.

Sauce Poivrade

Makes about 2³⁄₄ cups (675 mL)

- Strainer, lined in cheesecloth

¹⁄₃ cup	sunflower oil	75 mL
10 oz	game meat trimmings	300 g
3 tbsp	wine vinegar	45 mL
¹⁄₃ cup	white wine	75 mL
²⁄₃ cup	Marinade (page 346)	175 mL
2	shallots, minced	2
1	carrot, finely diced	1
1¹⁄₄ cups	thickened brown game stock (demi-glace) or store-bought equivalent	300 mL
6	black peppercorns, crushed	6
	Salt and freshly ground black pepper	
¹⁄₃ cup	butter	75 mL
3 tbsp	Armagnac or Cognac	45 mL

1. Heat oil in a skillet over medium heat. Sauté game meat trimmings. Remove from skillet and set aside.

2. Deglaze skillet with vinegar, white wine and marinade and reduce by 90 percent. Add trimmings, shallots, carrot and game stock. Cook over low heat for 1 hour.

3. Skim, then add peppercorns. Cook for 10 minutes, then pour through cheesecloth-lined strainer, pressing down thoroughly on ingredients.

4. Season with salt and pepper to taste. Whisk in butter and add Armagnac.

Sauce Diane

Makes about 3¹⁄₂ cups (875 mL)

³⁄₄ cup	heavy or whipping (35%) cream	175 mL
2¹⁄₂ cups	Sauce Poivrade (page 355)	625 mL
²⁄₃ cup	hard-boiled egg whites, finely diced	150 mL
2¹⁄₄ tbsp	finely minced truffle	34 mL
	Salt and freshly ground black pepper	

1. Whip cream until firm.

2. Heat Sauce Poivrade over low heat for 2 to 3 minutes before serving cooked game. Gently add whipped cream, then egg whites and minced truffle. Season with salt and pepper to taste and serve immediately

Grand Veneur Sauce

1⅔ cups	raw or cooked marinade with its vegetables (page 346)	400 mL
1¼ cups	thickened brown game stock (demi-glace) or store-bought equivalent	300 mL
⅓ cup	butter	75 mL
2 tbsp	gooseberry jelly	30 mL
⅓ cup	Cognac or Armagnac	75 mL
	Salt and freshly ground black pepper	

1. Reduce marinade over medium heat with its vegetables by 90 percent. Add game stock and cook, about 10 minutes. Pour through a fine-mesh strainer. Add butter, gooseberry jelly and Cognac. Season with salt and pepper to taste.

Tips

The traditional grand veneur sauce is made with the blood of game. Here is an adapted version of the recipe. If, however, you have game that was killed by a bullet, its muscles will inevitably contain blood. The blood will have an effect on the sauce when it is cooked because it will thicken faster, so watch carefully on how much it is reduced.

The famous chef Auguste Escoffier added cream to this sauce.

Venison Sauce

⅓ cup	unsalted butter	75 mL
2	shallots, minced	2
14 oz	game meat trimmings	420 g
3 cups	red wine	750 mL
3¼ cups	Sauce Poivrade (approx.) (page 355)	800 mL
	Salt and freshly ground black pepper	

1. Heat butter in a skillet over medium heat. Add shallots and sweat. Add game meat trimmings and cook, stirring, until firm, but not browned. Add red wine and reduce by 90 percent. Add Sauce Poivrade and cook, 20 to 30 minutes. Pour through a fine-mesh strainer. Season with salt and pepper to taste.

Variations

You can add 1 tbsp (15 mL) gooseberry jelly and 2½ tbsp (37 mL) port wine.

Sour Cherry Sauce

Tip

Sour cherries are small and red, with soft flesh, and are very tart. In Canada, they are grown in the Niagara valley. They can be replaced by small wild cherries.

- Strainer, lined in cheesecloth

2	shallots, finely minced	2
2 cups	red wine	500 mL
¾ cup	cherry juice (from cherries in jar)	175 mL
Pinch	ground cinnamon	Pinch
¾ cup	thickened brown game stock (demi-glace) or store-bought equivalent	175 mL
	Salt and freshly ground black pepper	
6 tbsp	butter	90 mL
⅔ cup	chopped fresh white bread	150 mL
1 cup	drained pitted sour cherries (from jar)	250 mL
2 tbsp	finely chopped lemon zest	30 mL

1. Place minced shallots, red wine, cherry juice and cinnamon in a saucepan over medium heat and reduce by 90 percent. Add brown game stock. Season with salt and pepper to taste. Pour through a cheesecloth-lined strainer.

2. When ready to serve, whisk in butter. Add chopped fresh white bread, pitted cherries and chopped lemon zest.

Pine Nut Sauce

¾ cup	pine nuts	175 mL
2½ tbsp	unsalted butter	37 mL
⅔ cup	white wine	150 mL
¼ cup	white wine vinegar	60 mL
⅓ cup	superfine (instant dissolving) sugar	75 mL
1⅔ cups	thickened brown game stock (demi-glace) or store-bought equivalent	400 mL
	Salt and freshly ground black pepper	
2½ tbsp	Armagnac or Cognac	37 mL

1. Toast pine nuts in warm butter and set aside.

2. Heat white wine, vinegar and sugar in a saucepan over medium heat and reduce by 90 percent. Add brown game stock. Season with salt and pepper to taste.

3. When ready to serve, add pine nuts and Armagnac.

Salmis Sauce

Makes about 2¼ cups (550 mL)

¼ cup	unsalted butter	60 mL
½ cup	finely diced carrots	125 mL
½ cup	finely diced celery	125 mL
¼ cup	minced shallots	60 mL
1¼ lbs	game meat trimmings	625 g
½ cup	white wine	125 mL
1¼ cups	full-bodied thickened game stock or store-bought equivalent	300 mL
1	bouquet garni	1
3	cloves garlic	3
	Salt and freshly ground black pepper	
¼ cup	duck or other blood (see Caution, below)	60 mL
2½ tbsp	Armagnac or Cognac	37 mL

1. Heat butter in a skillet over medium heat. Sweat carrots, celery and shallots. Add game meat trimmings and cook, stirring, without browning. Add white wine and reduce by 90 percent. Add game stock, bouquet garni and garlic. Simmer gently over low heat for 30 minutes.

2. Pour through a fine-mesh strainer. Season with salt and pepper to taste and finish thickening with blood and Armagnac.

Caution

This is a traditional recipe that uses uncooked blood. For food safety, it is important to know where your food has come from and that it has been safely stored and not contaminated in any way.

Sweet-and-Sour Highbush Cranberry Sauce

Makes about 3½ cups (875 mL)

- Juicer

1 cup	fresh or frozen highbush cranberries	250 mL
⅔ cup	superfine (instant dissolving) sugar	150 mL
1¼ cups	thickened brown game stock (demi-glace) or store-bought equivalent	300 mL
½ cup	finely diced celery	125 mL
⅓ cup	highbush cranberries	75 mL
⅓ cup	unsalted butter	75 mL
	Salt and freshly ground black pepper	

1. Extract juice from highbush cranberries. Place in a saucepan over medium heat, add sugar and cook until caramelized, about 10 minutes. Stop cooking by adding a little cold water to caramel (taking care not to spatter).

2. Heat game stock over low heat. Add diced celery and cook for 15 minutes.

3. Add reduced juice and cranberries. Whisk in butter. Season with salt and pepper to taste.

Orange Sauce

Makes about 3 cups (750 mL)

Tip
You can also add blanched orange zest.

⅔ cup	fresh orange juice	150 mL
⅓ cup	white wine	75 mL
¼ cup	apple cider vinegar	60 mL
½ cup	superfine (instant dissolving) sugar	125 mL
1⅓ cups	thickened brown game bird stock (demi-glace) or store-bought equivalent	325 mL
	Salt and freshly ground black pepper	
⅓ cup	Grand Marnier	75 mL

1. Combine orange juice, wine, vinegar and sugar in a saucepan over medium heat and cook until caramelized, about 10 minutes. Stop cooking by adding a little cold water to caramel (taking care not to spatter).

2. Heat brown game stock over low heat. Add orange juice mixture. Season with salt and pepper to taste. Add Grand Marnier.

Truffle Sauce Périgueux

Makes about 5 cups (1.25 L)

- Strainer, lined with cheesecloth

¼ cup	finely minced shallots	60 mL
½ cup	unsalted butter, divided	125 mL
⅔ cup	red port wine	150 mL
¾ cup	Madeira wine	175 mL
4 cups	thickened game bird or game meat stock (demi-glace) or store-bought equivalent	1 L
¼ cup	truffle juice	60 mL
1	black truffle, finely julienned	1

1. Sweat shallots over very low heat in half the butter. Add port wine and Madeira wine and reduce by 90 percent.

2. Add game stock. Simmer for about 10 minutes then pour through a cheesecloth-lined strainer.

3. Fifteen minutes before serving, whisk in remaining butter. Add truffle juice and julienned truffle.

Gribiche Sauce

Makes about 1¾ cups (425 mL)

4 tsp	Dijon mustard	20 mL
6	egg yolks	6
⅓ cup	red wine vinegar	75 mL
1⅔ cups	olive oil	400 mL
1 tsp	minced parsley	5 mL
2 oz	chopped sour pickles	60 g
1 tsp	chopped chervil	5 mL
½ tsp	chopped tarragon	2 mL
⅓ cup	chopped capers	75 mL
3	hard-boiled egg whites, chopped	3
	Salt and freshly ground black pepper	

1. Slowly whisk together Dijon mustard and egg yolks. Incorporate vinegar, then olive oil. Add parsley, pickles, chopped chervil, tarragon, capers and cooked egg whites. Season with salt and pepper to taste.

Caution

This recipe contains raw eggs. If you are concerned about the food safety of raw eggs, substitute ¼ cup (60 mL) pasteurized liquid egg yolks.

Techniques for Preparing Game Birds and Poultry

Top left: male mule duck; *right:* female

Bottom left: stuffed male mule duck; *right:* female

Top row, from left to right: goose, female mule duck, turkey poult, guinea fowl, pheasant

Middle row, from left to right: small chicken or chick, partridge, northern bobwhite, pigeon

Bottom row: quail of different sizes

Poultry cut into 4 portions

Poultry cut into 8 portions

Clockwise from left: turkey, mule duck, goose, Muscovy duckling

Deboned duck breasts (suprêmes), according to size (male and female Pekin duck, Muscovy duck, mule duck, male and female mallard duck)

Duck thighs, according to size (male and female Pekin duck, Muscovy duck, mule duck, female and male mallard duck)

Small game birds, according to size (duck, wild goose, grouse, ptarmigan, partridge, woodcock, quail)

Breasts of stuffed mule duck (magret)

Breasts and thighs of stuffed mule duck

Mule duck magret and foie gras

Aiguillettes sliced from the breast of a stuffed male mule duck

Sliced breast of a stuffed male mule duck

How to remove parts and debone

How to debone the thigh of poultry or a game bird

 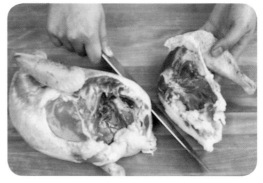

How to remove a breast or a deboned breast (suprême)

How to debone a chicken thigh or game birds

How to truss

How to truss poultry or a game bird

How to bard and split

How to bard poultry or a game bird

How to split and flatten poultry for cooking

How to lard and stuff

How to lard poultry or a game bird

How to prepare poultry with condiments under the skin and vegetables inside

Cooking Basics

Cooking Methods

BRAISE

- Sauté at high heat to brown the meat.
- Remove any surplus fat.
- Deglaze with wine and cook to extract the alcohol.
- Half steep the meat in the stock of your choice.
- Add seasoning ingredients.
- Cover hermetically.
- Cook at a constant and regular temperature.

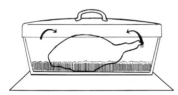

GRILL

- Carefully wipe the piece to be grilled.
- Lightly brush with oil.
- Season with salt and pepper.
- Place the piece to be grilled (skin-side down for game birds) on a hot grill.
- Rotate the piece a quarter turn to get the criss-cross grilled pattern.
- Rotate similarly on the other side.
- Finish cooking on very low heat.

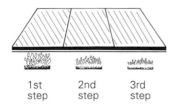

1st step   2nd step   3rd step

POACH

- Rinse game under running water (to remove impurities).
- Place in cold water and bring to the boil.
- Skim.
- Add a seasoning garnish: carrots, onions, cloves, leek greens, celery, bouquet garni, garlic and peppercorns.
- Season with coarse salt.
- Boil and skim frequently during the cooking time.
- Leave to cook on very low heat.
- As soon as cooked, remove the piece from the stock.

FRY

- Place the piece of meat over the stove, uncovered.
- Brown the first surface.
- Turn the piece over to brown the other parts.
- Add a little garnish: carrots, onions and bouquet garni.
- Once the piece is nicely browned and nearly at the end of the cooking time, add (according to the recipe) wine and stock.
- As soon as cooked, remove from the heat.

Thick pieces in a skillet so as to retain a minimum amount of moisture.

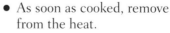

ROAST

- Preheat the oven.
- Turn the piece over to brown it.
- Reduce the temperature of the oven.
- Baste frequently during the cooking period.
- At the end of the cooking period, remove the piece of meat.
- Place the tray on the stovetop to caramelize the meat juices.
- Remove fat.
- Pour in a little brown poultry stock and deglaze.

SAUTÉ

- Heat the fat in a skillet.
- Place the pieces, skin-side down, in the hot fat.
- Brown (according to the recipe).
- Turn the pieces over as soon as they are brown.
- Cover and leave to cook on low heat.
- Remove the cooked pieces.
- Finish cooking the largest pieces.
- Remove all the pieces.
- Defat thoroughly.
- Deglaze with wine (according to the recipe).
- Let reduce gently.
- Add the stock (according to the recipe).
- Leave to reduce for a few minutes.
- Check the seasoning.
- Strain the sauce through a fine-mesh strainer.

Thin piece of meat in a skillet so as to rapidly eliminate any moisture.

About Thermometers

Use of Thermometers

When I started out, 50 years ago, our chef taught us the cooking temperatures for meat or fish "by touch." It was impossible to be precise because, depending on the quality of the meat or its aging, there could be wide variations in cooking time. Today, a thermometer is an indispensable tool in controlling the temperature of a piece of meat or fish, or to determine the actual temperature of your oven. As for me, I rarely specify cooking times.

To better understand the point of a thermometer, you only need to appreciate how our parents and grandparents were tormented by the fear of salmonella; they also overcooked chicken to kill harmful bacteria. It was the same story with pork and beef, to kill off taenia—or tapeworm—eggs.

Were they right? In a sense, yes! Henhouse, pigsty and stable hygiene was not the principal concern of farmers in the last century, but nowadays we know how to control parasites and bacteria.

Slow Cooking with a Thermometer

There have been no new inventions in cooking for hundreds of years, with the exception of new technologies and precision cooking tested by specialists. There is currently much talk of low-temperature cooking, which, it must be said, constitutes genuine progress.

But is it really progress? Andiron cooking in huge hearths during the feudal era was in fact low-temperature cooking.

During my apprenticeship, we served sumptuous meals to the Chevaliers du Tastevin at the Château du clos de Vougeot.[1] On one occasion, we slow-roasted wild boar piglet in hearths of embers.

Closer to modern times, not so long ago, when the entire family left for the fields during hay-making time, the mother would place a heavy cast-iron cooking pot on the wood stove, in which a succulent stew would simmer, emitting irresistible aromas upon the family's return. Such cooking was no doubt low-temperature cooking!

It is important to observe hygiene rules for game that has been hunted. These precautions allow us to enjoy a wonderful culinary experience while showing respect for the animal. In order to keep up with modern technology, and as with several recipes in this book, I have adopted non-traditional temperature-controlled cooking. What an adventure for an old-school chef like me!

This is an experience that will let you see for yourself the importance of cooking with a thermometer in a modern kitchen. Once, for a gourmet meal for two hundred at a benefit dinner, I cooked Boileau deer loins in water, which is not normally done and borders on sacrilege! Nevertheless, the dinner guests loved them. You will understand this better once you have attempted this adventure yourself.

To summarize, the morning before the reception, I sautéed the deer loins very quickly on both sides at high heat in a roasting dish, in order to brown them nicely, and then I let them cool in the refrigerator. I seasoned them with salt and pepper and added a sprig of thyme and a bay leaf, and then I wrapped them up in five or six layers of plastic wrap, so as to make them waterproof. I pierced a few little holes (four or five) with a pin

so that the air could escape, and then I started cooking them for the evening meal. I steeped the loins in a pot of water, the temperature of which was between 130°F (54°C) and 135°F (57°C) (between rare and medium). It should be mentioned here that the thermometer must be constantly in the water, and that the temperature must not fluctuate.

The loins cooked very, very slowly. This cooking method respects the hygiene rules of Quebec Department of Agriculture, Fisheries and Food (Ministère de l'Agriculture, des Pêcheries et de l'Alimentation—MAPAQ), namely that all bacteria be eliminated from rare meat, with a core temperature maintained at 130°F (54°C) for 121 minutes.

Just before serving, I removed the plastic wrap and gave the loins a "burst of heat" by putting them in the oven at 500°F (260°C) in order to crisp the surface. (This step is optional.) Then, I served the Boileau deer loins with a Sauce Poivrade.

This recipe is a gift for cooks: no cluttering up of the kitchen, no excessive heat, perfect cooking results (the meat is the same color all over), no waste, and most of all—exceptional tenderness.

Have you ever thought of cooking meat in water? I suggest you try this with chicken, but at a cooking temperature of 180°F (82°C), or with pork, at 184°F (84°C). Let me know how it turns out!

Hotels and restaurants use high-tech, expensive equipment and cook with sous-vide bags at the same temperatures as above. Now you understand the importance of cooking with a thermometer.

1. The Château du clos de Vougeot, surrounded by vineyards, was built in the 12th century by Cistercian monks. In 1945, the brotherhood of the Chevaliers du Tastevin acquired the castle and has since gathered periodically to partake in large feasts.

Glossary of Culinary Terms

À coeur
Degree of cooking at the core of a piece of meat.

Age
Hang game or feathered poultry for some time in a fresh place to tenderize it.

Aiguillette
Primarily duck breast filet, sliced thinly and long, with the grain.

À la goutte de sang
When the breast of a poultry or game bird is cooked medium-rare, pricking it with a pin will produce a drop of blood forming at the center of the fat.

Aromatic ingredients
Any herb, plant or root that gives off a pleasant scent.

Au piqué
The meat is considered cooked once the tip of a knife can easily be inserted and removed.

Bard
Thin slice of pork fatback.

Bard
To wrap a piece of meat in slices of pork fatback.

Blanc de cuisson
Mix of water and flour to which lemon juice or white vinegar is added.

Blanch
Procedure consisting of boiling food in a certain quantity of liquid for a given period of time in order to remove certain impurities or tenderize it.

Bouquet garni
Seasoning ingredients composed of celery, sprigs of thyme, stalks of parsley and bay leaves, tied up together. Used to impart a pleasant aroma to dishes.

Braise
Cook in a hermetically covered braising pan or saucepan with a small amount of liquid. As this cooking method is lengthy, measures must be taken to ensure that the cooking liquid does not evaporate, hence the importance of using a cooking pan that seals hermetically.

Bread
Dip an item in a beaten egg yolk, then in fresh or dry bread crumbs before frying it.

Brunoise (to finely dice)
Vegetables chopped into cubes of approximately $\frac{1}{8}$ inch (3 mm).

Clarify
Melt butter in a saucepan, then decant it into a container, taking care that the buttermilk or whey stays at the bottom of the saucepan.

Caul fat
Fatty and transparent membrane that envelops animal giblets.

Daube
Stew of certain meats and vegetables with stock and seasoning.

Deglaze
Dissolve the cooking juices that have caramelized at the bottom of a cooking dish with a base or a liquid.

Degorge (to soak)
Soak an item in cold water to remove any impurities.

Degrease
Remove excess fat from a product, a preparation or a cooking vessel.

Denerve
Remove nerves and tendons from a piece of raw meat.

Dress
Prepare meat before cooking.

Essence of vegetables or game
Infuse ingredients to obtain a seasoning liquid (without thickener).

"Étouffée" cooking method
Cook a food in a hermetically sealed saucepan, in a sous-vide bag or in terra-cotta.

Fry
Slowly cook in an open receptacle with some fat, a seasoning garnish and a small amount of liquid (water, stock, wine, etc.). Or rapidly cook a thin piece of meat in a pan.

Grill
Cook a food by exposing it to direct heat, whether by radiation or contact: embers, flat stone or very hot cast-iron plate or grill.

Hang (age)
Leave a non-gutted game bird to age. Proceed with extreme caution.

Julienne
Food (meat or vegetables) cut into thin slices of 1 to 2 inches (2.5 to 5 cm) in length.

Lard
Using a larding-needle, insert strips of lard into meat to "nourish" it. This is especially done for cuts of meat that have a tendency to be drier (external parts of thighs).

Larding needle
Small instrument that resembles a large needle used to insert strips of lard into meat.

Lever
To de-bone a breast or to filet.

Macerate (to soak or steep)
Leave fruit, vegetables or meat to soak for a certain amount of time in alcohol or seasoning liquid.

Macis
The branching and fleshy part of the nutmeg casing ground to powder, used as a seasoning.

Magret
Breast muscle of a fattened goose or duck.

Marinate
Leave meat or poultry to soak in a marinade to tenderize it and give it more flavor.

Mirepoix
Vegetables (carrots, onions, celery, leek) and sometimes pork fatback or ham chopped into 1-inch (2.5 cm) dice serving as the base for a sauce or mixture.

Noisette potatoes
Little balls of potato pulp shaped with a noisette spoon and sautéed.

Parings
Unused parts of a food.

Parisian potatoes
Balls of potato pulp formed with a melon baller and sautéed.

Poach
Cook food in a varying amount of liquid, while maintaining a very light simmer.

Polenta
In Italy, a porridge made of cornmeal.

Reduce
Boil or simmer a sauce or stock. Evaporation will render the preparation darker and more concentrated.

Roast
Cook a meat with a certain quantity of fat by exposing it directly to the heat of a fire or the radiating heat of an oven or rotisserie.

Sauté
Cook on high heat in fat and while shaking the skillet so as to make the items "jump" (sauter) and thus not stick to the pan.

Sealing Pastry
Mixture of flour with egg white or water, in varying quantities, according to requirements. This mixture is used to seal a saucepan lid.

Sear
Cook a meat in very hot fat so as to contract the flesh (as opposed to sautéing at high heat, which consists of browning).

Simmer
Cook slowly on low heat.

Skim
Procedure consisting of removing, with a spoon or a slotted spoon, any impurities released to the surface of a liquid (sauce base) during slow boil.

Stuff
Fill the interior of poultry or a piece of meat with stuffing.

Suprême
Term designating poultry breast or game fillet. Some sophisticated dishes are also referred to as "supreme."

Sweat
Cook a vegetable on relatively high heat in a fat in order to lose some of its natural water content and concentrate its juices.

Testicles or Rocky Mountain Oysters
Animal testicles.

Trim or Pare
Eliminate the non-usable parts of a piece of meat, fish or vegetables during preparation in order to improve the presentation.

Whisk in butter
Sprinkle a sauce with knobs of softened butter and incorporate them by whisking until a homogenous mix is obtained.

Acknowledgments

It is impossible to produce a book on the game birds and game animals of our beautiful province without the support of countless people. I wish to extend my heartfelt thanks to them for their encouragement.

- Lucille Daoust, Director General of the ITHQ.
- Paul Caccia, in charge of publishing at the Institut de tourisme et d'hôtellerie du Québec;
- My usual production team (see photo below);
- All the family at Les Éditions de l'Homme;
- My friend Serge Yelle, distinguished hunter, for supplying much of the game;
- The Himbeault family, Le Boucher du Chasseur, in Saint-Stanislas-de-Kostka;
- Michel Busch, Director (retired), Food & Beverage at the Fairmont Queen Elizabeth, for supplying the bear;
- Louis Normand, chef and professor, for supplying the woodcocks and partridge;
- Christina Blais, Department of Nutrition at the Université de Montréal;
- Hélène Thiboutot, food microbiologist;
- Nicolas Gauthier, Laies Marcassins du Rieur Sanglier, in Yamachiche;
- Jean-Pierre Marionnet, master butcher;
- *Aventure, chasse et pêche (Adventure, Hunting and Fishing magazine);*
- Maison Hector Larivée, for supplying the fruits and vegetables;
- Mark Hills of British Columbia, for supplying the muskox;
- Josée Toupin and Alain Demontigny, for supplying the bison;
- Jean-François Gosselin of the Institut Maurice-Lamontagne, for supplying the seal;
- Patrick Matheys, owner of the charcuterie Les Cochons Tout Ronds;
- Denis Ferrer, for supplying the Boileau deer;
- The Therrien family of Canabec, for supplying game;
- Monas & Co. Ltd, for equipment and various supplies;
- Sanelli Knives;
- Coranco, registered distributor of the Lagostina brand;
- Quebec's Ministry of Natural Resources and Wildlife;
- Olivier and Emmanuel Nassans of Élevages Périgord (1993) Inc.;
- Linen Chest, for table linens and accessories;
- La Maison d'Émilie, for table linens and accessories;
- Canada Beef Inc.

The team, from left to right: Pierre Beauchemin, food photographer at the ITHQ; Luce Meunier, props stylist; Myriam Pelletier, food stylist; Jean-Paul Grappe, chef

References

Assiniwi, Bernard. *Recettes typiques des Indiens*, Montréal, Leméac, 1972.

Blandin, Charles. *Cuisine et chasse de Bourgogne et d'ailleurs*, Lyon, Éditions Horvath, 1948.

Chaudieu, Georges. *Dictionnaire de boucherie et boucherie-charcuterie*, Paris, Éditions Peyronnet, 1970.

Collectif. *Secrets et vertus des plantes médicinales*, Sélection du Readers Digest, 1985.

Delannoy, Dominique. *Animaux de la ferme*, Paris, Éditions Artemis, 2000.

Dubois, Urbain. *Nouvelle cuisine bourgeoise pour la ville et la campagne*, Bernardin, Béchet et Fils.

Durantel, Pascal. *Les gibiers*, Chamalières, Losanges, 1997.

Frentz, Jean-Claude. *La charcuterie en toute simplicité*, Montréal, Éditions La Presse, 1989.

Gélinas, Pierre. *Répertoire des microorganismes pathogènes*, Saint-Hyacinthe, Fondations des Gouverneurs, Edisem, 1995.

Godfrey, W. Earl. *Les oiseaux du Québec*, Montréal, Éditions de l'Homme, 1990.

Grappe, Jean-Paul. *Champignons*, Montréal, Éditions de l'Homme, 2007.

Kayler, Françoise and André Michel. *Cuisine amérindienne*, Montréal, Éditions de l'Homme, 1996.

Lenoir, Jean. *Le nez du vin*, Carnoux, Éditions Jean Lenoir, 1998.

Madge, S. and H. Burn. *Guide des canards, des oies, des cygnes*, Paris, Lausanne, Delachaux et Nestlé, 1995.

Meilleures recettes de Tante Rosalie, Bruxelles, Société des journaux du Patriote, 1937.

Ministère de l'Agriculture, des Pêches et de l'Alimentation (MAPAQ). *Votre guide du consommateur*.
——. *Guide du manipulateur d'aliments*.

Pomiane, Edouard de. *Bien manger pour bien vivre, Essai de gastronomie théorique*, Paris, Albin Michel, 1922.

Prescott, Jacques and Pierre Richard. *Mammifères du Québec et de l'Est du Canada*, Waterloo, Éditions Michel Quintin, 1996.

Vayssière, Marie. *Noix, châtaignes, champignons*, Paris, Éditions du Laquet, 1998.

Wolff, J. M., J. P. Lebland, N. Soleilhac. *Technologie culinaire à la carte*. Paris, Éditions, J. Lanore, 1997.

Photo Credits

Despite numerous attempts, we have not been able to reach all rights holders of the documents reproduced. People who have additional information on this subject are kindly asked to contact Les Éditions de l'Homme at the following e-mail address: edhomme@groupehomme.com. Almost all of the photos reproduced in this book were taken by Pierre Beauchemin, except for the following:

Cover image background: © Ultramarinfoto/iStockphoto.com

p. 2: © Doran_S/iStockphoto.com

p. 6: © IngaL/iStockphoto.com

p. 8: © Joshandaly/iStockphoto.com

p. 11: © HuntImages/iStockphoto.com

p. 12: © Elenathewise/iStockphoto.com

p. 15 (left): © Robyn Mackenzie/Shutterstock.com

p. 16: © Oliver Childs/iStockphoto.com

p. 21: © Paul Tessier/iStockphoto.com

p. 28: © Silver-John/Shutterstock.com

p. 31: © Mikedabell/iStockphoto.com

p. 33 (right): © Natures pic's

p. 34 (left): © Natures pic's

p. 35 (left): © Isidor Vila Verde

p. 35 (right): © David Pigeon

p. 36 ((left): © Maren Winter

p. 36 (right): © Robin Arnold

p. 37 (right): © Daniel Mar/iStockphoto.com

p. 38 (left): © Richard Bartz

p. 38 (right): © Roy Patton

p. 39 (left): © Alan Wilson

p. 40: © Jurate Lasienne/Shutterstock.com

p. 41 (left): © Roger Whiteway/iStockphoto.com

p. 41 (right): © Frank Leung/iStockphoto.com

p. 42 (right): © Patrick Laporte

p. 43 (left): © Arpingstone

p. 43 (right): © Olvier Klein

p. 44 (left): © Jean-Michel Bernard

p. 45 (left): © Davee

p. 46: © Elli/Shutterstock.com

p. 48 (left): © Paul Tessier/iStockphoto.com

p. 50 (left): © Hereby

p. 50 (right): © Gerhard Theron

p. 51 (left): © Mdf

p. 51 (right): © Richard Bartz

p. 52: © Lepro/Shutterstock.com

p. 54 (left): © Brianna May/iStockphoto.com

p. 54 (right): © BS Thurner Hof

p. 56 (left): © Joaquim Antunes

p. 56 (right): © Dimus

p. 57 (left): © Delphine Bouvry

p. 57 (right): © Lupin

p. 58: © Kokhanchikov/Shutterstock.com

p. 59 (right): © Andreas Trepte/Marburg

p. 60 (right): © Marek Szczepanek

p. 61 (left): © Ow Johnson

p. 61 (right): © Mike Baird

p. 62: © Nassyrov Ruslan/Shutterstock.com

p. 104: © Moremi/Shutterstock.com

p. 133: © YinYang/iStockphoto.com

p. 134: © Youra Pechkin/Shutterstock.com

p. 166: © Jaroslav Machacek/Shutterstock.com

p. 176: © Sharan D/Shutterstock.com

p. 179: © Sethislav/iStockphoto.com

p. 182 (bottom): © Len Tillim/iStockphoto.com

p. 183 (top): © Ronsan4D/iStockphoto.com

p. 183 (bottom): © Dawnn/iStockphoto.com

p. 186: © Betty4240/iStockphoto.com

p. 187: © Andy Krakovski/iStockphoto.com

p. 189: © Anna39/iStockphoto.com

p. 191: © Steverts/iStockphoto.com

p. 192: © Marcel Jancovic/Shutterstock.com

p. 193 (top): © Sue Feldberg/iStockphoto.com

p. 193 (bottom): © Paul Reeves Photography/iStockphoto.com

p. 194 (top): © Jokos78/iStockphoto.com

p. 194 (bottom): © Neosummer/iStockphoto.com

p. 195: © SPrada/iStockphoto.com

p. 196: © Puchan/Shutterstock.com

p. 254: © Jiri Vondracek/Shutterstock.com

p. 274: © Kavram/Shutterstock.com

p. 287: © XXX/iStockphoto.com

p. 288: © TTphoto/Shutterstock.com

p. 300: © Jeffrey Van Daele/Shutterstock.com

p. 308: © Jason Vandehey/Shutterstock.com

p. 315: © Common mushrooms/Luchschen/iStockphoto.com

p. 315: © Oyster mushrooms/Michael Thompson/iStockphoto.com

p. 315: © Shiitake mushrooms/YinYang/iStockphoto.com

p. 316: © Jeffrey VanDaete/Shutterstock.com

p. 330: © Elenathewise/iStockphoto.com

p. 335: © AtWaG/iStockphoto.com

p. 336: © Graham Prentice/Shutterstock.com

p. 361: © Patricia Hofmeester/Shutterstock.com

Index

N

O

P

Library and Archives Canada Cataloguing in Publication

Grappe, Jean-Paul
[Gibier à poil et à plume. English]
The complete wild game cookbook : includes 165 recipes / Jean-Paul Grappe.

Includes index.
Translation of: Gibier à poil et à plume.
ISBN 978-0-7788-0516-8 (pbk.)

1. Cooking (Game). 2. Cookbooks. I. Title. II. Title: Gibier à poil et à plume. English.

TX751.G7213 2015   641.6'91   C2015-903327-6